Extended Prelude to Programming: Concepts and Design

Stewart Venit

California State University, Los Angeles

Scott/Jones, Inc., Publishers
P.O.Box 696, El Granada, CA 94018
Voice: (650) 726-2436; Fax: (650) 726-4693
E-mail: marketing@scottjonespub.com
Web: www.scottjonespub.com

Extended Prelude to Programming: Concepts and Design
Stewart Venit

Copyright © 2002 by Scott/Jones, Inc.

ISBN 1-57676-066-9   2 3 4 5   X Y Z

Book design: Stewart Venit
Book composition: nSight, Inc.
Book production: Audrey Anderson, Blue Room Graphics
Book manufacturing: Von Hoffmann Graphics
Cover design: Martie Sautter

Scott/Jones Publishing Company

The publisher wishes to acknowledge the memory and influence of James F. Leisy. Thanks, Jim. We miss you.

Publisher: Richard Jones
Editorial group: Richard Jones, Michelle Windell, Patricia Miyaki
Production management: Heather Bennett
Marketing and Sales: Vickie Chamberlin Judy, Page Mead, Hazel Dunlap,
     Donna Cross, Michelle Windell
Business operations: Michelle Robelet, Cathy Glenn, Natascha Hoffmeyer

Printed on recycled paper.

Additional Titles by Stewart Venit from Scott/Jones

A Short Prelude to Programming: Concepts and Design (257 pp)
The Windows 2000 Professional Textbook (689 pp)
The Windows 98 Textbook: Extended Edition (706 pp)
The Windows 98 Textbook: Standard Edition (470 pp)
A Short Course in Windows 98 (303 pp)

Forthcoming in 2002—*The Windows XP Textbook*

Stewart Venit is also consulting editor for:

Comprehensive Windows 2000 Professional Step-by-Step by L. Hardin and D. Tice
Essential Windows 2000 Step-by-Step by L. Hardin and D. Tice

Additional Titles of Interest from Scott/Jones

The Windows 2000 Server Lab Manual by Gerard Morris
Access 2000 Guidebook (3rd ed.) by M. Trigg and P. Dobson

C

Contents

Preface

Extended Prelude to Programming: Concepts and Design is intended for use in a language-independent, introductory programming course. The purpose of the text is, in a language-free context, to help students learn

1. General programming topics, such as the use of control structures, data types, files, arrays, and subprograms.

2. Structured programming principles, such as top-down modular design and proper program documentation and style.

3. How to use certain basic tools and algorithms, such as data validation, defensive programming, calculating sums and averages, and searching and sorting lists.

4. About other programming paradigms, such as object-oriented and event-driven programming.

No prior experience with computers or programming is necessary, nor is any special knowledge of mathematics, finance, or any other discipline.

Organization of the Text

Although we have ordered the chapters according to our preference, the text has been organized to allow as much flexibility as possible in the presentation of the material. The first six chapters form the core of the text, covering basic programming topics, as well as introducing relatively advanced material such as data files, subprograms, and object-oriented and event-driven programming. The last three chapters of the text return to these advanced topics, covering them in greater depth.

The first four chapters should be covered prior to any of the others, but Chapters 3 and 4 are independent of one another, except for a few clearly marked examples and problems in the latter chapter. Similarly, once the core material (Chapters 1–6) has been covered, Chapter 7, 8, or 9 could be done next. We recommend, however, that Section 7.1 be considered a prerequisite for Chapter 9 and that Section 7.5 be read prior to Section 9.5. A complete Chapter Dependency Flowchart is shown on the facing page.

Many sections throughout the text are optional and may be omitted, if so desired. For example, the first three sections of Chapter 1 contain optional material about computer hardware and software, and other chapters contain algorithms that could be skipped at the discretion of the instructor.

Features of the Text

Programming concepts in ths everyday world

1. Each chapter after the first begins with a discussion of how the material in that chapter relates to "the everyday world." These features are entitled *Programming in the Everyday World*, *Loops in the Everyday World*, and so on, and provide an easy-to-read introduction to the chapter.

Chapter overview/ summary

2. We have tried to unify the material in each chapter so that it forms a cohesive whole. To help in this regard, a list of objectives appears at the beginning of every chapter and a comprehensive review is provided at its end.

Diverse and plentiful exercises

3. The text contains a diverse selection of exercises:

   - At the end of each section is a "Self-Test" consisting of a few short questions (with answers given in the appendix).

   - At the end of each chapter is a relatively long set of short-answer questions of various types that provide further review (with answers to the odd-numbered ones in the appendix).

   - Also at the end of each chapter is a set of "programming problems" that require the student to design programs which use the material learned in that and certain earlier chapters.

Chapter
Dependency
Flowchart

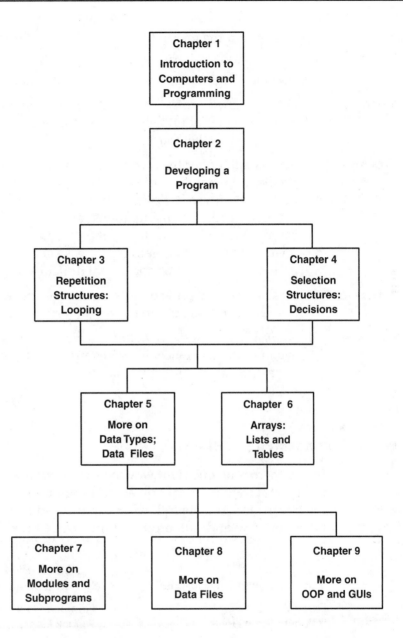

Emphasis
on program
design

4. Modular program design is introduced in Chapter 2 and empha-
    sized throughout the text. Pseudocode and hierarchy charts are the
    primary design tools, but flowcharts appear frequently, usually to
    clarify a program's logical flow.

Style
Pointers

5. The concepts of programming style and documentation are also
    introduced in Chapter 2. Style Pointers appear, when appropriate,

throughout the text to further illustrate these ideas.

TIPs

6. TIPs appear periodically throughout the text. These short notes provide insight or specialized knowledge about the topic at hand.

Programming Pointers

7. Other frequent notes, known as Programming Pointers, describe how the material under discussion relates to programming in actual high-level languages.

Focus on Problem Solving

8. Each chapter after the second contains a section entitled "Focus on Problem Solving." In these sections, we present a programming problem, analyze it, design a program to solve it, discuss any appropriate coding considerations, and indicate how the program could be tested. In so doing, the student not only sees a partial review of the chapter material, but also gets to work through a programming problem of non-trivial difficulty.

Margin notes

9. Occasional brief phrases in the margin of the text make it easy for the reader to find subtopics and important concepts.

Supplements

10. An *Instructor's Resource Manual*, which includes the answers to the even-numbered Review Exercises and a test bank of additional questions, is available directly from the publisher.

Acknowledgments

Just as there is no one right way to teach programming, there is no one right way to write a textbook about programming. I was fortunate in this regard to have the following experienced instructors offer varied points of view and numerous helpful suggestions for the developing manuscript:

Colin Archibald
Valencia Community College

Heather K. Bloom
Santa Fe Community College (Florida)

David W. Boyd
Valdosta State University

Ramona Coveny
Patrick Henry Community College

Linda Denney
Sinclair Community College

Elizabeth A. Dickson
Northern Virginia Community College

Judy Dunn
Laramie County Community College

Daniel L. Edwards
Ohlone College

Susan Fulton
College of Dupage

Carol Grimm
Palm Beach Community College

Bill Hammerschlag
Brookhaven College

John W. Miller
Pennsylvania College of Technology

Carol M. Peterson
South Plains College, Lubbock

Patty Santoianni
Sinclair Community College

Catherine D. Stoughton
Laramie County Community College

Daniel R. Terrian
Indian Hills Community College

Marilyn Wildman
Belmont Technical College

I am grateful to my publisher, Richard Jones, who suggested that I undertake this project and who gave it his enthusiastic and unwavering support. I am also indebted to Audrey Anderson, who guided the text through production, and to Cathy Stoughton and Judy Dunn, who class-tested it and wrote the *Instructor's Resource Manual*.

I would like to thank my wife, Corinne, and my daughter, Tamara, for their patience and understanding; they never complained about the countless hours I spent seemingly glued to the keyboard. I'd also like to thank my dog Maggie and my cat Smokey, who frequently kept me company, sleeping next to the humming computer.

1

An Introduction to Computers and Programming

OVERVIEW   Just sixty years ago, electronic computers didn't exist. Today, computers are everywhere. You can find them in homes, schools, and offices; in supermarkets and fast-food restaurants; on airliners and the space shuttle. They are used by the young and the old, by filmmakers and farmers, and by bankers and baseball managers. By taking advantage of a wealth of diverse and sophisticated software (programs), we are able to use computers in almost limitless ways: for education, entertainment, money management, product design and manufacture, and to run our businesses and institutions.

In this chapter, we will provide an introduction to computers and the programming process. You will learn about:

1. The history of the computer [Section 1.1].

2. The components that make up a typical computer system—its central processing unit, internal memory, mass storage, and input and output devices [1.2].

3. The types of software used by a modern computer [1.3].

4. Types of programming languages [1.3].

5. The basic building blocks—input, process, and output—of a typical computer program [1.4, 1.5].

6. The basic arithmetic operations employed in a program [1.5].

1.1 A Brief History of Computers

What Is a Computer?

Calculators, devices that increase the speed and accuracy of numerical computations, have been around for a long, long time. The *abacus,* which used rows of sliding beads to perform arithmetic operations, has roots that date back more than 5,000 years to ancient Babylonia. More modern mechanical calculators, using gears and rods, have been in use for almost 400 years. In fact, by the late nineteenth century, calculators of one sort or another were relatively commonplace. However, these machines were by no means *computers* as we now use the word.

A **computer** is a mechanical or electronic device that can efficiently store, retrieve, and manipulate large amounts of information at high speed and with great accuracy. Moreover, it can execute tasks (and act upon intermediate results) without human intervention by carrying out a list of instructions called a **program.**

Early Computers

Although we tend to think of the computer as a recent development, an Englishman named Charles Babbage designed and partially built a true computer in the mid-1800s. Babbage's machine, which he called an *Analytical Engine,* contained hundreds of axles and gears and could store and process 40-digit numbers. Babbage was aided in his work by Ada Augusta Byron, who grasped the importance of his invention and helped to publicize the project. (Ada Augusta, the daughter of the poet Lord Byron, is sometimes referred to as "the world's first programmer," and has had a major programming language named after her.) Unfortunately, Babbage never finished his Analytical Engine. His ideas were too advanced for the existing technology, and he could not obtain enough financial backing to complete the project.

Serious attempts to build a computer were not renewed until nearly 70 years after Babbage's death (in 1871). Around 1940, Howard Aiken at Harvard, and John Atanasoff and Clifford Berry at Iowa State, built machines that came close to being true computers. However, Aiken's Mark I could not act independently on its intermediate results, and the

Atanasoff-Berry computer required the frequent intervention of an operator during its computations.

Just a few years later, in 1945, a team at the University of Pennsylvania led by John Mauchly and J. Presper Eckert completed work on the world's first fully-operable electronic computer. Mauchly and Eckert named it ENIAC, an acronym for Electronic Numerical Integrator and Calculator. ENIAC (Figure 1) was a huge machine—80 feet long, 8 feet high, and weighing 33 tons—that contained over 17,000 vacuum tubes in its electronic circuits and consumed 175,000 watts of electricity. For its time, ENIAC was a truly amazing machine, performing up to 5,000 additions per second with incredible accuracy. However, by current standards, it would be exceedingly slow; a modern run-of-the-mill personal computer can exceed 100,000,000 operations per second!

For the next decade or so, all electronic computers used vacuum tubes to do the internal switching necessary to perform computations. These machines, which we now refer to as first generation computers, were large by modern standards (although not as large as ENIAC) and required a climate-controlled room and lots of tender loving care to

FIGURE 1

The ENIAC Computer (U.S. Army Photo)

keep them operating. By 1955, about 300 computers—built mostly by IBM and Remington Rand—were being used, primarily by large businesses, universities, and government agencies.

By the late 1950s, computers had become significantly faster and more reliable. This was due primarily to the replacement of their large, heat-producing vacuum tubes by relatively small transistors. The *transistor,* one of the most important inventions of the twentieth century, was developed at Bell Labs in the late 1940s by William Shockley, John Bardeen, and Walter Brattain, who later shared a Nobel Prize for this achievement. Due to their low energy needs and diminutive size, transistors could be packed close together in a compact enclosure. In the early 1960s, Digital Equipment Corporation (DEC) took advantage of small, efficient packages of transistors called *integrated circuits* to create the **minicomputer,** a machine roughly the size of a filing cabinet. As these computers were not only smaller but also less expensive than their predecessors, they were an immediate success. Nevertheless, sales of the larger computers, now being called **mainframes,** also increased rapidly, led by IBM's innovative System 360. The computer age had clearly arrived.

Personal Computers

Despite its increasing popularity, it was not until the late 1970s that the computer became a household appliance. This development was made possible by the invention (in the 1960s) of the *microchip,* a piece of silicon about the size of a postage stamp, packed with thousands of electronic components. The microchip and its more advanced cousin, the *microprocessor,* led to the creation in 1974 of the world's first **personal computer** (PC), a relatively inexpensive machine, small enough to fit on a desk top. This landmark computer, the Altair 8800 microcomputer, was unveiled in 1975. Although it was a primitive and not very useful machine, the Altair did inspire thousands of people, hobbyists and professionals alike, to become interested in personal computers. Among these were Bill Gates and Paul Allen, who later founded Microsoft Corporation, now one of the world's largest companies.

The Apple II and IBM PC   The Altair also captured the imagination of two young Californians, Stephen Wozniak and Steven Jobs. Determined to build a better, more useful computer, they founded Apple Computer, Inc. and in 1977 brought out the Apple II, which was an immediate hit. With the overwhelming success of this machine and Tandy Corporation's TRS-80, companies which were manufacturing the larger minicomputers and mainframes began to take notice. In 1981, IBM introduced the wildly popular IBM PC (Figure 2), and the personal computer's future was assured.

FIGURE 2

Two Historic
Computers

IBM Personal Computer   Apple Macintosh

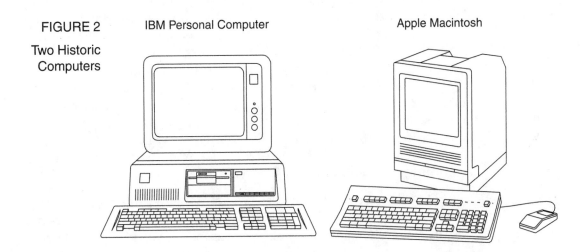

Many companies, hoping to benefit from the success of the IBM PC, brought out computers that could run the same programs as this machine, and these "IBM-compatibles" soon dominated the market. Even the introduction in 1984 of Apple's innovative and easy-to-use Macintosh (see Figure 2) could not stem the tide of the IBM compatibles, which now account for about 95% of the personal computer market. These computers, which almost all make use of Microsoft's Windows operating system, have also spawned a huge array of *software*—computer programs—of types never dreamed of by the manufacturers of the original mainframes. This software includes, to name just a few, word processors, photo editing programs, Web browsers, and a seemingly infinite variety of computer games.

Today's
computers

The computer market today comprises a vast array of machines. Personal computers are everywhere, ranging in price from a few hundred to a few thousand dollars. Their manufacturers are, for the most part, billion dollar companies: IBM, Dell, Gateway, Compaq, and

Apple. Although PCs are small and inexpensive, they produce a remarkable amount of computing power. Today's personal computer is more powerful than a typical mainframe of the mid-1970s, a machine that then cost hundreds of times as much as a PC does now.

Minicomputers have also found their niche. These machines, unlike personal computers, can be used by a number of people (typically, 16 or more) working simultaneously at separate remote *terminals* consisting of a keyboard and display screen. Minicomputers have become the mainstay of many small businesses and universities. They range in price from about $20,000 to $300,000. Mainframe computers are by no means dinosaurs. These relatively large and costly ($500,000 to $10,000,000) machines supply their users with tremendous power to manipulate information. **Supercomputers** are even more powerful than mainframes, and can process well over one billion instructions per second. For a special effects company, like Industrial Light and Magic, or a government agency like the Internal Revenue Service, there is no substitute for a mainframe or supercomputer.

The Internet
Despite all the recent advances in computer technology, the most significant development in the last ten years has been the phenomenal rise in popularity of the Internet. The **Internet** is a world-wide collection of *networks*, interlinked computers that are able to share resources and data via cable or phone lines. The Internet has roots that date back to a United States Defense Department project in the late 1960s. Over the last three decades, the Internet has grown from a small collection of mainframe computers used by universities and the military to a smorgasbord of millions of computers, whose users range from grade-school students to billion-dollar corporations.

The two main attractions of the Internet are e-mail and the World Wide Web. **E-mail,** which is short for *electronic mail*, allows anyone with access to the Internet to use his or her computer to exchange messages— almost instantaneously and at little or no cost—with another Internet user anywhere in the world. The **World Wide Web** (or, more simply, the Web), which originated in 1989, is a vast collection of linked documents (*Web pages*) created by Internet users and stored on thousands of Internet-connected computers. Although accessing (or *browsing*) the polyglot of information available on the Web can often be frustrating, its potential seems boundless. Some computer visionaries believe that the Internet, and especially e-mail and the World Wide Web, will ultimately play a more important role in our everyday lives than any other aspect of computer technology.

Self-Test 1.1 *

1. What characteristics of a computer distinguish it from

    a. a simple (non-programmable) calculator?
    b. a programmable calculator?

2. Complete each of the following statements:

    a. A _____ is a list of instructions to be carried out by the computer.
    b. The first fully-operative electronic computer was called _____.
    c. The fastest computers in use today are called _____.
    d. The _____ is a world-wide collection of interlinked networks.

3. Determine whether each of the following statements is true or false.

    a. The first personal computers were produced in the 1970s.
    b. Transistors, which eventually replaced early computers' vacuum tubes, were invented in the 1940s.
    c. Minicomputers and mainframe computers have become obsolete; they are no longer in use.
    d. The two most widely used features of the Internet are e-mail and the World Wide Web.

4. Match the people listed in the first column with the corresponding computer from the second column:

Charles Babbage and Ada Byron	ENIAC
J. Presper Eckert and John Mauchly	Apple II
Steven Jobs and Stephen Wozniak	Analytical Engine

1.2 Computer Basics

Components of a computer

As its definition implies, a computer must have the ability to input, store, manipulate, and output data. These functions are carried out by the five main components of a computer system:

1. The central processing unit (or CPU)

2. Internal memory (consisting of RAM and ROM)

---

*The answers to the Self-Tests are given in Appendix A.

3. Mass storage devices (primarily disk drives)

4. Input devices (primarily the keyboard and mouse)

5. Output devices (primarily the monitor and printer)

In the remainder of this section, we will describe these components as they are implemented on a modern personal computer.

In a personal computer, the CPU, internal memory, and most mass storage devices are located in the **system unit** (see Figure 3). The input and output devices are housed in their own enclosures and are connected to the system unit by cables. Components like these, that are used by a computer but located outside the system unit, are sometimes referred to as **peripherals.** All the physical equipment that makes up the computer system is known as **hardware.**

The Central Processing Unit

The **central processing unit** (also called the **processor** or **CPU**) is the brain of the computer. It receives all program instructions, performs the arithmetic and logical operations necessary to execute them, and controls all the other computer components. In a personal computer, the processor consists of millions of transistors residing on a single microchip about the size of a postage stamp and plugged into the computer's main circuit board, the *motherboard*.

FIGURE 3
A Typical
Computer

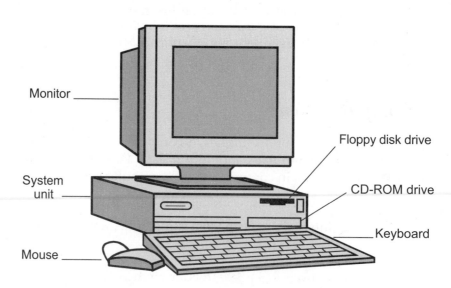

Monitor

Floppy disk drive

CD-ROM drive

System unit

Keyboard

Mouse

More than any other component, the CPU distinguishes one computer from another. A primary factor in determining the power of a processor is its speed, measured in *megahertz* (MHz). For example, the Pentium III microprocessor, which is made by Intel Corporation for use on PCs, is a chip that, as of this writing, is produced in several variations that run at speeds from about 600 MHz to 1200 MHz. Roughly speaking, the latter version processes data at twice the speed of the former. However, due to various factors, some processors are more powerful than others running at the same speed. For example, a Pentium III runs modern programs faster than Intel's Celeron chip of the same speed rating.

Internal Memory

A computer uses its **internal memory** to store the instructions and data to be processed by the CPU. In a personal computer, memory resides on a series of chips either plugged directly into the motherboard or into one or more smaller circuit boards connected to the motherboard.

There are two types of internal memory: ROM and RAM. **ROM** stands for *Read-Only Memory*. It contains an unalterable set of instructions that the computer consults during its start-up process and certain other basic operations. **RAM** (*Random-Access Memory*), on the other hand, can be both read from and written to. It is used by the computer to hold program instructions and data. (Think of ROM as a reference sheet, while RAM is a scratchpad—a very large scratchpad.) Whereas ROM is a permanent form of memory storage, all the information stored in RAM is lost when the computer is turned off.

The basic unit of memory is the **bit,** which can store only two different values (a 0 or a 1), but memory is usually measured in *kilobytes* and *megabytes.* One **byte** consists of eight bits and is the amount of memory used to store one character of information. (Loosely speaking, a *character* is any symbol you can type, such as a letter, a digit, or a punctuation mark.) One **kilobyte,** which is abbreviated *KB,* is 1,024 (= 2^{10}) bytes and one **megabyte** (*MB*) is 1,024 kilobytes. For example, a personal computer with 64 MB of RAM, a typical amount nowadays, can store 67,108,864 (= 64 × 1,024 × 1,024) characters of information.

Mass Storage Devices

In addition to ROM and RAM, a computer needs **mass storage,** another form of memory, which stores programs and data semi-permanently.

(They remain in mass storage until you decide to erase them.) However, to make use of any information stored on a mass storage device, the computer must first *load* (copy) that information into RAM.

Hard and floppy disk drives

The primary type of mass storage device is the **disk drive.** Most PCs contain a *hard disk drive* and a *floppy disk drive* housed within the system unit. A hard disk drive stores information on a constantly spinning magnetic platter—the **hard disk**—which is sealed within the drive. A floppy disk drive, on the other hand, makes use of **floppy disks** (or **diskettes**) that are stored away from the computer and, when needed, are inserted into the drive through a slot in its front. Most personal computers use floppy disks that are 3½ inches in diameter and can store up to 1.44 megabytes of data. Hard drives hold much more data than floppies. Modern personal computers are equipped with hard drives that have at least several gigabytes of storage capacity, where each **gigabyte** (GB) represents 1,024 megabytes.

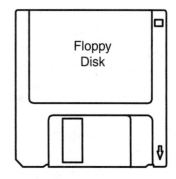

You may be wondering why computers contain both hard and floppy drives. Typically, the hard drive is used to store most of the programs and data to be used by a PC. Floppy drives, which are much slower in operation, are typically used for the following purposes:

- To transfer newly purchased programs from the distribution disks to the computer's hard disk.

- For *backup* purposes—to make copies of valuable hard disk data in the event that the hard disk becomes damaged.

- To help transfer information from one computer to another.

- For *archival* purposes—to move information from the hard disk to floppies when it is unlikely to be needed in the foreseeable future.

CD-ROM drives

Virtually all personal computers sold today are equipped with a third type of mass storage device, the **CD-ROM drive.** These drives use disks that are similar to audio compact discs (hence the "CD" in the name). Like floppies, CD-ROMs are removable and portable, but, unlike floppies, they hold large amounts of information—about 600 MB each. Because CD-ROM drives are read-only devices (hence the "ROM" in the name), they are used primarily:

- To distribute large applications to the computer user (instead of using dozens of floppies).
- To run applications that require a very large amount of storage space, such as encyclopedias and graphics-intensive games.

However, even CD-ROMs do not have the capacity needed to run certain modern computer applications, such as those that use large amounts of video and sound. For this reason, the *digital versatile disk*, or DVD, was developed. A DVD has more than seven times the storage capacity of a CD-ROM. **DVD drives,** which can also read CD-ROMs, are slowly replacing the latter in computer systems.

Other mass storage devices

Floppy disk, CD-ROM, and DVD drives are referred to generically as *removable media* devices because, unlike hard drives, their disks are inserted into the drive before use and removed from it afterwards. Other types of removable media drives have recently become popular; they have large storage capacities, yet preserve the floppy's ability to *write* data to the disk. The most common of these is the *Zip* drive made by Iomega Corporation, which holds 100 megabytes or more of information. Other drives of this type can store as much as two *gigabytes* of data.

Another fairly common mass storage device is the **tape drive,** which uses media that resemble audio cassettes. It can be used to copy (back up) the entire contents of a hard disk onto a magnetic tape. Should the information on the hard disk become inaccessible for any reason, the data could then be retrieved from the backup tape. A tape drive works slowly, but this isn't too important considering its intended role.

Input Devices

The computer uses its **input devices** to receive data from the outside world. For this purpose, every computer includes a typewriter-like **keyboard** to allow you to enter information into a program. The characters you type will simultaneously appear on the computer's display screen.

Computer keyboards contain quite a few keys not found on a typewriter. These "extra" keys include: *function keys,* which perform special tasks that vary from program to program; *cursor control keys* that allow you to move the *cursor* (which indicates the current typing position) around the screen; and many other specialized keys.

Another standard input device is the **mouse,** a hand-held object containing one, two, or three buttons, which (together with the cable that connects it to the computer) vaguely resembles a long-tailed rodent. When you roll the mouse around on the desk top, a pointer moves correspondingly on the screen. For example, if you roll the mouse to the left, the pointer moves left. Once the pointer is positioned appropriately on the screen, pressing a mouse button (*clicking the mouse*) performs a program function. The mouse can speed up many input operations, but it lacks the versatility of the keyboard.

Output Devices

Whereas input devices allow us to communicate with the computer, **output devices** make it possible for the computer to communicate with us. The most common output devices are *monitors* and *printers*.

A **monitor** is a high resolution television-like screen enclosed in a case and controlled by circuitry—the *video adapter*—within the computer. (The screens on portable computers use an entirely different technology; they are usually *LCD*—liquid crystal display—*panels.*) As is the case with televisions, monitor size is measured along the screen's diagonal. The most common screen sizes for desktop computers are 15 and 17 inches, but other sizes are also available. Another characteristic that affects the quality and cost of a monitor is its *resolution*—the number of *pixels* (tiny dots of light) it uses to create images. Nowadays, screen resolutions of 1024 × 768—768 horizontal rows, each containing 1,024 pixels—are commonplace. This kind of resolution puts all but the finest of televisions to shame.

Unfortunately, output to the screen is both impermanent (it disappears when the power is turned off) and not terribly portable (you'd need a pretty long extension cord to take your screen output home from school). If you want to make a permanent copy (a *hard copy*) of a program's output on paper, you need to use a **printer.**

The text and pictures produced by virtually all printers are composed of tiny dots of ink or an ink-like substance. The size of these dots and how closely they are packed together determine the quality of the output. Currently, two types of printers dominate the market:

- *Laser printers* have become the standard for business use. They produce excellent-looking black-and-white text and graphics at a high rate of speed, and are remarkably reliable. Laser prices start at about $300, and they cost relatively little to run and maintain. *Color laser printers* are not as common as their monochrome brethren, mainly because of their considerable cost.

- *Ink jet printers* spray incredibly tiny drops of ink on the paper creating surprisingly clear images. Most ink jets produce relatively good color output as well. Although, generally speaking, ink jet printers cost less to buy than lasers, they are slower and have a higher cost of operation. For these reasons, ink jets are more common in the home than in the office.

Self-Test 1.2

1. Name the five basic components that make up a typical computer system.

2. Give the function of

   a. The central processing unit (CPU).
   b. Mass storage devices.

3. Determine whether each of the following statements is true or false.

   a. The speed of a processor is usually measured in *megahertz*.
   b. A "bit" is another name for one byte of memory.
   c. Disk drives are a type of mass storage device.
   d. If a computer has good enough input devices, it has no need for output devices.

4. a. Name two input devices.
   b. Name two output devices.

5. Give one advantage and one disadvantage of a laser printer compared to an ink jet printer.

1.3 Software and Programming Languages

The most powerful hardware cannot accomplish anything by itself. It needs **software**—computer programs—to bring it to life. Software provides instructions for the central processing unit and, in so doing, allows the computer user to write letters, calculate loan balances, draw pictures, play games, and perform countless other tasks. In this section, we will describe some types of software and discuss the means by which this software is created.

Types of Software

Software can be divided into two general categories: applications software and system software.

Applications Software   **Applications** are programs you use to enhance your productivity, solve problems, supply information, or provide recreation. To be able to run programs like these is the reason one learns to use a computer.

Here are some of the more popular kinds of applications:

- *Word processors* help you create, edit, and print documents such as letters, reports, and memos.

- *Database managers* allow you to enter, access, and modify large quantities of data. You might use a database program to create a personal phone directory. A business can use this kind of application to maintain customer lists and employee records.

- *Spreadsheet programs* simplify the manipulation and calculation of large amounts of tabular data (spreadsheets). These programs are often used by businesses to try to foresee the effect of different strategies on their bottom line.

- *Painting programs* allow you to use the computer to draw pictures (*graphics*) on the screen and print them on paper.

- *Web browsers* and *e-mail programs* allow you to make use of the Internet to view a limitless variety of electronic documents and communicate with others around the world.

Applications are developed and published by many different companies and are sold in retail stores, by mail order firms, and over the Internet. Each software package contains one or more diskettes or CDs that contain the application *files*—the programs, data, and documents needed by the application. Before you can use a piece of software, it must be *installed*—the computer must copy files from the floppies or CDs to your computer's hard disk and supply certain information about the application to the operating system.

System Software   The second general software type is **system software,** the programs used by the computer to control and maintain its hardware and to communicate with the user. The most important piece of system software is the **operating system** (or OS)—the computer's master control program. A computer must use an OS written especially for it, although the computer owner may be able to choose from among several available operating systems. For example, if you use an IBM-compatible computer, you are probably using some version of the Microsoft Windows operating system, but you could install the Linux OS (a variant of Unix) or even DOS, the original operating system used with IBM computers.

The operating system has two general functions:

1. It helps the application you are using to communicate with the computer hardware. Applications are written to run under a specific operating system, which supplies easy ways for the programmers to access the computer's disk drives, memory, and so on.

2. It provides an *interface*—a link—between you and the computer that allows you to install and start up applications, manipulate disk files, and perform other very basic tasks.

Programming Languages

Just as a book must be written in a particular language, such as English, Spanish, or French, programs must be written in a particular programming language. A **programming language** is a set of symbols and the rules governing their use that is utilized in constructing programs.

Types of Programming Languages   Programming languages are of three fundamental types:

1. Machine languages

2. Assembly languages

3. High-level languages

A **machine language** program consists of a sequence of bits—zeros and ones. The numbers specified, and the order in which they appear, tell the computer what to do. Machine language, which differs considerably from one type of computer to another, is the only language the computer can understand directly. However, as you might imagine, it is very difficult for humans to read or write machine language programs. For this reason, **programmers** (those who write programs) normally use either *assembly* or *high-level* languages.

Assembly language is a symbolic representation of machine language. There is usually a one-to-one correspondence between the two; each assembly language instruction translates into one machine language instruction. However, assembly language uses easily recognizable codes, which make it a lot easier for people to understand. For example, the following instruction adds two numbers on a certain minicomputer.

Machine Language Instruction:
0110110111110111 0000000100000000 0000000100000000

Assembly Language Equivalent:
ADD A, B

Before a computer can carry out an assembly language program, it must be translated (by the computer) into machine language. This is done by a special program called an *assembler*.

High-level languages usually contain English words and phrases; their symbols and structure are far removed from those of machine language. High-level languages have several advantages over machine or assembly languages. They are easier to learn and use, and the resultant programs are easier to read and modify. A single instruction in a high-level language usually translates into many instructions in machine language. Moreover, a given high-level language does not differ very much from computer to computer; a program written on one machine can usually be modified relatively easily for use on another. On the negative side, high-level languages are usually less powerful and produce less efficient programs than their assembly language counterparts. High-level languages, like assembly languages, must be translated into machine language before they can be understood by the computer.

Examples of
high-level
languages

The first high-level language, FORTRAN (which stands for FORmula TRANslator), was developed in the mid-1950s, primarily for engineering and scientific applications. Since then, there has been a flood of high-level languages. A few of these are:

- Ada (named after Ada Augusta Byron)—used mostly for programs written under U.S. Department of Defense contracts

- BASIC (Beginner's All-purpose Symbolic Instruction Code)—a popular, easy-to-learn language developed at Dartmouth College in the mid-1960s

- C++—currently, one of the most popular languages; used for efficient programming of many different types of applications

- COBOL (COmmon Business Oriented Language) — once the most popular language for business-related programming applications; it is still used for writing such programs

- Java—another very popular modern language, especially for Web applications

- Pascal—a popular language to use as a basis for teaching programming

- Visual Basic—a version of BASIC that is well-suited for software that runs on graphical user interfaces (GUIs), such as Windows and Macintosh computers

Writing Programs To write a program in a high-level language, you must first have access to the appropriate software on your computer or on the network (if any) to which your computer is connected. This software usually consists of several programs that work together to help you create the finished product, including a *text editor* in which you type and *edit* (modify) the program statements (instructions), a *debugger* that helps you to find errors in your program, and a *compiler* or *interpreter* that translates your program into machine language. This software is readily available for many programming languages; it is sold in most campus bookstores, in retail stores, and over the Internet.

To use the programming language software package (once it is installed on your computer or on your network), you first start it up as you would any application. Then, you type the program *statements* (instructions) and *run* the program (execute its statements) to see if it is working properly. If not, it is necessary to revise the program and run it again.

Of course, writing an appropriate program to solve a specific problem requires a good deal of knowledge about programming concepts in general and a specific language in particular. It is the purpose of this text to present the relevant programming concepts; once you have mastered them, learning a programming language should prove to be relatively easy.

Self-Test 1.3

1. What is the difference between applications software and system software?
2. Briefly describe three types of applications.
3. Name the three basic types of programming languages.
4. Since high-level languages are easier to use, why would a programmer want to write a program in assembly language?
5. What was the first high-level language? When was it developed?
6. Why do you think that there are so many different kinds of programming languages?

1.4 Basic Programming Concepts—Data and Data Types

In Sections 1.4 and 1.5, we will discuss some basic programming concepts. In this section, we present a simple programming problem and then use it to illustrate the notions of data input, variables, and data types.

A Simple Program

Suppose that a friend of yours is planning a trip to England and wants an easy way to convert a price in the local currency, British pounds, into U.S. dollars. To help your friend, you look in the business section of the newspaper to determine the conversion factor and discover that one British pound is equivalent to $1.62. Then, you give the following instructions for using a simple calculator to perform the computation:

Enter the price of the item in pounds into the calculator's display.
Press the multiply (×) key.
Enter 1.62 into the display.
Press the equals (=) key. (The price in dollars will appear in the display.)

Of course, these instructions are to be executed (carried out) in the order in which they appear.

The instructions shown here are not very different from those in a computer program designed to perform this task. The *Price Conversion* program instructions might look like this:

The *Price Conversion* program

Input the price of the item, PoundPrice, in pounds
Compute the price of the item in dollars:

Set DollarPrice = 1.62 * PoundPrice
Write DollarPrice

Program instructions (or **statements**) are executed in order, unless one of the statements indicates otherwise.

Programming Pointer Although, in this text, we will sometimes refer to a list of instructions like the one above as a "program," it is not really a program in the strict sense of the word. Programs are written in programming languages and follow an exact *syntax*— rules of usage that determine whether an instruction (statement) is or is not valid. In fact, the list of instructions above is referred to as *pseudocode;* the prefix *pseudo* (pronounced "sue-dough") means "not real." An example of an actual program (in the BASIC language) that would solve our problem is:

```
INPUT PoundPrice
LET DollarPrice = 1.62 * PoundPrice
PRINT DollarPrice
END
```

Our simple price conversion "program" illustrates the basic structure of the vast majority of computer programs—they input data, process it, and output the results. In this context, *data* may be numbers (as it is here), words (as in a word processing program), or for that matter, any collection of symbols.

Data Input, Variables, and Data Types

The **input** operation transmits data from an outside source to the program. Often, this data is typed at the computer keyboard (at the appropriate time) by the person using the program. For example, the INPUT statement of the BASIC program shown in the Programming Pointer above causes the execution of this program to pause and displays a question mark symbol (?) on the screen. The question mark is an indicator—a **prompt**—telling the user to enter data. At this point, we might type, for example, 100 (indicating that the price of an item is 100 pounds). To cause program execution to resume (in this BASIC program), we then press the Enter key. These actions are referred to as "entering data from the keyboard."

Use Prompts Unlike BASIC, most programming languages do not display a prompt (such as a question mark) when execution pauses for input. It is the responsibility of the programmer to provide the prompt. This is done by placing (prior to the Input statement) a statement in the program that displays a message on the screen telling the user what kind of data to input.

For example, in the price conversion program we should use the following pair of statements to prompt for and input the desired data:

Write "Type the price in pounds and then press the Enter key."
Input PoundPrice

The first (Write) statement causes the message in quotation marks to appear on the screen; the second (Input) statement causes execution to pause. Now, the user understands full well what to do; he or she types the appropriate number and presses the Enter key. Then, execution resumes.

Other forms of data input

While input from the keyboard is very common, data may be input into a program by other means, as well. In some programs, the user inputs information by clicking or moving the mouse. For example, to draw a straight line in a graphics program, the user might click on a symbol (*icon*) representing a line, then click on the locations of the line's endpoints. Still another common form of input does not involve the user at all—data can be transmitted to a program from a data file stored on disk.

Since, when writing a program, we do not know what specific data the user will enter while running the program, we assign the input data to a program **variable,** a quantity that can change value during the execution of a program. Then, to refer to the input data in a subsequent program statement, we simply refer to its variable name. At this point, the *value* of the variable—the number or other data it represents—will be used in this statement. For example, the input variable in our price conversion program is PoundPrice. If, in running the program, the user enters 100, this value is assigned to PoundPrice. Then, if later in the program, the expression

1.62 * PoundPrice

occurs, the computer will multiply 1.62 by 100.

Use Meaningful Variable Names   Although most programming languages have rules that govern the form of the name of a program variable (for example, blank spaces are usually not allowed), the name you choose is otherwise up to you. To illustrate, we could have used X or PP or even George to represent the price of the item in pounds. However, to minimize confusion, especially if your program is to be read by others, the names you give to variables should be meaningful. So, instead of PoundPrice, we might have used PriceInPounds or perhaps just Pounds. But, you must be consistent! If you use PriceInPounds in the Input statement, then the name of this variable in the next statement, currently,

Set DollarPrice = 1.62 * PoundPrice

must also be changed to PriceInPounds.

Types of data   There are two fundamental types of data:

- *Numeric* data consists of numbers. This type of data is usually sub-divided into *integer* data, which is any whole number, such as –3, 0, or 4, and *floating point* data, which is made up of those numbers that contain a decimal point, such as 3.21 or –5.0.

- *Character* (or *alphanumeric*) data is made up of *characters*—basically, all the symbols you can type at a keyboard. Character data is usually enclosed in quotation marks, such as "J" or "#". (Note that the blank, or space, is a valid character, " ".)

Programming Pointer Due to the fact that a computer stores integer, floating point, and character data in different ways, a program must identify the kind of data that is represented by a given variable. This is handled differently by different programming languages. Nevertheless, most languages require that all variables be identified (or *declared*) before their first use. For example, in C++, the integer variables Num1 and Num2 and character variable Initial are declared by using the statements:

```
int Num1, Num2;
char Initial;
```

In this text, we will normally not explicitly declare variables. But, when we do, we will use pseudocode like the following to do so:

```
Declare Num1, Num2 As Integer
Declare Initial As Character
```

Self-Test 1.4

1. What are the three main components that make up the basic structure of most computer programs?

2. Write a pair of statements, the first of which is an appropriate prompt, to input a temperature in degrees Fahrenheit. (Use F for the variable.)

3. Suppose a program is to calculate the maturity (final) value of an investment given the amount invested, the rate of interest, and the length of time that the money is invested.

    a. What data must be input to this program?
    b. Give (reasonable) names for each of the input variables.

4. For each of the variables listed in your answer to Problem 3b, is that variable of numeric or character type?

1.5 Basic Programming Concepts—
Data Processing and Output

In this section, we will continue the discussion of the fundamental building blocks—input, processing, and output—that make up a program. In Section 1.4, we concentrated on data input; here, we will discuss the processing and output components.

Processing Data

In the Price Conversion program of Section 1.4,

The *Price*
Conversion
program

Input the price of the item, PoundPrice, in pounds
Compute the price of the item in dollars:
    Set DollarPrice = 1.62 * PoundPrice
Write DollarPrice

after the user has input the value of PoundPrice, the instruction

Compute the price of the item in dollars:
    Set DollarPrice = 1.62 * PoundPrice

is executed. This statement comprises the *processing* part of the program, and accomplishes two things:

1. It multiplies the value of PoundPrice, the price of the item in pounds, by 1.62. (Notice that we use, as do all major programming languages, the asterisk, *, for the multiplication symbol.)

2. It assigns the resulting value of the expression on the right of the equals sign to the variable on the left. (For this reason, this kind of statement is called an *assignment statement*.)

For example, if the value of PoundPrice is 100 when this statement is executed, the expression on the right side is computed to be 162 and is assigned to the variable DollarPrice.

Programming
Pointer

A program variable is actually the name for a storage location in the computer's internal memory (see Section 1.2); the value of the variable is the contents of that location. It might help to think of the storage locations as mailboxes, each variable as the name printed on a mailbox, and the value of a variable as the contents of a mailbox. Thus, a "picture" of the computer's memory before and after the statement

Set DollarPrice = 1.62 * PoundPrice

is executed would look like this:

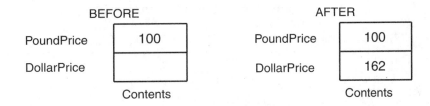

	BEFORE			AFTER
PoundPrice	100		PoundPrice	100
DollarPrice			DollarPrice	162
	Contents			Contents

Notice that the value of PoundPrice does not change when it appears on the right side of an assignment statement. DollarPrice, however is *undefined* (has no value) before the statement is executed, as indicated by the "empty mailbox" in the figure above, and takes on the assigned value after execution.

Assignment statements can sometimes look a little strange. For example, a not uncommon program statement looks like this:

Set Counter = Counter + 1

Although this looks confusing, if we take it slowly, it's easy to see what happens here. First, the right side is evaluated, and 1 is added to the current value of the variable Counter. Then, this new value is assigned to the variable on the left, Counter. The net result is to add one to the previous value of Counter. So, if the value of Counter were equal to 23 prior to this statement, its value would be 24 afterwards.

Programming Pointer

What happens if a variable that already has a value is assigned a new one? For example, suppose a program contains the statements:

Set X = 45
Set X = 97

In such a case, the latest value assigned to the variable (in our example, 97) replaces the previous one. In terms of storage locations, when the second of the two assignment statements is executed, the value currently stored in location X (45) is erased and the new value (97) is stored there in its place.

Arithmetic Operators

The symbol, *, that we use to denote multiplication is an example of an *arithmetic operator*. Many programming languages use five basic arithmetic operators—addition, subtraction, multiplication, division, and exponentiation (taking a number to a power)—see Table 1*.

TABLE 1

The Five Basic Arithmetic Operations

Operator	Symbol	Example	Result
Addition	+	2 + 3	5
Subtraction	−	7 − 3	4
Multiplication	*	5 * 4	20
Division	/	12 / 3	4
Exponentiation	^	2 ^ 3	8

For example, to convert a temperature in degrees Fahrenheit to degrees Celsius, we use the formula:

$$C = \frac{5\,(F - 32)}{9}$$

In this text (and in a programming language), however, we write this formula as: C = 5 * (F − 32)/9. Then, to determine the value assigned to the variable C when the value of F is (say) 77, we proceed as follows:

C = 5 * (77 − 32)/9 = 5 * (45)/9 = 225/9 = 25

Hierarchy of Operations   Notice that if the parentheses were missing in the last example, we get a different result:

5 * 77 − 32/9 = 385 − 32/9, which is approximately 381.4.

This is due to the fact that the rules of arithmetic tell us that the order in which arithmetic operations are performed (that is, their *hierarchy*) is:

- First, perform the operations in parentheses (from the inside out, if there are parentheses within parentheses).

- Next, perform exponentiations (take numbers to powers).

---

*The "standard" Pascal and C++ languages are exceptions; they do not contain an exponentiation operator.

- Then, do multiplications and divisions (from left to right if there is more than one).

- Finally, do additions and subtractions (from left to right if there is more than one).

To illustrate these rules, let us *evaluate* (that is, find the value of) the expression:

$$3 * (6 + 2) / 12 - (7 - 5) \wedge 2 * 3$$
$$= 3 * 8 / 12 - 2 \wedge 2 * 3 \quad \text{[evaluate parentheses first]}$$
$$= 3 * 8 / 12 - 4 * 3 \quad \text{[perform exponentiations next]}$$
$$= 24 / 12 - 4 * 3 \quad \text{[do multiplications and divisions next,}$$
$$= 2 - 12 \quad \text{from left to right]}$$
$$= -10 \quad \text{[do additions and subtractions last]}$$

Data Output

A program's **output** is data sent from memory to the screen, printer, or sometimes another destination, such as a disk file. The output normally consists, at least in part, of the results of the program's processing component. In the Price Conversion program, the output is produced by the statement

Write DollarPrice

We will use this kind of statement to indicate that the value of the variable (in this case, DollarPrice) is displayed on the screen and then the *cursor* (an indicator of the current typing position) moves to the beginning of the next line.

In addition to outputting numbers, it is often useful to output *text*—words and other symbols. For example, if the user has input 100 (for the price of an item in pounds) into the Price Conversion program, the only output that currently appears on the screen is the number 162. It would be much more informative to instead display the following:

    The price of the item in dollars is 162

We will accomplish this in our programs by using the statement:

Write "The price of the item in dollars is ", DollarPrice

This statement displays the text included between the quotation marks followed by the value of the variable. If, on the other hand, we want the displayed output to appear on two separate lines on the screen:

```
The price of the item in dollars is
100
```

we will use two statements in our program:

Write "The price of the item in dollars is"
Write DollarPrice

(Of course, each programming language has its own special statements to create the kinds of screen output described above.)

Annotate Your Output   If the output of your program consists of numbers, also output enough explanatory text (that is, *annotate* your output) so that the user will understand the significance of these numbers. For example, if your program computes the temperature in degrees Celsius (C) when degrees Fahrenheit (F) is input, the output statements might look like this:

Write "Degrees Fahrenheit: ", F
Write "Degrees Celsius: ", C

Self-Test 1.5

1. If the temperature is 95 degrees Fahrenheit, use the formula in the this section to find the resulting temperature in degrees Celsius.

2. If $X = 2$ and $Y = 3$, give the value of each of the following expressions:

   a. $(2 * X - 1) \wedge 2 + Y$
   b. $X * Y + 10 * X / (7 - Y)$
   c. $(4 + (2 \wedge Y)) * (X + 1) / Y$

3. If Number has the value 5 before the execution of the statement

   Set Number = Number + 2

   what is the value of Number after the execution of this statement?

4. If PoundPrice = 100 and DollarPrice = 162, write statements that will produce the following output on the screen:

   a. ```
   The price of the item is 162 dollars.
   ```
   b. ```
   The price in pounds is 100
   The price in dollars is 162
   ```

5. Write a program (like the Price Conversion program of this section) that inputs a temperature in degrees Fahrenheit (F) and outputs the corresponding temperature in degrees Celsius (C). (*Hint:* Use the formula given in this section of the text.)

Chapter Review and Exercises

Key Terms *

Computer	Program
Minicomputer	Mainframe
Personal computer (PC)	Supercomputer
Internet	E-mail
World Wide Web (Web)	System unit
Peripherals	Hardware
Central processing unit (CPU)	Processor
Internal memory	Read-only memory (ROM)
Random-access memory (RAM)	Bit
Byte	Kilobyte (KB)
Megabyte (MB)	Mass storage
Disk drive	Hard disk
Floppy disk (diskette)	Gigabyte (GB)
CD-ROM drive	Tape drive
Input device	Keyboard
Mouse	Output device
Monitor	Printer
Software	Application
System software	Operating system
Programming language	Machine language
Programmer	Assembly language
High-level language	Program statement
Input	Input prompt
Variable	Output

Chapter Summary

In this chapter, we have discussed the following topics:

1. The history of computers, including:

   - Early computers, such as the Analytical Engine and ENIAC.

   - The development of the mainframe, minicomputer, and personal computer.

---

*Key terms are listed (from left to right) in their order of appearance in the text, where they are shown in boldface type.

- The rise of the personal computer—the Altair 8800, Apple II, IBM PC, and Macintosh.

2. The basic components that make up a typical computer system:
   - The central processing unit—the brain of the computer.
   - Internal memory—its RAM and ROM.
   - Mass storage devices, including hard and floppy disk drives, CD-ROM drives, Zip drives, and tape drives.
   - Input devices such as a keyboard or mouse.
   - Output devices such as a monitor or printer.

3. Types of software (computer programs):
   - Applications such as word processors, spreadsheet programs, database managers, graphics programs, and Web browsers.
   - System software such as the computer's operating system—the master control program—and the utilities that support it.
   - Programming languages for creating applications—machine language, assembly languages, and high-level languages (BASIC, C++, Java, Pascal, etc.).

4. The basic building blocks of a computer program:
   - Input statement—to transmit data to the program from an outside source.
   - Processing—manipulating data to obtain the desired results.
   - Output statements—to display the results on the screen, printer, or another device.

5. Basic arithmetic operations (addition, subtraction, multiplication, division, and exponentiation)—the way they are represented in a programming language and the order in which they are performed.

Review Exercises *

1. Fill in the blank: A nineteenth century computing pioneer, _____ , designed a computer called the *Analytical Engine*.

2. Fill in the blank: The first fully-operable electronic computer was named _____ .

---

* The answers to the odd-numbered exercises appear in Appendix B.

3. Fill in the blank: The invention of the _____ helped make smaller computers by replacing the larger, less efficient vacuum tubes in their electronic circuits.

4. Fill in the blank: Until the appearance of the _____ in the mid-1960s, only large mainframe computers were available.

5. List the following personal computers in the order in which they were introduced:
   a. Apple II
   b. Altair 8800
   c. Macintosh
   d. IBM PC

6. The founders of Microsoft Corporation were
   a. John Mauchly and J. Presper Eckert.
   b. Steve Jobs and Stephen Wozniak.
   c. Bill Gates and Paul Allen.
   d. Richard Rodgers and Oscar Hammerstein.

7. List the following types of computers in order of increasing size and power.
   a. Mainframes
   b. Minicomputers
   c. Personal computers
   d. Supercomputers

8. Which operating system is now used by almost all IBM-compatible computers?
   a. DOS
   b. Windows
   c. Linux
   d. Macintosh OS

9. Fill in the blank: The physical components of a computer system are referred to as its _____.

10. Fill in the blank: A personal computer's main circuit board is called its _____.

11. Fill in the blank: One byte of memory consists of _____ bits.

12. Fill in the blank: One kilobyte is equal to _____ bytes.

13. Fill in the blank: Some examples of mass storage devices are floppy disk drives, hard disk drives, and _____ drives.

14. Fill in the blank: Of the various types of printers, the highest quality output is produced by a _____ printer.

15. True or false: Computer components housed outside the system unit are called peripherals.

16. True or false: The contents of a computer's ROM are lost when the power is turned off.

17. True or false: Floppy disk drives access data more slowly than hard disk drives.

18. True or false: A CD-ROM drive can be used for backup purposes.

19. True or false: Computer keyboards contain fewer keys than a standard typewriter.

20. True or false: Inexpensive laser printers are especially good at producing color output.

21. Which of the following components is *not* contained within the system unit of a typical PC?
    a. The motherboard
    b. A floppy disk drive
    c. Random access memory (RAM)
    d. None of the above answers is correct.

22. The computer's central processing unit
    a. Processes program instructions.
    b. Performs arithmetic and logical operations.
    c. Controls the other components of the computer.
    d. Performs all of the above functions.

23. Which of the following is an input device?
    a. A monitor
    b. A keyboard
    c. A CPU
    d. Read-only memory (ROM)

24. Which of the following is an output device?
    a. A monitor
    b. A keyboard
    c. A CPU
    d. Read-only memory (ROM)

25. One advantage of a floppy disk over a hard disk is that
    a. It can be used to transfer data between computers.
    b. It holds more data.

   c. Data can be retrieved from it more quickly.

   d. None of the above answers is correct.

26. Fill in the blank: Software is divided into two broad categories: _____ software and system software.

27. Fill in the blank: The master control program that oversees the computer's operations is called its _____.

28. Which of the following is an example of applications software?

   a. The computer's RAM

   b. The computer's operating system

   c. A programmable calculator

   d. A word processor

29. Which of the following is an example of system software?

   a. The computer's RAM

   b. The computer's operating system

   c. A programmable calculator

   d. A word processor

30. Fill in the blank: High-level programming languages are translated into machine language by means of either an interpreter or a _____.

31. Fill in the blank: The first high-level programming language was known as _____, which stands for "formula translator."

32. Which of the following is *not* a type of programming language?

   a. Natural language

   b. Assembly language

   c. Machine language

   d. High-level language

33. Fill in the blank: The three basic building blocks of a program are input, _____, and output.

34. Fill in the blank: The first of the following two statements

   Write "Enter your weight in pounds:"
   Input Weight

provides a(n) _____ for the input.

35. Suppose $X = 3$ and $Y = 4$. Give the value of each of the following expressions:

   a. $X * Y \wedge 2 / 12$

   b. $((X + Y) * 2 - (Y - X) * 4) \wedge 2$

36. What is the output of the following program?

      Set Num1 = 4
      Set Num1 = Num1 + 1
      Set Num2 = 3
      Set Num2 = Num1 * Num2
      Write Num2

Programming Problems

For each of the following problems, write a program (like the Price Conversion program of Section 1.4) to solve the problem. Include appropriate input prompts and annotate output.

A. Write a program that computes a 15% tip when the price of a meal is input by the user. [*Hint:* The tip is computed by multiplying the price of the meal by 0.15.]

B. Write a program that converts a temperature input in degrees Celsius (C) into degrees Fahrenheit (F) using the formula $F = (9/5)C + 32$.

C. Write a program that computes the batting average for a baseball player when the user inputs the number of hits and at bats for that player. [*Hint:* Batting average is computed by dividing the number of hits by the number of at bats.]

D. Write a program that computes the total interest (I) and final value (FV) of an investment when the user inputs the original amount invested (P), the rate of interest (R, as a decimal), and the number of years the money is invested (T). Use the formulas $I = P*R*T$ and $FV = P + I$.

Programming in the Everyday World

As you know, a computer program is nothing more than a list of instructions. It may be long, complex, and hard to read for the beginner, but it's still just a list at heart. The basic structure is no different from the instructions for assembling a bicycle or building a bookshelf, or the recipe for baking a cake.

Unfortunately, the world is chock full of poorly written and hard to use instructions. The clocks on too many video cassette recorders flash "12:00" for years on end because their owners couldn't understand the manual. "Some assembly required" strikes fear into numerous people because they know how difficult it usually is to follow the directions. Writing a good list takes time, patience, discipline, and organization, and it's something you must learn before diving into the details of programming.

Consider the person writing the cookbook you'd use to bake that cake mentioned above. Initially, you might suspect that the author simply wrote down some recipes and sent them to a publisher. If you ponder this a little more, though, you'd realize that this is a poor way to solve the "write a cookbook" problem. The potential for trouble is just too great, and there is a real risk that the organization of the cookbook would be haphazard. A much better approach would be for the writer to:

1. Spend a good deal of time just thinking about the book and the recipes it will contain. Look at some other cookbooks and talk to some cooks.

2. Write down a plan for the basic organization of the various chapters in the book, then write the recipes within each chapter.

3. Take the cookbook into the kitchen and try all the recipes. After that, have a friend or two do the same thing to get a result independent of any bias.

4. Taste all the food and determine which recipes work and which need to be fixed, either because there are errors or the process is confusing. It's natural and normal to encounter some mistakes, and they have to be corrected— even if it means a lot of rewriting and further testing in the kitchen.

The basic process of thinking about a solution, composing a solution, trying the solution, and checking the results works very well and is a natural way of proceeding. Be warned, though, that you may sometimes be tempted to take shortcuts in carrying out this process. Cutting corners can leave you with a cake that tastes like cardboard, and who wants that?

2

Developing a Program

OVERVIEW   In Sections 1.4 and 1.5, we introduced some basic programming concepts and gave an example of a very simple program. In this chapter, we will discuss at length the process of developing a program. To be more specific, you will learn

1. About the overall program development process of problem analysis, program design, program coding and documenting, and program testing [Section 2.1].

2. About the principles of top-down modular program design [2.2].

3. To construct hierarchy charts and use pseudocode to implement a program design [2.2].

4. How to properly document a program [2.3].

5. How to test a program and about the kinds of errors that can occur during the testing process [2.3].

6. About flowcharts and flowchart symbols [2.4].

7. About the three fundamental control structures and how to represent them using flowcharts [2.4].

8. About other approaches to program design—event-driven programming for a graphical user interface (GUI) and object-oriented programming [2.5].

2.1   *The Program Development Cycle*

In Section 1.4, we gave an example of a very simple computer program —first in a generic form and then supplying the corresponding BASIC code. Once you gain some experience at programming, you will find writing programs of this sort to be relatively easy. However, most real-world programs are considerably more complicated. In this section, we will describe a general systematic approach to programming that works well regardless of the complexity of the given problem.

In developing a computer program to solve a given problem, we follow some time-honored problem-solving principles. We must

- Completely understand the problem.
- Devise a plan to solve it.
- Carry out the plan.
- Review the results (to see how well our plan has worked).

When this approach is applied to program writing, it entails carrying out the following tasks.

1. Analyze the problem. (Make sure you completely understand it.)
2. Design the program. (Devise a plan to solve the problem.)
3. Code the program. (Carry out the plan.)
4. Test the program. (Review the results.)

This process is called the **program development cycle.** The word *cycle* is used here because we often have to return to previous steps and make modifications before the process is complete. For example, in the testing phase, we may find errors in the design process which require us to redesign, recode, and retest the program. In fact, in commercial programs, the cycle is rarely ever complete. These programs are continually evaluated and modified to meet changing demands or increasing competition.

Throughout the remainder of this chapter we will consider the steps of the program development cycle in greater detail and illustrate each of them by considering the following example.

Brewster's Thousands Problem   John Brewster has just inherited some money. He wants to invest it in a certificate of deposit (CD) at his local bank. The bank offers various types of CDs, with varying terms (the length of time the money must be left in the CD), rates of interest, and compounding frequencies (the number of times per year interest is added to the account). John would like to have a computer program to compute, for any given initial investment, the final (maturity) value of the CD.

Analyzing the Problem   First, we must study the given problem until we fully understand it. To a large extent, this step entails acquiring all the facts concerning the problem specifications. In doing so, we ask ourselves

- What results are we trying to obtain; what is the required *output?*

- What data are given; what is the supplied *input?*

- How will we obtain the required output from the given input?

Notice that these questions are directly related to the three main building blocks of most programs—input/process/output—but they are considered in a different order; in analyzing a problem, we begin by considering the desired *output*.

At this stage in the program development process, we choose variables to represent the given input and the required output. We also start thinking about what formulas or logical processes we will have to carry out in order to get the desired results. In this way, our analysis of the problem will lead us naturally into the second step of the cycle, that of designing the program.

For the *Brewster's Thousands* example, the required output is the final value of the certificate of deposit. The data input are the initial amount of the investment (the *principal*), the interest rate, the frequency of compounding (a given number of times per year), and the term of the investment. To find a relationship among these quantities, we consult an algebra or finance textbook. The appropriate relation is called the *compound interest formula*, which is usually written as

The compound interest formula

$$FV = P(1 + r/n)^{nt}$$

where:

- P and FV are the initial and final amounts

- r is the annual rate of interest expressed as a decimal (for example, a 5% interest rate would appear in the formula as .05)

- n is the number of times per year that compounding takes place

- t is the number of years the money is invested (investment term)

In our program we will use the following variable names, which are more descriptive than those given in the formula above.

- Principal—the amount invested (P in the formula)

- Rate—the rate of interest as a decimal (r in the formula)

- Frequency—the number of times per year that compounding takes place (n in the formula)

- Term—the investment term in years (t in the formula)

- FinalValue—the value of the investment at the end of the term (FV in the formula)

In terms of these variable names, the compound interest formula becomes:

FinalValue = Principal * (1 + Rate / Frequency) ^ (Frequency * Term)

Here, FinalValue is an output variable; all the other variables could be taken as input variables. However, it is more natural to take the *percentage* rate of interest (for example, 10%) as input, and then compute the decimal rate (in this case, 0.10) from it using the formula:

Rate = PercentageRate / 100

We will now briefly describe the other steps of the program development process. A more detailed description of each step, and how it relates to the *Brewster's Thousands* problem, will be presented in later sections of this chapter.

Designing the Program   In this phase of the program development cycle, we create an outline of our program; we construct a framework on which to build the code. The program design consists of a step-by-step procedure—an **algorithm**—for solving the original problem. (In fact, the resulting computer program may be considered a very detailed description of this algorithm.) Algorithms abound in programming, mathematics, and the sciences, and are common in everyday life as well. For example, you are making use of an algorithm when you follow a recipe to bake a cake or go through the process of using a bank's ATM. We will discuss program design in detail in Section 2.2.

Coding the Program   Once you have designed a suitable program to solve a given problem, you must write the **program code;** that is, you must write instructions in a particular programming language (such as BASIC, Pascal, C++, or Java) that puts the design into usable form. As we discussed in Section 1.3, coding the program entails using the appropriate software to enter the program *statements* (instructions) into the computer's memory (and, ordinarily, save them to disk). Since this text does not make use of a specific programming language, our comments about coding programs will usually be general in nature. We will, however, have more to say about this topic in Section 2.3.

Testing the Program   Testing the program ensures that it is free of errors and that it does indeed solve the given problem. Testing actually takes place throughout the program development cycle; at each step you should check your work for mistakes. For example, in the design phase, you should imagine that *you* are the computer and run through the algorithm using simple input data to see if you get the expected results. (This is sometimes referred to as *desk-checking* or *walking through* a program.) The ultimate test, however, is to **run** the program—have the computer, with the aid of the programming language software, execute its statements—to see if it works correctly. We will discuss testing a program again in Section 2.3.

Self-Test 2.1

1. Name the four fundamental phases of the program development cycle.

2. Briefly describe, in your own words, what takes place during each phase.

3. Determine whether each of the following statements is true or false.

   a. If you completely understand a given problem, you should skip the design phase of the program development cycle.
   b. Program design provides an outline for the program code.
   c. Testing a program is only necessary for very complex programs.

4. Suppose you want to write a program that will input a temperature in degrees Celsius and output the equivalent degrees Fahrenheit. Analyze this problem: give the input and output variables, as well as the formula that will produce the required output from the given input. [*Hint:* The necessary formula is: F = 9 * C / 5 + 32]

2.2   *Program Design*

The design phase of the program development cycle (see Section 2.1) is arguably the most important aspect of developing a program, especially in the case of complex problems. A good, detailed design makes it much easier to write good, usable program code. Rushing into coding too quickly would be like trying to build a house without a complete set of plans; it may result in a lot of hard work being torn out and redone.

Modular Programming

A good way to begin the job of designing a program to solve a particular problem is to identify the major tasks that the program must accomplish. In designing the program, each of these tasks becomes a **program module.** Then, if need be, we can break each of these fundamental, high-level tasks into subtasks. The latter are called *submodules* of the original, or *parent*, module. Some of these submodules might be divided into submodules of their own, and this division process can be continued as long as seems necessary to identify the tasks needed to solve the given problem. This process of breaking down a problem into simpler and simpler subproblems is called **top-down design;** identifying the tasks and various subtasks involved in the program design is called **modular programming.**

To illustrate the modular approach, let us return to the *Brewster's Thousands* problem of Section 2.1. For the sake of convenience, we restate it here.

The *Brewster's Thousands* Problem

John Brewster has just inherited some money. He wants to invest the money (the *principal*) in a certificate of deposit (CD) at his bank. The bank offers various types of CDs, with varying *terms* (the length of time the money must be left in the CD), rates of interest, and *compounding frequencies* (the number of times per year interest is added to the account). John would like a program to compute, for any given initial investment, the final (maturity) value of the CD.

There are three fundamental tasks we must perform to solve this problem*:

1. Input Data—input the variables Principal, PercentageRate, Term, and Frequency

---

*The program variables used here are described in Section 2.1 in the subsection entitled "Analyzing the Problem."

2. Perform Calculations—compute the rate of interest

   Set Rate = PercentageRate / 100

   and the final value of the investment

   Set FinalValue = Principal *
   (1 + Rate / Frequency) ^ (Frequency * Term)

3. Output Results—Display the FinalValue of the investment

We could, if we want, further divide the second task into two subtasks, computing the Rate in one and the FinalValue in the other. This raises the question: How do we know when to stop breaking the submodules into more submodules? This leads to the more basic question: What makes a module a module? A module has these characteristics:

Characteristics of a program module

- A module performs a single task. For example, an *input module* prompts for, and then inputs data from the user.

- A module is self-contained and independent of other modules.

- A module is relatively short; ideally, it should not exceed one page in length. Brevity enhances readability because it allows one to see all the module's statements at once.

Calling a Module In a complex program, there might be dozens of program modules and submodules. To execute a particular submodule, we place a statement in the parent module that **calls** the submodule into action; that is, which causes the first statement of the latter to be executed. (We sometimes describe this action by saying that the call "transfers program control" to the beginning of the submodule.) Then, when the submodule has completed its task, execution returns to the calling (parent) module—to the statement *after* the one that caused the transfer of control. Here's a picture of the situation:

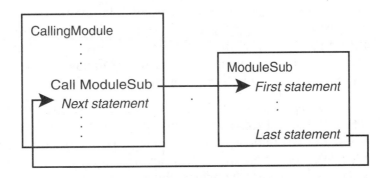

Every program has one special module, called its **main module,** which is where program execution begins. The main module is the only program module that is not a submodule of another; it is the parent module of the program's highest-level modules, those that perform the most fundamental of tasks. Consequently, these modules are called into action by the main module.

Programming Pointer   When the program is coded, the main module becomes the *main program*, and all other modules are known as, depending upon the programming language, *subprograms, procedures, subroutines,* and/or *functions.*

Benefits of Modular Programming   Our discussion so far has concentrated on what a program module is and how modules interact. Before we proceed to the next topic, let us point out why the modular approach to program design is important. It has the following benefits:

1. Program readability is improved. This, in turn, reduces the time needed to locate errors in a program or make revisions to it.

2. Programmer productivity is increased because it is easier to design, code, and test the program one module at a time than all at once.

3. Different program modules can be designed and/or coded by different programmers, an essential feature in large, complex programs.

4. In some cases, a single module can be used in more than one place in the program. This reduces the amount of code in that program.

5. Modules performing common programming tasks (such as sorting data in order) can be used in more than one program. Creating a *library* of such modules reduces design, coding, and testing time.

Hierarchy Charts

As you know, a program may contain a large number of modules. We can keep track of a program's modules and the relationships among them in a visual way through the use of a **hierarchy chart.** A hierarchy chart describes these relationships in the same way that an organization chart determines who's responsible to whom in a business firm.

Figure 1 depicts a typical hierarchy chart. Notice that the main module sits at the top of this chart (think of it as the "chairman of the code"). Recall that the main module is where program execution begins. Below the main module are the highest-level submodules (labeled A, B, and C, in Figure 1), those that perform the most fundamental of program tasks.

Finally, the modules B1 and B2 are submodules of the parent module B. In other words, a line drawn down from one module to another indicates that the former is the parent; it calls the latter into action. A hierarchy chart for the Brewster's Thousands program is shown in Figure 2.

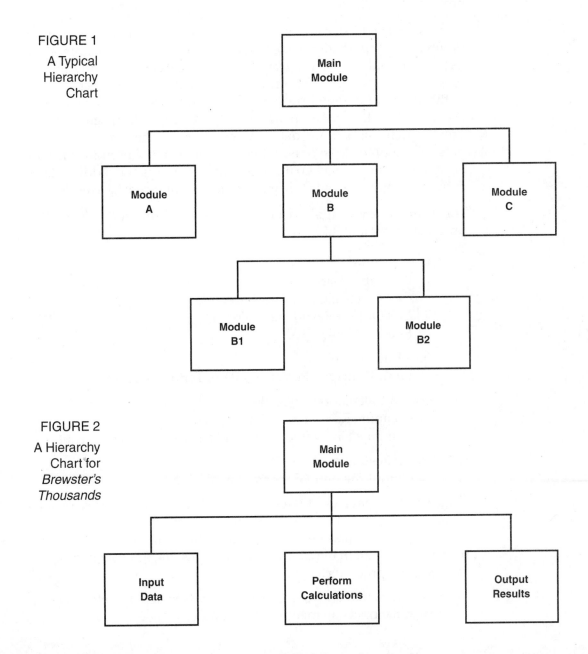

FIGURE 1

A Typical Hierarchy Chart

FIGURE 2

A Hierarchy Chart for *Brewster's Thousands*

Pseudocode

Once we have identified the various tasks our program needs to accomplish and have constructed a hierarchy chart to represent the relationships among them, we must fill in the details of the program design—for each module, we must provide specific instructions to perform that task. We supply this detail using pseudocode.

Recall that **pseudocode** (which was introduced in Section 1.4 and is pronounced "sue-dough-code") uses short, English-like phrases to describe the outline of a program. It is not actual code from any specific programming language, but sometimes strongly resembles actual code. In the spirit of top-down program design, we often start with a rough pseudocode outline for each module and then refine the pseudocode to provide more and more detail. Depending on the complexity of a program module, little or no refinement of its initial pseudocode may be necessary, or we may go through quite a few versions, adding detail each time until it becomes clear how the resulting code should look.

For example, the initial pseudocode for the Brewster's Thousands program might look like this:

        Main module
            Call Input Data module
            Call Perform Calculations module
            Call Output Results module
            End Program

        Input Data module
            Input Principal, PercentageRate, Term, Frequency

        Perform Calculations module
            Compute Rate from PercentageRate
            Compute FinalValue from Principal, Rate, Term, and Frequency

        Output Results module
            Output the input data and FinalValue

Notice that we have used the word "Call," followed by the name of a module, to call that module into action. Recall that this kind of statement causes the named module to be executed, after which control returns to the next statement in the calling module. Thus, the flow of execution in this program proceeds as follows:

1. The statement *Call Input Data module* is executed, transferring control to the first statement in that module.

2. All statements in the Input Data module are executed and then control transfers to the statement *Call Perform Calculations module* in the Main Module, which transfers control to the first statement in the Perform Calculations module.

3. After the last statement in Perform Calculations is executed, control transfers to the statement *Call Output Results module* in the Main Module, which transfers control to the first statement in the Output Results module.

4. After the last statement in Output Results is executed, control transfers to the *End Program* statement in the main Module and execution terminates.

We now refine (add detail to) each module, which gives us this final version of the pseudocode:

Main module
    Display program title and brief description of the program
    Call Input Data module
    Call Perform Calculations module
    Call Output Results module
    End Program

Input Data module
    Prompt for Principal, PercentageRate, Term, Frequency
    Input Principal, PercentageRate, Term, Frequency

Perform Calculations module
    Set Rate = PercentageRate / 100
    Set FinalValue = Principal *
        (1 + Rate / Frequency) ^ (Frequency * Term)

Output Results module
    Write Principal, PercentageRate, Term, Frequency
    Write FinalValue

Provide a Welcome Message at the Beginning of Your Program   The first few lines, or perhaps the first screen, the user sees when running your program should provide some general information about the program. This includes the title of the program and perhaps a brief description of it. Commercial programs—those sold for profit—would also display a copyright notice at this point. The welcome message can be placed in the main module or in a module of its own, called from the main module.

Let us recall (from Sections 1.4 and 1.5) a few things concerning this pseudocode:

- The term *prompt* means to display a message on the screen that tells the user (the person running the program) what kind of data to input.

- When an Input statement is executed, program execution pauses to allow the user to enter data (in this case, numbers) from the keyboard, and this data is assigned to the listed variables.

- When a Write statement is executed, the values of the listed variables are displayed on the screen (and then the cursor is moved to the beginning of the next line).

Echo-print the Input Variables Notice that, in the Output Results module, we display not only the value of the output variable FinalValue, but also the values of all input variables. This is called *echo-printing* the input, and is a good programming practice because it reminds the user what data have been entered and allows him or her to check it for mistakes.

Programming Pointer When code is written for the OutputResults module, it is important to display text that clarifies the meaning of the numbers being output. For example, a reasonable way to display the output is as follows (expressions like xxxx indicate the numbers that were input or calculated):

```
Compound Interest Calculation

Investment principal (in dollars):  xxxx.xx
Rate of interest (in percent):  xx.x
Term of investment (in years):  xx
Number of times per year compounded:  xx

Value of investment at maturity:  xxxx.xx
```

Self-Test 2.2

1. List the characteristics of a program module.

2. What are three benefits of modular program design?

3. Write a sequence of Write statements (as in Section 1.5) that will display the output of the Brewster's Thousands program as shown in the Programming Pointer above. [*Hint:* Use the statement

    Write

(just the word *Write,* nothing else) to skip a line in the output.]

4. Given the statements

Call Cancer Cure module
Write "My job here is done!"

what statement is executed immediately after

a. The Call statement?
b. The last statement in the Cancer Cure module?

5. Suppose the Perform Calculations module in the Brewster's Thousands program is broken into two submodules, Compute Rate and Compute Final Value. Construct the corresponding hierarchy chart.

2.3 Coding, Documenting, and Testing a Program

In this section, we will discuss the last two steps of the program development cycle (see Section 2.1)—coding the program and testing the program. We will also introduce the notion of **documenting** a program—providing explanatory material about the program for other programmers and/or users. Detailed program documentation is essential for commercial programs, but even relatively simple programs can benefit by having some documentation.

Coding and Documenting a Program

Once a suitable program design has been created to solve a given problem (see Section 2.2), it is time to **code** the program—translate the pseudocode of the design into the corresponding statements in a particular programming language. The result is a program that can be run (executed) on your computer. Of course, in order to carry out this phase of the program development cycle, you must be familiar with the syntax and structure of a programming language such as BASIC, Pascal, C++, or Java, and also have access (on your computer or network) to the software that allows you to work with this language. Although this is obviously a crucial step in developing a program, this text presents programming concepts in a language-free environment, and we will normally have little to say about the translation of the design into actual code.

However, one aspect of the coding process is of importance regardless of the language used—annotating (explaining the purpose of) portions of code within the program itself. This kind of annotation is known as *internal documentation,* and is made up of *comments.* A **comment** is text inserted into the program for explanatory purposes, but ignored by the computer when the program is run. Comments are not seen by the program's user; they are intended solely for those reading the code itself.

Programming Pointer
In processing the program statements, how does the computer know that comments are to be ignored? The answer is simple: A certain symbol or combination of symbols (which depends on the programming language you are using) indicates to the computer that what follows, or what lies between them, is not to be processed. For example:

- In BASIC, an apostrophe (') anywhere on a line, or the letters REM at the beginning of a line, indicates that all text following these symbols is to be ignored by the computer.

- In Pascal, all text contained between the symbols (* and *), or between the symbols { and }, is to be ignored.

- In C++, two consecutive forward slashes (//) anywhere on a line indicate that all text following these symbols is to be ignored; moreover, all text contained between the symbols /* and */ is ignored, as well.

For example, a BASIC program to solve the Brewster's Thousands problem of Section 2.1 might begin as follows:

```
'   Compound Interest Calculations
'   Programmer: S. Venit - California State University
'   Version 1.0 -- January 1, 2001

'   This program uses the compound interest formula to
'   compute the maturity value of a given investment.

'   Variables used:
'      FinalValue - Value of investment at maturity
'      Frequency  - Number of times per year
'                   compounding takes place
```

... and so on.

Comments have two fundamental purposes:

1. *Header comments,* which appear at the beginning of a program or program module, provide general information about that program or module. The comments in the preceding Programming Pointer are an example of typical program header comments.

2. *Step comments* appear throughout the program to explain the purpose of specific portions of code. For example, if your program includes code that finds the average of the numbers input, a step comment might precede this code that reads: "Find the average of numbers input."

Include Comments in Your Program Since comments are not processed by the computer and are not seen by the user of the program, they in no way affect the way the program runs. Good comments do, however, make it easier for another programmer to understand your code. Nevertheless, do not "over comment"—in particular, don't explain every line of code. A good rule of thumb is to write enough step comments so that *you* will be able to easily read your program a year after you have written it.

Programming Pointer

Every *commercial* program—one sold for profit—includes another form of documentation to help customers learn to use the software. This kind of documentation may be supplied in written form, as a user's guide, or as on-screen help that is accessed while running the application (or as a combination of the two). In either case, this kind of explanatory material is known as *external documentation*.

Testing a Program

As we mentioned in Section 2.1, it is necessary to **test** a program (or program-to-be) at every phase of the program development cycle to ensure that it is free of errors. The final, and most important, testing takes place when the code has been completed—we run the program with various sets of input data (*test data*) until we are convinced that our program is working properly.

For example, once the Brewster's Thousands program of Sections 2.1 and 2.2 has been coded, we use the appropriate software to run the program, perhaps entering the following input data:

    Principal = 1000
    PercentageRate = 12
    Frequency = 4
    Term = 6

We would then compare the output with the result obtained by using, say, a business calculator. If the two figures agree, we would try a few more sets of input data and again check our results. Although program testing of this sort does not *guarantee* that a program is error-free, it does give us confidence that this is indeed the case.

Programming Pointer

Commercial programs are often so complex that the testing phase lasts for several months or more. For example, when Microsoft develops a new version of its Windows operating system, testing the software is a major project in itself that usually takes more than a year to complete. First, the code is tested, module by module, "in-house" by Microsoft employees. Then, the completed software is put through its paces, running on a wide range of different computers using different peripherals, both in-house and at a limited number of selected non-Microsoft sites. This phase of the process is known as *alpha testing*. Once the software is reasonably reliable, it is sent to thousands of *beta test* sites. In both the alpha and beta testing, users report problems to Microsoft and necessary changes are made to the code. (During alpha and early beta testing, features are added and/or revised as well.) Finally, when problem reports dwindle to what Microsoft considers an acceptable level, the code is finalized and the software is put into production.

Types of Errors If a test run turns up problems with the program, we must **debug** it—eliminate the errors. This may be relatively easy or very difficult, depending on the type of error and the debugging skill of the programmer. The two fundamental types of errors that can arise in coding a program are syntax errors and logic errors.

A **syntax error** is a violation of the programming language's rules for creating valid statements. It can be caused, for example, by misspelling a keyword or by omitting a required punctuation mark. Syntax errors are normally detected by the language software either when you type the invalid statement or when the program is translated by the computer into machine language (see Section 1.3). When the software detects a syntax error, it normally issues a message and highlights the offending statement. For these reasons, syntax errors are the easiest to find and correct.

A **logic error** results from failing to use the proper combination of statements to accomplish a certain task. It may occur due to faulty analysis, faulty design, or failure to code the program properly. Here are a few kinds of logic errors:

- Using an incorrect formula to produce a desired result.

- Using an incorrect sequence of statements to carry out an algorithm.

- Failing to allow for input data that may lead to an "illegal" operation (such as division by zero) when the program is run.

Unlike syntax errors, logic errors are not detected by the programming language software. They can be found only by a careful reading of the program specifications and design, or by running the program with test data. In the latter case, a logic error usually causes the program to give incorrect results or to fail to proceed beyond a certain point (the program may *crash* or *hang*). Extensive testing is the best way to ensure that a program's logic is sound.

Self-Test 2.3

1. Briefly describe the two basic types of comments (internal documentation).

2. What is meant by external documentation for a program?

3. Fill in the blank: After a program is coded, it must be _____.

4. Briefly describe the difference between syntax errors and logic errors.

2.4   Structured Programming

Structured programming is a method for designing and coding programs in a systematic, organized manner. In this chapter, we have already discussed some structured programming principles: following the steps of the program development cycle, designing a program in a top-down, modular fashion, and using comments to document a program. In this section, we will introduce a couple more aspects of structured programming: designing each module as a sequence of control structures and using good programming style. We begin by discussing the use of flowcharts in program design.

Flowcharts

In Section 2.2, we introduced two devices to aid in the design of a program: hierarchy charts and pseudocode. Each of these techniques has its place in program design—hierarchy charts identify the program modules and show the relationships among them; pseudocode fills in the details of how the modules are to be coded.

Another common program design tool is the flowchart. A **flowchart** is a diagram that uses special symbols (see Figure 3) to display pictorially the flow of execution within a program or program module. For example, a flowchart for the Brewster's Thousands problem of Section 2.1 is shown in Figure 4; to read it (or any flowchart), start at the top and follow the arrows.

FIGURE 3

Flowchart Symbols

Symbol	Name	Description
(rounded rectangle)	**Terminator**	Represents the start or end of a program or module
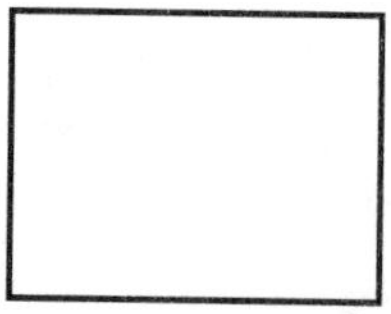 (rectangle)	**Process**	Represents any kind of processing function; for example, a computation
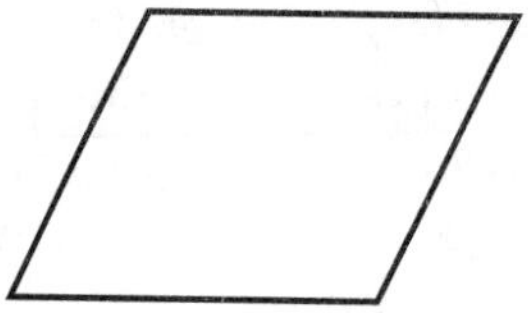 (parallelogram)	**Input/output**	Represents an input or output operation
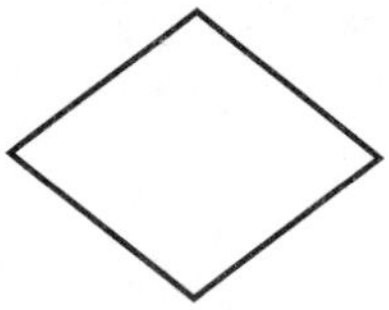 (diamond)	**Decision**	Represents a program branch point
 (circle)	**Connector**	Indicates an entry to, or exit from, a program segment

FIGURE 4

The Flowchart
for Brewster's
Thousands

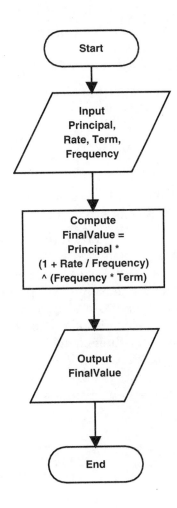

Control Structures

To help create a well-structured program design, each module should consist of a series of properly organized groups of statements known as **control structures,** which are of three basic types:

1. The sequential structure

2. The loop (or repetition) structure

3. The decision (or selection) structure

A **sequential structure** consists of a sequence of consecutive statements, executed in the order in which they appear. In other words, none of the statements in this kind of structure causes a **branch**—a jump in the logical flow of execution—to another part of the program module. The general form of a sequential structure is:

> Statement
> Statement
> .
> .
> .
> Statement

Note that all the program modules you've seen so far consist of a single sequential structure.

Unlike sequential structures, loop and decision structures contain *branch points*—statements that cause a branch to take place. A **loop structure** (also known as a **repetition structure**) contains a branch *back* to a previous statement in the program module. This results in a block of statements that can be executed many times; it will be repeated as long as a given condition within the loop structure (for example, "Is X > 0?") causes the branch to be taken. A flowchart of a typical loop structure is shown in Figure 5. Notice that the diamond-shaped "decision" symbol is used to indicate a branch point. If the condition within the diamond is true, follow the "Yes" arrow; if not, follow the "No" arrow.

FIGURE 5

A Loop
Structure

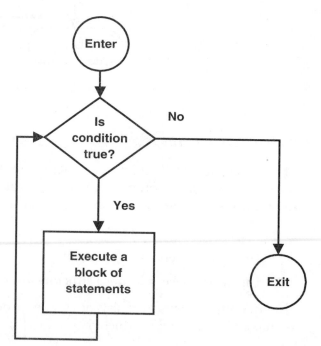

In a **decision structure** (also known as a **selection structure**), there is a branch *forward* at some point, causing a portion of the program to be skipped. Thus, depending upon a given condition at the branch point, a certain block of statements will be executed while another is skipped. The flowchart for a typical decision structure is shown in Figure 6.

FIGURE 6

A Decision
Structure

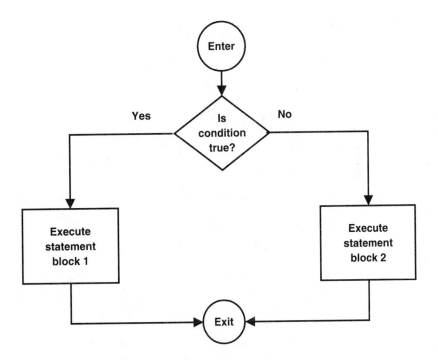

Programming Style

Most of the structured programming principles we've discussed so far have dealt with the design of a program. A well-structured design leads, in a natural way, to well-structured, easy-to-read code. In fact, one of the goals of structured programming is to create a program that is easy for programmers to read (and understand) and for users to run. The elements of a program that affect its readability and ease of use are grouped together under the general heading of **programming style.** Some of the guidelines for developing a good programming style have already been discussed, and we will review them in the form of *Style Pointers* in the remainder of this section. Additional Style Pointers will appear, whenever appropriate, throughout the text.

Write Modular Programs   Design a program as a collection of modules. In doing so, you will reap the benefits of modular programming described in Section 2.2. The more complex the program, the greater the benefit.

Use Descriptive Variable Names   To improve program readability, variable names should remind the reader (of the code) of what they represent. For example, FinalValue is a better name than F or Amount. (See Section 1.4.)

Provide a Welcome Message for the User   The first few lines, or the first screen, displayed by your program should contain a *welcome message,* which typically contains the program title, programmer's name and affiliation, date, and possibly a brief description of the program.

Use a Prompt before an Input   Before requesting input data from the user, display a message on the screen that states the type of input desired. If you don't issue a prompt, in most programming languages, the user will not even be aware of the fact that execution has paused for input. (See Section 1.4.)

Identify Program Output   The output produced by your program should stand on its own; it should make sense to someone who has no knowledge whatsoever of the code that produced it. In particular, never output numbers without an explanation of what they represent. (See Section 1.5.)

Document Your Programs   Use comments within your program—internal documentation—to provide general information about a program or program module (header comments) or to explain the purpose of blocks of code (step comments). Moreover, if your program is to be run by others, provide external documentation in the form of on-screen help or a user's guide to provide information about the program. (See Section 2.3.)

Self-Test 2.4

1. List three principles of structured programming.

2. Draw and label the following flowchart symbols.
   a. Process
   b. Decision
   c. Input/output

3. What are the three basic control structures?

4. In one sentence, explain why using good programming style is important.

5. List four principles of good programming style.

2.5   *An Introduction to GUIs and OOP*

In the first four sections of this chapter, we have concentrated on the notion of structured programming and the top-down, modular approach to program design. In recent years, two other program design models, event-driven programming and object-oriented programming, have become popular and are now used extensively. These approaches to programming look at the design process from other viewpoints yet still retain the basic principles of structured programming—the use of program modules, fundamental control structures, good programming style, and rigorous program testing.

GUIs and Event-driven Programming

The **graphical user interface** (or **GUI**), popularized by the Apple Macintosh computer in the mid-1980s (see Section 1.1), is now the standard for all personal computers and other, more powerful machines. The basic purpose of a GUI is to make the computer and software easier to learn and use. It achieves this goal, in part, by allowing the user to make choices and initiate actions with the help of mouse-activated icons, menus, and dialog boxes.

Writing a program for a graphical user interface requires a different way of approaching the programming process. The appearance of the program's output becomes the first concern. The program is designed as a sequence of inter-related *screens* (windows and dialog boxes), each having a certain specific function. The actions of the user, such as pressing keys on the keyboard or positioning and clicking the mouse, determine the flow of program execution. These actions are referred to as *events*, and this type of programming as **event-driven programming.**

As an example, let's take a look at the Paint application, which is packaged as part of the Microsoft Windows operating system. When you start Paint (typically, by clicking the mouse on a menu item on the main Windows screen), a window like the one in Figure 7 (on the next page) is displayed.

This screen provides the user with a large number of options. You can

- Display a menu by clicking the mouse on one of the names on the menu bar.

- Select a tool from the toolbox by clicking on its icon.

Title bar —
Menu bar —

Toolbox —

Color palette —

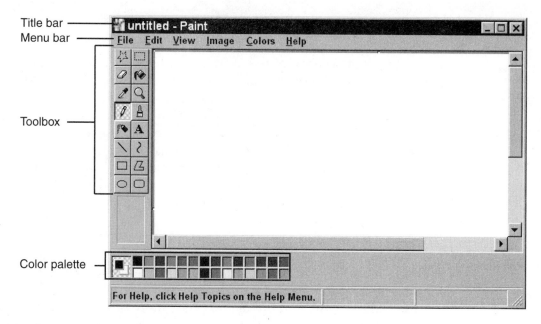

FIGURE 7   Windows Paint

- Select a drawing color by clicking on one in the color palette.
- Draw a shape by "dragging" the mouse in the main screen area.

Regardless of the action you take (regardless of the *event* that occurs), the program must recognize that it has taken place and respond in the proper way; it must transfer execution to the appropriate module of code. For example, suppose you click on the word File on the menu bar. The program responds by displaying the File menu, a list of basic options. If you then click on the menu item labeled Print, the program will display a new screen—the dialog box shown in Figure 8.

Dialog box
basics

A dialog box, like the one in Figure 8, provides options for the user in the form of *controls*—command buttons, options buttons, text boxes, and so on. Each control has its own attributes (size, shape, etc.) and events to which it responds (mouse click, key press, etc.). For example:

- Clicking on the triangle on the right-end of the *drop-down list* displays a list of names. To select one of them, the user clicks on that name.
- Clicking inside a *check box* turns on that option; clicking in the check box again turns it off.
- Clicking on an *option button* (also known as a *radio button*) turns on

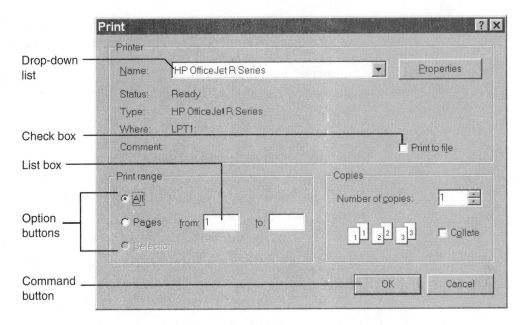

Drop-down list

Check box

List box

Option buttons

Command button

FIGURE 8   A Typical Dialog Box

that option and also turns off the other options in that group. For example, the "bullet" inside the *All* option button in Figure 8 indicates that all pages should be printed; it is not the case that certain specified Pages or a Selection of pages are to be printed.

- To use a *text box*, you type a number, name, or other text inside it.

- Clicking on a *command button* causes an action to take place. The dialog box will be removed from the screen and (depending on the function of the command button) something else will happen.

Depending on the event (say, a mouse click in a certain location) that takes place in a dialog box, the program must respond appropriately. For example, in Figure 8, if the user clicks on the OK command button, the program must recognize this action and transfer the flow of execution to a program module that in turn sends a message to the printer to print the drawing.

Programming Pointer   Although event-driven GUI programming can be done from "scratch," some programming languages (such as Visual Basic and Visual C++) are designed specifically for this purpose and make the job much easier. For example, these kinds of languages provide tools that allow you to quickly place controls in a dialog box that automatically recognize when an event has taken place. However, the programmer still has to design, write, and test the code that determines what happens when an event occurs. Given the enormous array of options available in a typical event-driven program, this is not an easy task.

Designing a
GUI
program

Designing an event-driven program for a GUI involves the following general steps:

1. Design the appearance of the program's screens. This entails determining

   - The screens that are needed to handle the program's tasks and options.

   - The content (menus, controls, text, and other objects) of each screen.

   - The relationships among the various screens.

2. Assign properties to the objects on each screen. These properties include

   - The name of the object (so that it can be referred to in the code).

   - The position and size of the object.

   - Text displayed along with the object.

   - The actions that can be taken to activate the object.

3. Design and code modules (procedures) that are activated when an event (such as a mouse click) associated with an object takes place.

Object-oriented Programming

Top-down modular programming centers on the basic tasks that need to be performed to solve a given problem. **Object-oriented programming** (or **OOP**), on the other hand, focuses on the "objects" needed to solve the problem. An **object** is a structure composed of (or *encapsulating*) two parts—data associated with the object and procedures that operate on the object. (Remember that a procedure is the generic name for the code corresponding to a program module.) In the language of object-oriented programming, the data portion of an object is known as its *attributes;* the procedures are its *methods.*

Examples of
objects

Just about anything qualifies as an object. For example, a microwave oven is an object. Its attributes include its dimensions, its capacity, and its power output. Its methods are the operations you can perform on it; you can set its timer, start it, stop it, and so on. One other facet of a microwave oven is common to all objects—you can use it without understanding its inner workings. Here are some examples of programming-related objects:

- The windows, dialog boxes, and individual controls (command buttons, etc.) in a GUI program are objects. The attributes of, say, a dialog box include its title, size, and position on the screen. Its methods allow you to open (display) it, close it (remove it from the screen), change its position, and so on. A major part of GUI programming involves defining the attributes and methods of the many objects used in these kinds of programs.

- The automobiles in a motor vehicle database are objects. Their attributes include their make, model, year, color, and license plate number. Methods for this example would include procedures used to display, change, add, or delete data concerning a vehicle.

- The students listed in a course grading program are objects. Their attributes might be their names, test scores, and final grades for the course. Methods might include procedures to compute average test scores and assign grades for each student.

Object-oriented program design
  A programmer using the top-down, modular approach to program design begins by determining fundamental tasks. An object-oriented programmer, on the other hand, determines the fundamental objects associated with a problem. To be more specific, the basic steps at the heart of designing an object-oriented program are to:

1. Identify the objects to be used in the program.
2. Determine the objects' attributes.
3. Define the objects' methods.
4. Determine the relationships among the program's objects. For example, an object may make use of the attributes and/or methods of another object, in which case we say that the former has *access* to these data and procedures. As another example, one object may be a special case of another (say, a rectangle object relative to a polygon object), in which case the former could *inherit* properties of the latter.

To illustrate these steps, suppose that an instructor wants to create a program which calculates course grades for her classes.

1. Two fundamental types of objects are needed in this problem:
   - The classes that the instructor teaches.
   - The students who make up each class.

2. The attributes (data)

- For the student object are student name, test scores, average test score, and course grade. The first two would be input to the program; the last two are calculated from the input data.

- For the class object are its course name and number, the number of students in the class, and perhaps the grade distribution (number of As, Bs, etc.) for the class. The last attribute is calculated data.

3. The methods

- For the student object are procedures to compute average test score and, given this average, the course grade.

- For the class object might include procedures to compute a class average and to rank the students in terms of their test average.

4. The class object makes use of some of the attributes of the student object; it needs to be granted *access* to this data. In fact, the student object can be considered an attribute of the class object, in which case we can say that the class object *owns* the student object.

In writing the program, the instructor would use as many *instances* of the class object as she had classes to teach and as many instances of the student object as she had students in each class.

Everyone Needs Structured Programming   Keep in mind that whether you use a top-down, event-driven, or object-oriented approach to program design, you will need to learn the principles of structured programming. Each of these programming models needs systematic design, program modules, control structures, clear documentation, good programming style, and adequate program testing. Learning the principles and techniques stressed in this text will prepare you for programming using any approach and any language.

Self-Test 2.5

1. What do the letters GUI stand for?

2. Briefly describe what is meant by an event-driven program.

3. Name three types of controls found in dialog boxes and describe the purpose of each.

4. What entities form the two parts of an OOP object?

5. For an object found in everyday life but not mentioned in this text, give its attributes and methods.

Chapter Review and Exercises

Key Terms

Program development cycle	Algorithm
Program code	Designing a program
Top-down program design	Modular programming
Calling a module	Main module
Hierarchy chart	Pseudocode
Documentation	Coding a program
Comments	Testing a program
Syntax error	Logic error
Structured programming	Flowchart
Control structure	Sequential structure
Loop (repetition) structure	Decision (selection) structure
Graphical user interface (GUI)	Event-driven programming
Object-oriented programming (OOP)	Object

Chapter Summary

In this chapter, we have discussed the following topics:

1. The program development cycle:
   - Analyze the problem
   - Design the program
   - Code the program
   - Test the program

2. The top-down, modular programming approach to program design:
   - Break a program into modules and submodules that perform the basic tasks that the program must carry out.
   - Provide a pictorial representation of the modules using hierarchy charts.
   - Use pseudocode to fill in the details of each module and, if necessary, repeatedly refine the pseudocode.

3. Other aspects of modular programming:

- Calling a module into action—executing its statements and returning to the calling module

- The characteristics of a module: a module is self-contained, compact, and performs a single task

- The benefits of modular programming: program readability is improved and programmer productivity is increased

4. Documenting a program:

- Internal documentation (comments) is for the benefit of someone reading the program code. Header comments appear at the beginning of a program or program module and provide general information about it; step comments appear throughout the program to explain (annotate) portions of code.

- External documentation is for the benefit of someone running the program; it consists of on-screen help or a printed user guide.

5. Testing a program—running the program with various sets of input data (test data) to check it for errors:

- Syntax errors are caused by violations of the programming language's rules for statement structure.

- Logic errors are caused by combinations of statements that fail to carry out the desired task.

6. Structured programming principles:

- Solve a problem by following the steps of the program development cycle.

- Design the program in a modular fashion.

- Design and code each module as a series of control structures.

- Use good programming style—code the program in a way that enhances readability and ease of use. This includes the appropriate use of internal and, if necessary, external documentation.

- Test the program in a systematic way to ensure that it is free of errors.

7. Flowcharts and control structures:
   - Some flowchart symbols—terminator, process, input/output, decision, and connector (see Figure 3)
   - Using flowcharts to describe the three basic control structures: sequence, loop (repetition), and decision (selection)

8. The basics of programming for a graphical user interface (GUI):
   - The idea of event-driven programming—the user's actions (events) drive the flow of execution.
   - Typical objects used in programming for a GUI: windows, menus, dialog boxes, and controls (such as command buttons and text boxes).
   - The basic steps in event-driven GUI program design: design the appearance of the program's screens, determine the properties of the windows and controls, and write the procedures corresponding to each event.

9. The basic idea of object-oriented programming (OOP):
   - Objects are structures made up of data (attributes) and procedures (methods).
   - OOP program design focuses on the objects needed for a program, their attributes and methods, and the relationships among the objects.

Review Exercises

1. Fill in the blank: The process of solving a problem by analyzing it, designing an appropriate program, coding the design, and testing the code is known as the _____.

2. Fill in the blank: In analyzing a problem, we usually start by identifying the results we want the program to produce; that is, the program's _____.

3. True or false: Before we code a program, we should design it.

4. True or false: Top-down design refers to breaking a problem into simpler and simpler pieces.

5. Which of the following is *not* a characteristic of a program module?
   a. It performs a single task.
   b. It contains several submodules.
   c. It is self-contained.
   d. It is relatively small in size.

6. Which of the following is *not* a benefit of modular programming?

    a. It increases program readability.

    b. It increases programmer productivity.

    c. It allows for the creation of a "library" of common programming tasks.

    d. It allows one programmer to do the job of many in the same amount of time.

7. Fill in the blank: The _____ is the generic name for the module in which program execution begins.

8. Fill in the blank: To _____ a module (or subprogram) into action means to cause execution to transfer to that module.

9. Fill in the blank: A _____ is a pictorial representation of a program's modules and the relationships among them.

10. Fill in the blank: _____ makes use of short, English-like phrases to describe the design of a program.

11. Suppose the main module of a program contains the statements

        Call ModuleA
        Call ModuleB
        Call ModuleC

    Then, the statement that is executed *after* Call ModuleB is:

    a. Call ModuleA

    b. Call ModuleC

    c. The first statement in ModuleB.

    d. None of the above is correct.

12. Suppose the main module of a program contains the statements

        Call ModuleA
        Call ModuleB
        Call ModuleC

    Then, the statement that is executed after all statements in ModuleB have been carried out is:

    a. Call ModuleA

    b. Call ModuleC

    c. The first statement in ModuleB.

    d. None of the above is correct.

13. True or false: A welcome message for a program consists of a series of comments.

14. True or false: The contents of comments are ignored by the computer while running a program.

15. True or false: Program comments are also known as external documentation.

16. True or false: Program comments are intended to be read by someone running the program.

17. Fill in the blank: A _____ comment provides a general description of a program or program module.

18. Fill in the blank: A _____ comment provides an explanation of a portion of code.

19. True or false: If you are sure that you have coded a program correctly, then there is no need to test it.

20. True or false: Commercial programs, like those developed by Microsoft, do not normally require testing.

21. Fill in the blank: A _____ error is a violation of a programming language's rules for the structure of statements.

22. Fill in the blank: A _____ error results from statements that do not properly perform their intended task.

23. True or false: To debug a program means to correct its errors.

24. True or false: Structured programming is a method for designing and coding programs effectively.

25. True or false: A control structure is a means by which programmers control the user's input.

26. True or false: If you don't use good programming style, then your programs will not run.

27. Which of the following is *not* a principle of structured programming?

    a. Design the program in a top-down, modular fashion.
    b. Write each program module as a series of control structures.
    c. Code the program so that it runs correctly without testing.
    d. Use good programming style.

28. The flowchart symbol shown at the right is a(n)

    a. Process symbol.
    b. Input/output symbol.
    c. Decision symbol.
    d. Terminator symbol.

29. The flowchart symbol shown at the right is a(n)

    a. Process symbol.
    b. Input/output symbol.
    c. Decision symbol.
    d. Terminator symbol.

30. The flowchart symbol shown at the right is a(n)

    a. Process symbol.
    b. Input/output symbol.
    c. Decision symbol.
    d. Terminator symbol.

31. Which of the following is *not* a basic control structure?

    a. The process structure.
    b. The loop structure.
    c. The decision structure.
    d. The sequence structure.

32. Which of the following is *not* a principle of good programming *style*?

    a. Use descriptive variable names.
    b. Provide a welcome message.
    c. Identify, using text, the numbers output.
    d. Test the program.

33. Fill in the blank: GUI stands for _____.

34. Fill in the blank: A _____ is a special type of window that offers the user options by means of command buttons, text boxes, and other controls.

35. True or false: In programming for a GUI, we refer to a mouse click or a key press as an event.

36. True or false: In designing a program for a GUI, we begin by considering how we would like the program's screens to look.

37. Fill in the blank: OOP stands for _____.

38. Fill in the blank: An OOP object encapsulates _____ and _____.

39. Viewing an ordinary door as an OOP object, give two of its attributes and two of its methods.

40. True or false: In object-oriented program design, we focus on the objects to be used in the program, their attributes and methods, and the relationships among the objects.

41. True or false: In object-oriented programming, it is not possible for one object to use the methods of another object.

42. Suppose you want to write a program that computes the average (mean) of three numbers entered by the user.

    a. Give the input and output variables for this program.

    b. Draw a hierarchy chart for this program that reflects the following basic tasks:

        Display Welcome Message
        Input Data
        Calculate Average
        Output Results

    c. Write pseudocode for each program module, including the main module.

    d. Refine the Output Results module so that it will produce nice-looking output.

    e. Construct a flowchart for this program.

    f. Give an example of reasonable input data for testing it.

Programming Problems

Each of the following problems can be solved by a program that performs three basic tasks—Input Data, Process Data, and Output Results. For each problem, use pseudocode to design a suitable program for solving it.

A. Input a saleswoman's sales for the month (in dollars) and her commission rate (as a percentage) and output her commission for that month.

B. The manager of the Super Supermarket would like to be able to compute the unit price for products sold there. To do this, the program should input the price of an item and its weight in pounds and ounces. It should then determine and display the unit price (the price per ounce) of the item.

C. The owners of the Super Supermarket would like to have a program that computes the monthly gross pay of their employees. The input for this program is an employee ID number, hourly rate of pay, and number of regular and overtime hours worked. (Gross pay is the sum of the wages earned from regular hours and overtime hours; the latter are paid at 1.5 times the regular rate.)

D. Modify the program of problem C so that it also computes and displays the employee's net pay. Net pay is gross pay minus deductions. Assume that deductions are taken for tax withholding (30% of gross pay) and parking ($10 per month).

E. Sharon and Judy bowl as a team. Each of them bowls three games in a tournament. They would like to know their individual averages for their three games and the team score (the total for the six games).

F. Joe wants to buy a car. He would like to be able to compute the monthly payment (M) on a loan given the loan amount (P), the annual percentage rate of interest (r), and the number of monthly payments (N). The program should allow Joe to input P, r, and N, and would then compute and display M using the formula

$$M = P * R * (1 + R)^\wedge N / ((1 + R)^\wedge N - 1)$$

where R = r/1200, the monthly rate of interest expressed as a decimal.

Loops in the Everyday World

You may not remember it, but you probably learned to walk about the time you were one year old. With your first step, you had to figure out how to execute this process:

> Put one foot in front of the other

At some point, you did just that and it was a major accomplishment. Of course, this didn't get you very far. If you wanted to walk across the room, you needed to extend this process to:

> Put one foot in front of the other
> Put one foot in front of the other
> Put one foot in front of the other

and so on.

This is not a very efficient way to describe what you did; a detailed list of your actions as you ambled all over the house would get very long. Since you did the same thing over and over, a much better way to describe your actions would be:

> Repeat
> > Put one foot in front of the other
> Until you get across the room

This way is short, convenient, and just as descriptive. Even if you want to take hundreds or thousands of steps, the process can still be described in just three lines. This is the basic idea of a *loop*.

Walking is just one of many examples of loops in your daily life. For example, if you have a large family and need to prepare lunches for everyone in the morning, you can do this:

> Repeat
> > Make a sandwich
> > Wrap the sandwich
> > Place the sandwich in a lunch bag
> > Place an apple in the lunch bag
> > Place a drink in the lunch bag
> Until 7 lunches have been made

Where else would you encounter a looping process? How about in balancing your checkbook (one check at a time), or while brushing your teeth, or even when playing a compact disc song by song? After you read this chapter (one word at a time), you'll be ready to place loops in your programs as well.

3

Repetition Structures: Looping

OVERVIEW   In Section 2.4, we introduced the control structure known as a *loop*, or *repetition structure*—a block of statements that can be executed repeatedly. In this chapter, we will explore this topic in depth. We will discuss different types of loops, applications of loops, and using loops contained in other loops. To be more specific, you will learn about

1. The difference between pre-test and post-test loops [Section 3.1].

2. How to use relational operators in loop conditions [3.1].

3. Constructing counter-controlled loops [3.2].

4. Constructing sentinel-controlled loops [3.3].

5. Some applications of loops, including data input and validation, and computing sums and averages [3.3].

6. Using nested loops [3.4].

3.1 An Introduction to Repetition Structures

All programming languages provide statements to create a **loop** (or **repetition** structure)—a block of code that, under certain conditions, will be executed repeatedly. In this section, we will introduce some basic ideas about these structures.

A Simple Example of a Loop

We start with a simple example of a loop.

EXAMPLE 1   This program repeatedly inputs a number from the user and displays that number until the user enters 0. The program then displays the word *Done*.

> Repeat
>   Prompt for and input a
>   number, Num
>   Write Num
> Until Num = 0
> Write "Done"

In this pseudocode, the loop begins with the word *Repeat* and ends with the line containing the word *Until*. The **body of the loop**—the block of statements that will be executed repeatedly—consists of the statements between *Repeat* and *Until*. The body of the loop is executed until the **exit condition** following the word *Until* becomes true (in this case, until the number input by the user is 0). At that point, the loop is *exited*, and the statement that follows the loop is executed. A flowchart for this program is shown in Figure 1.

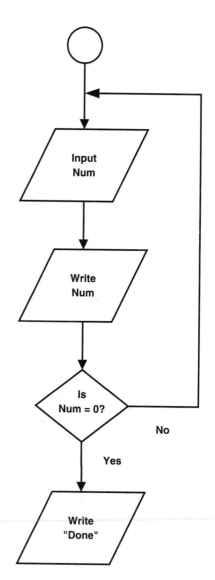

FIGURE 1   Flowchart for Example 1

Let us trace (follow) execution in Example 1, assuming that the user enters the numbers 1, 3, and 0, in that order:

- When execution begins, the loop is entered, the number 1 is input, and this number is displayed. These actions make up the first *pass* (time) through the loop. The exit condition, Num = 0, is now "tested" and found to be false (because, at this point, Num = 1), which causes the loop to be *reentered*—the body of the loop is executed again.

- On the second pass through the loop, the number 3 is input and displayed, and once again the condition Num = 0 is false, causing another pass through the loop to take place.

- On the third pass through the loop, the number 0 is input and displayed. This time, the condition Num = 0 is true, so the loop is exited—execution transfers to the statement after the loop (Write "Done").

- The word *Done* is displayed, and the program is complete.

Beware of Infinite Loops   If a loop's exit condition is never satisfied (in the case of a Repeat ... Until loop, if the condition never becomes true), then the loop will never be exited—it will become an *infinite loop*. It is therefore important to make sure, through a suitable prompt, how the user is to terminate the action of the loop. In Example 1, a suitable prompt would be:

Write "Enter a number; enter 0 to quit."

Relational Operators

The "condition" that determines whether a loop is reentered or exited is usually constructed with the help of six basic **relational operators:**

equal to (=)	not equal to (≠)
less than (<)	less than or equal to (≤)
greater than (>)	greater than or equal to (≥)

For example, suppose that in Example 1, the loop contained *any* of the following exit conditions:

$$Num \neq 0$$
$$or \quad Num > 0$$
$$or \quad Num \geq 0$$

Then, only one pass would have been made through the loop because each of these three conditions is true if the value of Num is 1 (as it was on the first pass in our example).

**Programming
Pointer**

The characters ≠, ≤, and ≥ cannot be typed on a standard computer keyboard. For this reason, most programming languages use a special pair of characters to represent each of these relational operators. Typically:

    <> represents *not equal to*
    <= represents *less than or equal to*
    >= represents *greater than or equal to*

In this text, we will use these symbols in the pseudocode to represent the corresponding operator.

The operators *equal to* and *not equal to* can be applied to characters as well as numbers*. For example, if the value of Response is "Y", then all of the following conditions are *true*:

    Response <> "N"
    Response <> "y"
    Response = "Y"

Pre-test and Post-test Loops

All repetition structures can be divided into two fundamental types: pre-test loops and post-test loops. The loop in Example 1,

    Repeat
        Prompt for and input a number, Num
        Write Num
    Until Num = 0

is an example of a **post-test loop**—one in which the exit condition occurs *after* the body of the loop is executed. In a **pre-test loop,** on the other hand, the exit condition appears at the top of the loop.

EXAMPLE 2   This is an example of a pre-test loop:

    While Num <> 0
        Write Num
        Input Num
    End While

In our pseudocode for a pre-test loop: the first statement begins with the word *While* and is followed by the exit condition (here, Num <> 0— Num "not equal to" 0); the last statement in the loop is *End While*. As

---

* In actuality, all six operators can be applied to characters, words, and other sequences of characters. We will discuss this topic in Section 5.2.

with post-test loops, all statements in between comprise the body of the loop. When the loop is entered, the exit condition is tested. If it is found to be *true*, the body of the loop is executed and control then returns to the top of the loop; if it is false, then the loop is exited and the statement following *End While* is executed next.

Suppose that in Example 2 the value of Num is 1 when the loop is entered, and that, on the next two passes through the loop, the user enters the numbers 3 and 0. Here's how execution flows in this case:

- The While statement is executed testing the exit condition, Num <> 0, which is found to be true (Num is initially equal to 1). Thus, the body of the loop is executed, 1 is displayed, and 3 is input. Then, control returns to the top of the loop.

- Again, the exit condition is tested, and since 3 is not equal to 0, a second pass is made through the loop. This time 3 is displayed and 0 is input, before control returns to the top of the loop.

- Once again, the exit condition is tested, and since Num is now equal to 0, it is found to be false. The loop is therefore exited and the statement following End While is executed next.

The flow of execution for Example 2 is illustrated under "pre-test loop" in Figure 2 (on the next page), which shows typical pre-test and post-test loops.

Differences between pre-test and post-test loops

There are three basic differences between pre-test and post-test loops:

1. By definition, a pre-test loop has its exit condition—the one that determines whether or not the body of the loop is executed—at the top; a post-test loop has its exit condition at the bottom.

2. The body of a post-test loop is always executed at least once. The body of a pre-test loop will not be executed at all, however, if its exit condition is false on the first pass.

3. Before a pre-test loop is entered, the variables that appear in its exit condition must be *initialized*—they must be assigned a value. (We say that we must *prime* a pre-test loop.) This is not necessary in a post-test loop; the exit condition variables may be initialized within the body of the loop. For example, the following program segment uses a pre-test loop to display the squares of numbers input by the user until he or she enters zero or a negative number (which is not displayed).

Input Number
While Number > 0
    Write Number ^ 2
    Input Number
End While

Notice that we initialize the variable Number by using an Input statement just prior to entering the loop. (Trace this pseudocode with the test data 3, 1, –1 to see, in detail, how it works.)

Either a pre-test or a post-test loop can be used to accomplish a given task, although, as you will discover, some tasks are easier to accomplish with pre-test loops; others with post-test loops.

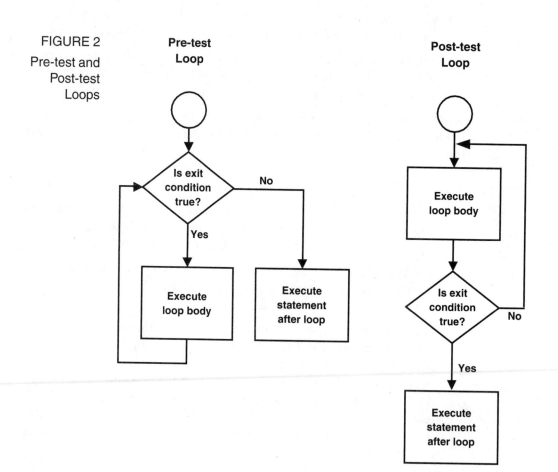

FIGURE 2

Pre-test and Post-test Loops

Style Pointer

Indent the Body of a Loop   To make it easier to read your pseudocode (and the corresponding program code), you should indent the body of a loop relative to its first and last statements. For example, compare the loop on the right, which is indented, to that on the left, which is not:

Not indented: Repeat
 Input Num
 Write Num
 Until Num = 0

Indented: Repeat
 Input Num
 Write Num
 Until Num = 0

Self-Test 3.1

1. What numbers will be displayed if code corresponding to the following pseudocode is run:

   a. Set Num = 1
     Repeat
       Write 2 * Num
       Set Num = Num + 1
     Until Num = 3

   b. Set Num = 1
     While Num < 3
       Write 2 * Num
       Set Num = Num + 1
     End While

2. Is each of the following conditions true or false?

   a. 5 = 5   b. 5 <> 5   c. 5 < 5
   d. 5 <= 5   e. 5 > 5   f. 5 >= 5

3. If C1 = "J" and C2 = "j", is each of the following true or false?

   a. C1 = C2   b. C1 <> C2   c. "J" <> "j"

4. List the main differences between pre- and post-test loops.

5. The following program is supposed to input numbers from the user and display them as long as 0 is not entered. A statement is missing; insert the missing statement.

   Input Number
   While Number <> 0
     Write Number
   End While

3.2   Counter-controlled Loops

In Section 3.1, we discussed two fundamental types of repetition structures, pre-test and post-test loops. In this section, we will discuss a special type of pre-test loop known as a counter-controlled loop. A **counter-controlled loop** is one that is executed a fixed number, N, of times, where N is known prior to entering the loop for the first time.

Constructing a Counter-controlled Loop

A counter-controlled loop is so-named because it contains a variable (the *counter*) that keeps track of the number of passes through the loop (the number of loop *iterations*). When the counter reaches a preset number, the loop is exited.

EXAMPLE 3   One common use of counter-controlled loops is to print "tables" of data. For example, suppose we want to display the squares of the first N positive integers, where N is to be entered by the user. The pseudocode for this process is:

Prompt for and input the positive integer N
Initialize the counter to 1: Set Count = 1
While Count <= N
    Write Count, Count ^ 2
    Add 1 to Count: Set Count = Count + 1
End While

Notice that to ensure that the counter Count correctly keeps track of the number of loop iterations:

1. We set Count equal to its first value—we initialize it to 1—before entering the loop.

2. We *increment* (increase) Count by 1 within the loop.

Thus,

- On the first pass through the loop, the number 1 and its square are displayed, and Count is incremented to 2.

- On the second pass through the loop, the number 2 and its square are displayed, and Count is incremented to 3.

This process continues until

- On the Nth pass through the loop, N and its square are displayed, Count is incremented to N + 1, and the loop is exited because the value of Count now exceeds N.

A flowchart corresponding to this pseudocode is shown in Figure 3.

FIGURE 3

Flowchart for
Example 3

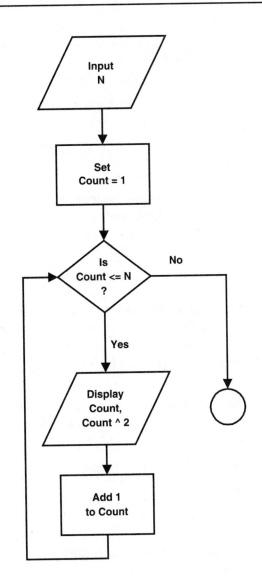

Built-in Counter-controlled Loops

Most programming languages contain a statement that makes it easy to construct a counter-controlled loop. We will use the following pseudocode to represent this statement, which creates a "built-in" counter-controlled loop:

For *Counter* = *InitialValue* Step *Increment* To *LimitValue*
    Body of the Loop
End For

In this typical For statement, Counter must be a variable, Increment must be a constant (a number), and InitialValue and LimitValue may be constants, variables, or expressions. For example, in the statement

For K = 1 Step 3 To N + 1

the counter is the variable K, the initial value is the constant 1, the increment is the constant 3, and the limit value is the expression N + 1.

The action of a For loop

A For loop works like this:

- Upon entering the loop, Counter is set equal to InitialValue and, if InitialValue is not greater than LimitValue, then the body of the loop is executed. If Counter is greater than LimitValue, the loop is skipped—the statement following End For is executed next.

- On each subsequent pass through the loop, Counter is increased by the value of Increment and, if the new value of Counter is not greater than LimitValue, the body of the loop is executed again. When the value of Counter exceeds that of LimitValue, the loop is exited and the statement following *End For* is executed next.

A flowchart depicting the action of a For loop is shown in Figure 4.

EXAMPLE 4 The following For loop has the same effect as the While loop we constructed in Example 3 at the beginning of this section—it displays a table of numbers from 1 to N and their squares.

```
Input a positive integer N
For Count = 1 Step 1 To N
    Write Count, Count ^ 2
End For
```

Here are a few more examples that illustrate additional features of For loops.

EXAMPLE 5 This program provides an example of a For loop with an increment value that is not equal to 1. It displays the odd numbers between 1 and 20.

```
For N = 1 Step 2 To 20
    Write N
End For
```

On the first pass through this loop, N is initialized to 1, displayed, and incremented by 2 (due to *Step 2* in the For statement). Thus, on the

FIGURE 4

The Action
of a
For Loop

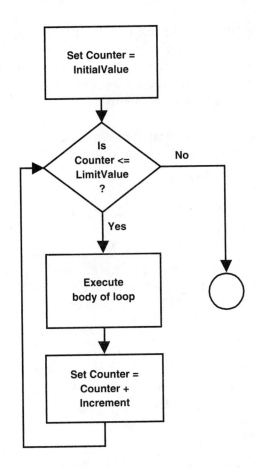

second pass, 3 is displayed and N is incremented by 2 again. This continues until the 10th pass. On this loop iteration, the value of N (19) is displayed and incremented to 21. Since N now exceeds the limit value (20), the loop is exited.

EXAMPLE 6   By using a negative value for the loop increment, we can "step backwards" through a loop; that is, have the counter variable *decrease* in value from iteration to iteration. For a negative increment, the loop is exited when the value of the counter becomes less than the loop's limit value. Here's an example:

```
For Index = 9 Step –2 To 5
    Write Index
End For
```

In the first pass through this loop, Index is initialized to 9, this value is displayed, and then –2 (the increment) is added to it. The value of Index is now 7. On the second pass, 7 is displayed; then Index is decreased to 5. Finally, on the third pass, 5 is displayed; then Index is set equal to 3. Since 3 is less than the limit value (5), the loop is exited.

EXAMPLE 7   If the loop increment is *positive* and the initial value is *greater than* the limit value, then the body of the loop is skipped.

> Write "Before loop"
> For K = 5 Step 1 To 4
>   Write "Help, I'm a prisoner in a For loop!"
> End For
> Write "After loop"

Since the initial value (5) is greater than the limit value (4) and the increment is positive (it is 1), the body of the loop is skipped. Thus, the output produced by code corresponding to this pseudocode is:

```
Before loop
After loop
```

Note that a For loop is also skipped when the increment is *negative* if the initial value is *less than* the limit value.

Self-Test 3.2

1. What numbers will be displayed when code corresponding to the following pseudocode is run:

    a. Set N = 3
        For K = N Step 1 To N + 2
            Write N, K
        End For

    b. For K = 10 Step –2 To 7
            Write K
        End For

2. What output will be displayed when code corresponding to the following pseudocode is run:

    a. Set N = 3
        For K = 5 Step 1 To N
            Write N
        End For

    b. For K = 1 Step 1 To 3
            Write "Hooray"
        End For

3. Write a program (pseudocode) that contains the statement

    For Count = 1 Step 1 To 3

and which would produce the following output if it were coded and run:

```
10
20
30
```

4. Rewrite the following pseudocode using a For loop instead of the While loop shown here.

```
Set Num = 1
While Num <= 10
    Input Response
    Write Response
    Set Num = Num + 1
End While
```

3.3 Applications of Repetition Structures

Throughout the rest of the text, you will see many examples of how the repetition (or loop) structure can be used in constructing a program. In this section, we will present a few basic applications of this fundamental control structure.

Using Sentinel-controlled Loops to Input Data

Loops are often used to input large amounts of data: on each pass through the loop, one item of data (or one set of data) is entered into the program. The exit condition for such a loop must cause it to be exited after all data have been input. Often, the best way to force a loop exit is to have the user enter a special item, a **sentinel value,** to act as a signal that input is complete. The sentinel item, or *end-of-data marker*, should be chosen so that it cannot possibly be mistaken for actual input data. For example, if a list of positive numbers is to be input, the sentinel value could be chosen to be the number −1. Here is a simple example of a **sentinel-controlled loop,** one that uses a sentinel value to determine whether or not the loop is to be exited.

EXAMPLE 8   Suppose that the input data for a program that computes employee salaries consists of the number of hours worked by each employee and his or her rate of pay. The following pseudocode could be used to input and process this data:

> Prompt for and input the number of hours worked (Hours)
> While Hours <> –1
>> Prompt for and input the rate of pay (Rate)
>> Set Salary = Hours * Rate
>> Write Hours, Rate, Salary
>> Prompt for and input Hours
> End While

It is crucial that the input prompts for the number of hours worked (one prompt prior to the loop, one within the loop) make it clear to users that they must enter the number –1 when all employees have been processed. Thus, a refinement of this pseudocode would be:

> Write "Enter the number of hours worked."
> Write "Enter –1 when you are done."
> Input Hours
> While Hours <> –1
>> Write "Enter the rate of pay."
>> Input Rate
>> Set Salary = Hours * Rate
>> Write Hours, Rate, Salary
>> Write "Enter the number of hours worked."
>> Write "Enter –1 when you are done."
>> Input Hours
> End While

In this program segment, if the value input for Hours is the sentinel value –1, the exit condition in the While statement is false, the loop is exited, and input is terminated. Otherwise the loop body is executed, inputting Rate, computing and displaying the salary, and again inputting Hours. Then, the process is repeated.

EXAMPLE 9 Another way to allow the user to signal that all data have been input is to have the program ask, after each input operation, whether or not this is the case. This technique is illustrated in the following program segment.

> Repeat
>> Write "Enter the number of hours worked."
>> Input Hours
>> Write "Enter the rate of pay."

> Input Rate
> Set Salary = Hours * Rate
> Write Hours, Rate, Salary
> Write "Process another employee? (Y or N)"
> Input Response
> Until Response = "N"

Here, the user enters the letter Y if there are more data to input, or N otherwise. (Hence, the variable Response must be of character type.) The exit condition, **Response** = "N", then determines whether or not the loop is reentered.

Data Validation

To have the user enter a positive number at some point during program execution, we use pseudocode similar to the following:

> Write "Enter a positive number: "
> Input Num

However, despite the input prompt, the user might enter a negative number or zero, which may cause an error when the program is run. To ensure that this does not occur, we should include statements in the program that check, or **validate,** the number input and request that the user reenter it if it is not in the proper range. The next two examples use loops to accomplish this task.

EXAMPLE 10 This pseudocode validates the number entered using a post-test loop.

> Repeat
>   Write "Enter a positive number ---> "
>   Input Num
> Until Num > 0

In this technique for validating data, the prompt

```
Enter a positive number --->
```

is repeated until the number entered (Num) is positive.

EXAMPLE 11 Sometimes, in validating data, we want to emphasize the fact that the user has made an error by displaying a message to this effect. We can do this with a pre-test loop, as illustrated in the following pseudocode.

> Write "Enter a positive number ---> "

```
Input Num
While Num <= 0
     Write "The number entered must be positive"
     Write "Please try again ---> "
     Input Num
End While
```

Notice that in validating input data with a pre-test loop, we use *two* Input statements (and accompanying prompts). The first is positioned before the loop and is always executed; the second is contained within the loop and is executed only if the data entered is not in the proper range. Although this means of validating input data is a little more complicated than that used in Example 10, it is also more flexible and user-friendly. Within the body of the data validation loop, you can provide whatever message best suits the situation.

Data validation is an example of *defensive programming*, writing code that checks during execution for improper data. We will demonstrate other defensive programming techniques in Section 4.4.

Style Pointer

Validate Input Data   Your programs should, whenever possible, *validate* input data; that is, check that it is in the proper range. A pre-test or post-test loop can be used for this purpose, as shown in Examples 10 and 11.

Computing Sums and Averages

When we use a calculator to sum a list of numbers, we add each successive number to the running total, the sum obtained so far. In effect, we are looping, repeatedly applying the addition operation until all the numbers have been added. To write a program to sum a list of numbers, we do essentially the same thing, as illustrated in the next example.

EXAMPLE 12   The following pseudocode adds a list of positive numbers entered by the user.

```
Initialize the sum to 0: Set Sum = 0
Prompt for and input Number
While Number > 0
     Add Number to Sum: Set Sum = Sum + Number
     Prompt for and input Number
End While
Write Sum
```

Upon exit from the loop, the variable Sum, which in this context is called the *accumulator,* contains the sum of all the positive numbers entered and is displayed. A flowchart for this example is shown in Figure 5.

To better understand how this algorithm works, let us trace execution of this pseudocode if input consists of the numbers 3, 4.2, 5, and 0:

FIGURE 5

Flowchart for
Example 12

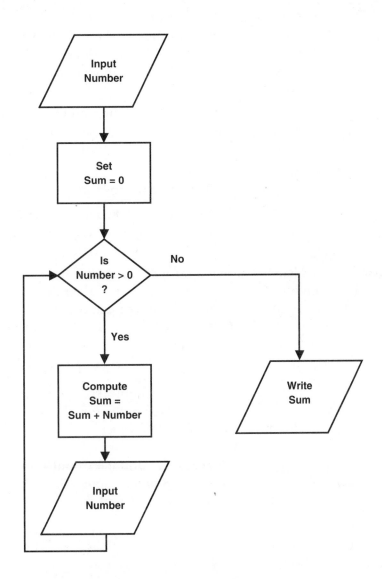

- Prior to entering the loop, we initialize the variable Sum; we set it equal to 0 so that it will not be an undefined variable (see Section 1.4) when the right side of the statement

    Set Sum = Sum + Number

    is evaluated. For the same reason, we input the initial value of Number from the user prior to entering the loop.

- On the first pass through the loop, Number equals 3, so the exit condition is true and the loop body is executed. Thus, the current values of Sum and Number are added and the result, 3, is assigned to Sum. Moreover, the next number (4.2) is input and assigned to Number.

- A second pass is now made through the loop with Number = 4.2, which is added to the current running total, 3, to increase the value of Sum to 7.2. In this pass, the number 5 is input.

- Since Number is still not 0, the loop body is executed once more assigning 12.2 to Sum and 0 to Number.

- Now, Number *is* 0, so the exit condition is true. The loop is exited and the current value of Sum, 12.2, is displayed.

Calculating an average
To calculate the average (or *mean*) of a list of numbers, we compute their sum and divide it by the number of data items on the list. Thus, the process of finding an average is similar to that of finding a sum, but here we need a counter to keep track of how many numbers have been entered.

The pseudocode for finding the mean of a list of positive numbers is:

    Initialize a counter: Set Count = 0
    Initialize an accumulator: Set Sum = 0
    Prompt for and input a Number
    While Number > 0
        Add 1 to Count: Set Count = Count + 1
        Add Number to Sum: Set Sum = Sum + Number
        Prompt for and input Number
    End While
    Set Average = Sum / Count

In this pseudocode, notice that:

- The While loop sums the numbers, but the mean is computed after the loop has been exited.

- If the first number entered by the user is negative or 0, when the statement

    Set Average = Sum / Count

    is executed, the value of Count will be 0, and a "division by zero" error will occur when the program is run. We will show how to avoid this situation by using defensive programming techniques in Section 4.4.

Self-Test 3.3

1. Write pseudocode using a post-test (Repeat ... Until) loop that inputs a list of characters from the user until the character * is input.

2. Suppose you want to input a number that should be greater than 100. Write pseudocode that validates input data to accomplish this task

    a. Using a pre-test (While) loop.
    b. Using a post-test (Repeat...Until) loop.

3. Use a For loop to sum the integers from 1 to 100.

4. Modify the program (pseudocode) of Problem 3 so that it finds the average of the first 100 positive integers.

3.4   Nested Loops

Programs sometimes employ one loop which is contained entirely within another. In such a case, we say that the loops are **nested.** The larger loop is called the *outer loop;* the one lying within it is called the *inner loop.*

Nested For Loops

The pseudocode in the following simple example contains nested For loops. It illustrates the order in which the loop iterations (passes through the loops) take place.

EXAMPLE   Each time the inner loop in this program is reentered, the values of the
13   counter variables for both loops are displayed.

```
For OutCount = 1 Step 1 To 2
    For InCount = 1 Step 1 To 3
        Write "Outer-", OutCount, " Inner-", InCount
    End For (InCount)
    Write
End For (OutCount)
```

When this program is executed, OutCount is set equal to 1 by the first
For statement, and control passes to the second For statement, the top of
the inner loop. The inner loop is then executed with InCount (and
OutCount) equal to 1, displaying the text

```
Outer-1 Inner-1
```

Then, control returns to the top of the inner loop and increments
InCount to 2. In this way (with OutCount still equal to 1), the inner loop
is executed two more times, with InCount equal to 2 and 3, displaying

```
Outer-1 Inner-2
Outer-1 Inner-3
```

Thus, for the initial value of OutCount (1), the inner loop is executed
successively for all values (1, 2, and 3) of its counter variable, InCount,
and then this loop is exited. At this point, the Write statement following
the end of the inner For loop displays a blank line, then control transfers
to the top of the outer loop and OutCount is incremented to 2.

Now, the body of the inner For loop is entered once again. InCount is
initialized to 1, and the inner loop is executed three more times—with
InCount successively equal to 1, 2, and 3 (and OutCount equal to 2).
Then, the inner loop is exited and this time, since OutCount has reached
its limit value, the outer loop is exited as well.

The complete output of this program segment is:

```
Outer-1 Inner-1
Outer-1 Inner-2
Outer-1 Inner-3

Outer-2 Inner-1
Outer-2 Inner-2
Outer-2 Inner-3
```

Figure 6 contains a flowchart that shows the flow of execution in this
example.

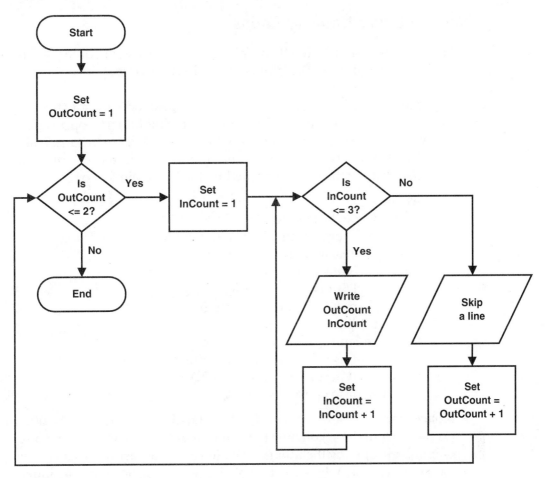

FIGURE 6   Flowchart for Example 13

Nesting For Loops If For loops have any statements in common, then one of them must be nested entirely within the other (they may not partially overlap) and their counter variables must be different. To illustrate this point, the following two sets of pseudocode show two different valid ways in which three For loops may be nested.

```
For I = . . .                    For I . . .
    For J = . . .                    For J = . . .
                                         For K = . . .
    End For (J)
    For K = . . .                    End For (K)
                                 End For (J)
    End For (K)              End For (I)
End For (I)
```

Nesting Other Kinds of Loops

So far, we have illustrated the nesting process only with For loops. The next example contains nested Repeat and While loops.

EXAMPLE 14   This pseudocode makes use of a post-test Repeat loop to allow the user to sum several sets of numbers in a single run. This (outer) loop, in effect, allows the entire program to be re-executed if the user so desires. It also contains statements that initialize the sum to 0, input the first number, and then display the sum computed by the inner While loop.

>   Repeat
>   Initialize the sum to 0: Set Sum = 0
>   Prompt for and input a number (Num) to be summed
>   (Use 0 as a sentinel value)
>   While Num <> 0
>   Set Sum = Sum + Num;
>   Prompt for and input Num
>   End While
>   Write Sum
>   Prompt user for another set of numbers to be summed
>   and input Response (Y or N)
>   Until Response = "N"

Notice that with the exception of its last statement, the body of the outer (Repeat...Until) loop contains the usual pseudocode for summing a set of numbers input by the user (see Section 3.3). The last statement in this loop queries (asks) the user if he or she would like to continue, inputs this response, and then uses it in the exit condition for the Repeat loop. Here's a refinement of this crucial step:

>   Write "Sum another list of numbers? (Y or N)"
>   Input Response

A flowchart tracing the flow of execution in this example is shown in Figure 7.

Style Pointer

Further Indent the Body of a Nested Loop   As you know, when writing pseudocode (or code) for any kind of loop, indenting the body of that loop enhances program readability. The same guideline applies to a loop that is nested within another. In this case, the Repeat, Until, While, End While, For, and/or End For statements for the *inner* loop align with the rest of the statements in the body of the *outer* loop and the statements in the body of the inner loop are indented relative to the outer loop. The examples in this section have illustrated this principle.

FIGURE 7

Flowchart for
Example 14

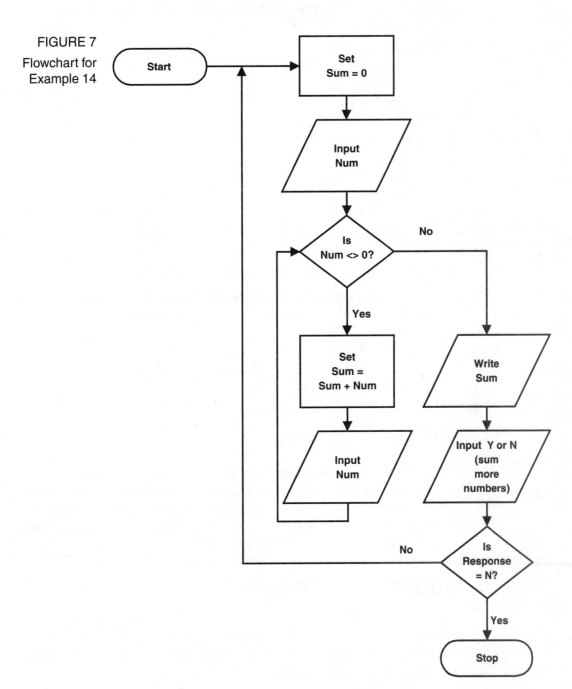

Self-Test 3.4

What is the output of the code corresponding to the pseudocode in Exercises 1 and 2?

1. For I = 2 Step 1 To 4
        For J = 2 Step 1 To 3
            Write I, " ", J
        End For (J)
    End For (I)

2. For I = 1 Step 3 To 5
        Set K = 2 * I – 1
        Write K
        For J = I Step 1 To I + 1
            Write K
        End For (J)
    End For (I)

3. Draw a flowchart corresponding to pseudocode of Exercise 1.

4. Write pseudocode that contains two nested Repeat loops which input and validate a number X that should be greater than 0 and less than 10.

3.5   *Focus on Problem Solving*

In this section, and in sections with the same title throughout the text, we develop a program that makes use of much of the material in the current chapter. The program here uses a counter-controlled loop to display a table of data. It also features data validation (using post-test loops) and finds the mean of a set of numbers.

A Cost, Revenue, and Profit Problem

The KingPin Manufacturing Company wants to compute its costs, revenue, and profit for various production levels of its only product, king pins. From past experience, the company knows that when *x* king pins are produced and sold:

- The total cost (in dollars), C, to the firm of producing them is

  $C = 100{,}000 + 12x$

- The total revenue (in dollars), R, received by the firm is

  $R = x(1000 - x)$

For example, if 100 king pins are produced and sold, then the

Total cost is: $C = 100{,}000 + 12(100) = \$101{,}200$
Total revenue is: $R = 100(1000 - 100) = \$90{,}000$

To gauge the effects of various production levels (x, in the formula) on its bottom line, the company would like to create a table of the costs, revenue, and profit (or loss) corresponding to a wide range of production levels. The company would also like to know the mean (average) profit for all these production levels.

Problem Analysis   As is often the case, the best way to attack this problem is to start with the desired output (the table of costs, revenue, and profit), and to then determine the input and formulas needed to produce this output. We will have the computer display a table with four columns: The first (left) column will list a range of different production levels (number of king pins produced); the other three columns will display the cost, revenue, and profit corresponding to each production level. Thus, the column headings and a couple of the table rows would look something like this:

```
Number     Cost   Revenue   Profit
------     ------  -------   ------
   100    101200    90000   -11200
   200    102400   160000    57600
```

The problem description does not specify the number of rows that the table is to contain, nor does it specify the range of production levels. So, upon further consultation with the KingPin company, we decide to input the following information from the user:

The number of production levels to be listed
(that is, the number of rows in the table), NumRows

The largest production level, MaxX, to appear

Then, in the left table column we will display evenly-spaced production levels, X, ranging from 0 to MaxX. For example, suppose that the user input is NumRows = 6 and MaxX = 500. Then, the left column of the displayed table would contain the following entries (values of X): 0, 100, 200, 300, 400, 500. (Notice that the spacing between these values is 100.)

In general, to determine the correct spacing between the values of X in the left table column, we divide MaxX by the number of spaces (intervals) between the values of X, which is NumRows – 1. That is:

Spacing = MaxX/(NumRows – 1)

To obtain the entries in any row of the Cost and Revenue columns, we substitute that row's value of X (from the left column) into the supplied formulas:

Cost = 100000 + 12 * X
Revenue = X * (1000 – X)

To find the Profit entry in any row, we just subtract:

Profit = Revenue – Cost

(If this figure is negative, it indicates a *loss.*) The mean (average) profit is obtained by adding all the individual profits, obtaining a figure we will call Sum, and then applying the formula:

Average = Sum / NumRows

Program Design   To design this program using a top-down modular approach, we first determine its major tasks. The program must perform the following operations:

- Input the necessary data
- Compute the table entries
- Display the table
- Display the average profit

We should also provide a *welcome message,* a general description of the program that is displayed for the user at the beginning of a program run. Moreover, since table values will be calculated and displayed one row at a time, the second and third tasks are done almost simultaneously. (The sum needed to determine the average profit is also computed at this time.) Taking these points into consideration, a better approach might be to create the following major modules:

1. Display a welcome message
2. Input data from the user
3. Display the table
4. Display the average profit

The third of these tasks makes up the bulk of this program, and perhaps should be further subdivided. In displaying the table, we must first do some "housekeeping" tasks (such as setting up the table, displaying titles, initializing variables, etc.) and then perform the necessary calculations to create the table entries. Thus, we break task 3 into two subtasks:

Do table housekeeping
Do table calculations

The second of these tasks actually does several small jobs—it computes the table entries, displays them, and accumulates the profits—and could be further subdivided. However, as you will see, all these operations are performed within a single loop, so we will let this task stand as it is. The hierarchy chart in Figure 8 shows the relationships among the program modules.

We now design, using pseudocode, each program module. First, we give a relatively rough outline of the program; then, we refine it as necessary.

Main Module   The main module need only call its immediate submodules; they will perform all the necessary program tasks. The

FIGURE 8

Hierarchy Chart for "A Cost, Revenue, and Profit Problem"

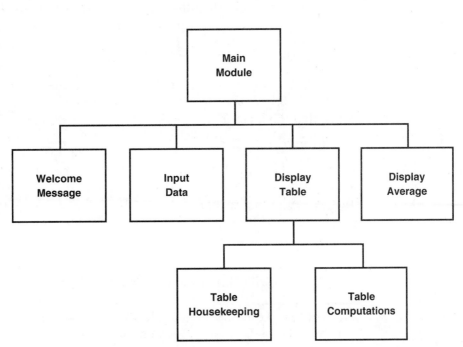

pseudocode is simply:

> Call Welcome Message module
> Call Input Data module
> Call Display Table module
> Call Display Average module

Welcome Message module   This module just displays information for the user:

> Briefly describe program

To be more specific (to *refine* this module):

> Display a title for the program ("A Cost/Revenue/Profit Table")
> Give a brief overall description of the program
> Describe, in general, how the user input affects the table

Input Data module   On the surface, this module is straightforward:

> Prompt for, input, and validate:
> > The number of rows desired in the table (NumRows)
> > The largest production level to appear in the table (MaxX)

We validate the first input value using a Repeat loop:

> Repeat
> > Write "Enter the number of desired production levels."
> > Write "It must be greater than 1."
> > Input NumRows
> Until NumRows > 1

The validation of MaxX is a little tricky. Of course, we want to ensure that MaxX is greater than 0, but there is also another requirement. Notice that the formula for revenue

$$\text{Revenue} = X * (1000 - X)$$

is not valid if $X > 1000$, because in this case $1000 - X$ would be negative, causing Revenue to be negative, and negative revenue makes no sense. Thus, we must ensure that MaxX > 0 and that MaxX <= 1000. We do this with two nested Repeat loops*:

> Repeat
> > Repeat
> > > Write "Enter the largest desired production level."

---

*After you read the material on logical operators in Section 4.2, you will see how to do this data validation using only one Repeat loop.

> Write "It must be greater than 0 and not exceed 1000."
> Input MaxX
> Until MaxX > 0
> Until MaxX <= 1000

Display Table module   This module just calls its submodules:

Call Table Housekeeping module
Call Table Computations module

Table Housekeeping module   This module does a few minor things in preparation for the computation and display of the table entries (which take place in the next module). It must

- Display the table title:
  Write "KingPin Manufacturing Company"

- Display the table headings:
  Write "Number   Cost   Revenue   Profit"

- Calculate the spacing for the values (X) in the left column:
  Set Spacing = MaxX / (NumRows – 1)

- Initialize the sum of profits to 0:
  Set Sum = 0

Table Computations module   This module is the heart of the program and contains the bulk of the computation. It consists of a single counter-controlled loop which, for each production value X:

- Calculates the corresponding values of Cost, Revenue, and Profit.

- Displays these values (on the same line).

- Adds the value of Profit to a running total, Sum (for use in computing the average profit).

Thus, the pseudocode is:

```
For X = 0 Step Spacing To MaxX
    Set Cost = 100000 + 12 * X
    Set Revenue = X * (1000 – X)
    Set Profit = Revenue – Cost
    Set Sum = Sum + Profit
    Write X, Cost, Revenue, Profit
End For
```

Display Average module   This module is very simple. It does the following:

> Set Average = Sum / NumRows
> Write Average

Program Coding The program code is now written using the design as a guide. At this stage, header comments and step comments (see Section 2.3) are inserted into each module, providing internal documentation for the program. Here are a few other points concerning the coding that are specific to this program:

Clearing
the screen

• When output is displayed on the screen, new lines are generated one after the other as specified by the code. When the screen is full, the next Write statement will cause the screen to *scroll up* (all text will move up one line with the top line of text disappearing from the screen) and the new text will be displayed at the bottom of the screen. It is often desirable, however, to "clear the screen" of all text, so that the data that follows is displayed all by itself at the top of the screen. Most programming languages contain a statement that clears the screen. It is advisable to use this statement at the beginning of every program. In this program, a clear screen statement would also be appropriate before printing the table of cost, revenue, and profit.

Integer
spacing
between
values of X

• In producing the table for this program, we generated rows of data (NumRows of them) with evenly-spaced production levels from $X = 0$ to $X = MaxX$. To calculate the spacing between production levels, we used the formula:

> Spacing = MaxX / (NumRows – 1)

Since the values on the right side of this equation are input by the user, it is possible that Spacing will not be an integer (whole number). For example, if NumRows = 8 and MaxX = 400, then Spacing is 400/7, which is approximately 57.14. But, it normally doesn't make sense to produce 57.14 of a product—we want the spacing to be an integer. Now, some programming languages automatically ignore the decimal part in this division, giving the integer result, 57. In other languages, it is necessary to insert a statement (after the one that computes Spacing) that accomplishes the same thing. (See Section 5.1 for more information about this topic.)

Formatting
the output

- Most programming languages contain statements that help the programmer to *format* output. For example, in this program, we would like our table to look as professional as possible. The data in the table should line up in columns, the dollar amounts should be rounded to the nearest dollar (or be displayed with two figures after the decimal point), and a dollar sign should precede them. If we just use basic Write statements to create the output, it might look like this:

```
Number    Cost   Revenue    Profit
------    ----   -------    ------
 800    109600    160000    504000
 900    110800     90000    -20800
1000    112000        0   -112000
```

However, using the special formatting statements that most languages supply, our table could look like this:

```
Number        Cost     Revenue       Profit
------        ----     -------       ------
   800    $109,600    $160,000    $  50,400
   900     110,800      90,000      -20,800
  1000     112,000           0     -112,000
```

Program Test To adequately test this program, we must run it with several sets of input data.

- To test the data validation loops, we input non-positive values of NumRows and MaxX. We also run the program with a value of MaxX for which MaxX > 1000.

- To verify that the computations are being done correctly, we make a program run using simple input data so that the results can be checked easily with a calculator. For example, a good choice would be:

  NumRows = 3 and MaxX = 1000

These values should produce a table that contains three rows, with production levels (values of X) equal to 0, 500, and 1000. This run tests the smallest and largest possible values for X (0 and 1000), which produce negative values for Profit, as well as an intermediate value (500), which produces a positive profit.

Self-Test 3.5

All problems in this Self-Test refer to "A Cost, Revenue, and Profit Problem" described in this section.

1. For each of the following production levels, calculate the corresponding Cost, Revenue, and Profit.

   a. $X = 0$ b. $X = 900$

2. For each of the following sets of input values, give the resulting value for Spacing and list the values of X displayed in the Number column of the resulting table.

   a. NumRows = 2, MaxX = 1000
   b. NumRows = 11, MaxX = 100

3. Replace the post-test Repeat loop that validates the input value of NumRows (in the Input Data module) with a pre-test While loop.

4. Replace the For loop in the Table Computations module with a While loop.

Chapter Review and Exercises

Key Terms

Loop (repetition) structure	Body of a loop
Exit condition	Post-test loop
Pre-test loop	Counter-controlled loop
Sentinel value	Sentinel-controlled loop
Validate data	Nested loops

Chapter Summary

In this chapter, we have discussed the following topics:

1. Pre-test and post-test loops:

   • Structure of a pre-test loop

         While *exit condition*
            Body of the Loop
         End While

- Structure of a post-test loop

    Repeat
       Body of the Loop
    Until *exit condition*

2. Differences between pre-test While and post-test Repeat loops:

   - For pre-test loops, the exit condition is at the top of the loop; for post-test loops, the exit condition is at the bottom.

   - Repeat loops are reentered as long as the exit condition is false; While loops are reentered as long as the exit condition is true.

   - The body of a post-test loop must be executed at least once; this is not true for a pre-test loop.

   - Variables appearing in the exit condition for a pre-test loop must be initialized prior to entering the loop structure; this is not true for a post-test loop.

3. The six relational operators:

   Equal to (=)   Not equal to (<>)
   Less than (<)   Less than or equal to (<=)
   Greater than (>)   Greater than or equal to (>=)

4. Counter-controlled loops:

   - Built-in counter-controlled loops have the form:

       For *Counter = InitialValue* Step *Increment* To *LimitValue*
           Body of the Loop
       End For

   - If the loop increment is positive, the body of a For loop is executed until the value of the counter exceeds the loop's limit value.

   - If the loop increment is negative, the body of a For loop is executed until the value of the counter becomes less than the loop's limit value.

5. Some applications of loops:

   - Inputting data until the user enters a sentinel value

   - Validating data—ensuring that they are in the proper range

   - Computing sums and averages

6. How to correctly nest loops; that is, use one loop inside another.

Review Exercises

1. Determine whether each of the following expressions is true or false.

   a. 3 <> 5   b. 5 <= 5   c. 5 > 5

2. If Num = 3, determine whether each of the following expressions is true or false.

   a. (Num * Num) >= (2 * Num)   b. (3 * Num − 2) >= 7

3. Determine whether each of the following expressions is true or false.

   a. "A" <> "E"   b. "E" = "E"   c. "E" = "e"

4. If N1 = "A" and N2 = "a", is:

   a. N1 = N2   b. N1 <> N2

5. Consider the following loop:

   ```
   Set Num = 2
   Repeat
       Write Num
       Set Num = Num – 1
   Until Num = 0
   ```

   a. Is this loop a pre-test loop or a post-test loop?
   b. List the statements in the body of the loop.
   c. What is the exit condition for this loop?

6. Give the output of the loop in Exercise 5.

7. Consider the following loop:

   ```
   Set Num = 2
   While Num <> 0
       Write Num
       Set Num = Num – 1
   End While
   ```

   a. Is this loop a pre-test loop or a post-test loop?
   b. List the statements in the body of the loop.
   c. What is the exit condition for this loop?

8. Give the output of the loop in Exercise 7.

9. Draw a flowchart for the pseudocode in Exercise 5.

10. Draw a flowchart for the pseudocode in Exercise 7.

11. True or false: The body of a pre-test loop must be executed at least once.

12. True or false: The body of a post-test loop must be executed at least once.

13. True or false: A counter-controlled loop cannot be constructed using a While statement.

14. True or false: A counter-controlled loop cannot be constructed using a Repeat statement.

15. Consider the counter-controlled loop:

    For K = 3 Step 2 To 8
        Write K
    End For

    a. What is the name of the counter variable?
    b. Give the values of the initial value, the increment, and the limit value.

16. Give the output of the loop in Exercise 15.

17. Fill in the blank: The counter variable in a For loop will decrease in value on each pass through the loop if the value of the loop's increment is _____.

18. Fill in the blank: If a For loop's increment is positive, then the body of the loop will not be executed if the initial value is _____ the limit value.

19. Fill in the blank: A special symbol that indicates the end of a set of data is called an end-of-data marker or a _____.

20. Fill in the blank: To _____ data means to ensure that they are in the proper range.

21. Add statements to the following pseudocode that create a post-test loop which validates the input data:

    Write "Enter a negative number: "
    Input Num

22. Redo Exercise 21 using a pre-test loop.

23. Complete each statement regarding the following pseudocode, which sums a set of numbers:

    Set A = 0
    For B = 1 Step 1 To N
        Set A = A + 2 * B – 1
    End For
    Write A

   a. The accumulator for this program is the variable _____.

   b. The counter variable for this program is _____.

24. If N = 4 in the pseudocode in Exercise 23, then what number is displayed when the corresponding code is run?

25. Rewrite the code in Exercise 23 using a While loop instead of the For loop.

26. Draw a flowchart corresponding to the pseudocode of Exercise 23.

27. Is the loop in Exercise 23 a pre-test loop or a post-test loop?

28. Add statements to the pseudocode of Exercise 23 that find the average of the N numbers A generated within the loop.

29. What is the output of the code corresponding to the following pseudocode?

```
For I = 1 Step 1 To 3
    For J = 4 Step 1 To 5
        Write I * J
    End For (J)
End For (I)
```

30. What is the output of the code corresponding to the following pseudocode?

```
Set N = 1
Repeat
    Repeat
        Write "Hello"
    Until N >= 1
    Set N = N + 1
Until N = 3
```

31. True or false: If one For loop is nested within another, then the counter variables for the two loops must be different.

32. True or false: If one For loop is nested within another, then the limit values for the two loops must be different.

33. True or false: A While loop may not be nested within a For loop.

34. True or false: Two non-overlapping loops may not be nested within a third loop.

Programming Problems

For each of the following problems, use the top-down modular approach and pseudocode to design a suitable program to solve it. Whenever appropriate, validate input data.

A. Find the sum of the squares of the integers from 1 to N, where N is input by the user.

B. Input a list of people's ages from the user (terminated by 0) and find the average age.

C. The number *N factorial*, denoted by N!, is defined to be the product of the first N positive integers:

$$N! = 1 \times 2 \times \ ... \ \times N$$

(For example, 5! = 1 × 2 × 3 × 4 × 5 = 120.) Find N!, where N is a positive integer input by the user. [*Hint:* Initialize a Product to 1 and use a loop to multiply that Product by successive integers.]

D. Allow the user to enter a sequence of temperatures in degrees Celsius (C) terminated by –999. For each one, find the corresponding temperature in degrees Fahrenheit (F). The conversion formula is F = 9 * C / 5 + 32.

E. A biologist determines that the approximate number, N, of bacteria present in a culture after T days is given by the formula

$$N = P * 2 \wedge (T \ / \ 10)$$

where P is the number present at the beginning of the observation period. Input P from the user and compute the number of bacteria in the culture after each of the first 10 days. Display the output in the form of a table with headings Day and Number.

F. Alberta Einstein teaches a business class at Podunk University. To evaluate the students in this class, she has given three tests. It is now the end of the semester and Alberta would like to have a program that inputs each student's test scores and outputs the average score for each student and the overall class average.

Decisions in the Everyday World

When was the last time you made a decision? A few seconds ago? A few minutes ago? Probably not longer than that, for the capability to choose a course of action is a built-in part of being human. It's a good thing, too, because it gives us the adaptability we need to survive in an ever-changing world. Examples of decisions you make on a daily basis are plentiful. Here are several simple ones which might sound familiar:

- IF it's the end of the month, THEN pay the rent.

- IF you're driving AND it's nighttime OR raining OR foggy, THEN turn on the headlights.

- IF the cat is chewing on the furniture, THEN chase him away; OTHERWISE give him a treat.

- IF the boss is approaching, THEN resume work; OTHERWISE continue playing computer games.

We call these *simple* decisions because they are both straightforward and limited. There is some condition (IF you're driving), which is either true or false, and you take action based on which one it is. The human brain can handle much more complicated choices as well, and deal with strange outcomes like "maybe" or "a little," but we will not consider these here. One thing is for sure, though—if you didn't have the ability to make decisions, you probably wouldn't get very far in this world.

Decision making is just as important within computer programs. After all, we want them to solve our problems for us, and our situations are usually far from simple. For example, if you were writing a payroll processing program for a large company, you would quickly discover that there are many different types of employees. Each worker type (salaried, hourly, temporary) might have his or her pay calculated by a different method. Without the variability that the IF statement provides, you would only be able to write a program that could process paychecks one way. This means you might need hundreds of different programs—some for people that worked overtime, some for people that didn't, some for employees due bonuses, and even more for individuals on differing pay scales. This approach is too horrible to even contemplate. Instead, you can use decisions (IF the employee worked overtime, THEN add extra pay) built right into one "flexible" program.

Read on—for IF you master the concepts within this chapter, THEN you will open the door to a very powerful programming technique!

Selection Structures: Making Decisions

OVERVIEW   One of a computer's characteristic qualities is its ability to make decisions—to select one of several alternative groups of statements. These groups of statements, together with the condition that determines which of them is to be executed, make up a **selection** (or **decision**) **control structure.** In this chapter, we will discuss the various types of selection structures, as well as some of their applications. To be more specific, you will learn

1. To construct single- and dual-alternative selection structures [Section 4.1].

2. About relational and logical operators [4.2].

3. To construct multiple-alternative selection structures [4.3].

4. Some applications of selection structures, including defensive programming and menu-driven programs [4.4].

5. To use a simple function, "built-in" to most programming languages [4.4].

4.1   An Introduction to Selection Structures

In this section, we will introduce the three basic types of selection (decision) structures and discuss two of them in greater detail.

Types of Selection Structures

A selection structure consists of a **test condition** together with one or more groups (or *blocks*) of statements. The result of the "test" determines which of these blocks is executed. A selection structure is called

1. A **single-alternative** (or **If-Then**) **structure** if it contains a single block of statements to be either executed or skipped.

2. A **dual-alternative** (or **If-Then-Else**) **structure** if it contains two blocks of statements, one of which is to be executed while the other is to be skipped.

FIGURE 1   **If-Then Structure**   **If-Then-Else Structure**

Flowcharts for Single- and Dual-alternative Selection Structures

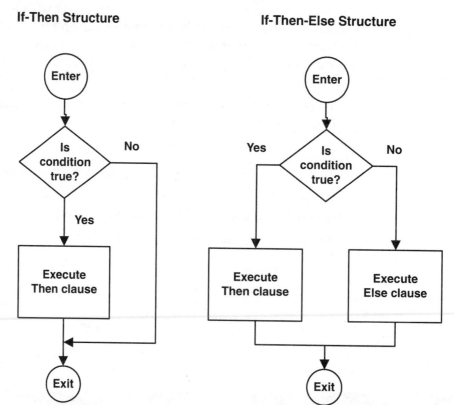

3. A **multiple-alternative structure** if it contains more than two blocks of statements, one of which is to be executed while the others are to be skipped.

Figures 1 and 2 show the flow of execution in each of the three types of selection structures. (Note that in Figure 1, the blocks of statements to be executed or skipped are referred to as the *Then* and *Else clauses.*)

Single- and Dual-alternative Structures

In this section, we will consider the single- and dual-alternative selection structures, more commonly called If-Then and If-Then-Else structures. Multiple-alternative structures will be discussed in Section 4.3.

The If-Then Structure The simplest type of selection structure is the If-Then, or single-alternative, structure. Using pseudocode, we can describe its general form as follows:

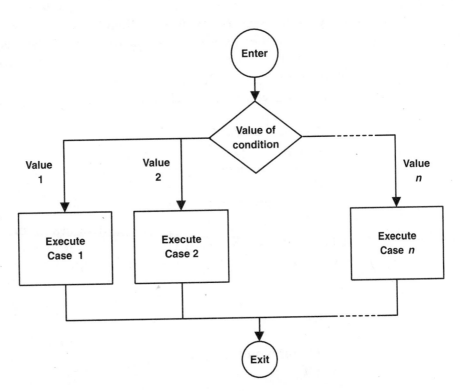

FIGURE 2

Flowchart for a Multiple-alternative Selection Structure

If *test condition* Then
    statement
    statement
      •
      •
      •
    statement
End If

In this pseudocode, *test condition* is an expression which is either true or false at the time of execution. (For example, a typical test condition is Number = 0, which is true if the value of Number is 0 and is false otherwise.) Here's how execution flows in this structure:

The action of the If-Then structure

- If the test condition is true, then the block of statements between the If-Then statement and the End If statement (the *Then clause*) is executed.

- If the test condition is false, then the block of statements between the If-Then statement and End If is skipped.

In either case, execution then proceeds to the program statement following End If. The next example illustrates this logic.

EXAMPLE 1

Suppose you are writing a program to collect information about the employees in a firm. You would like them to enter their name, address, and perhaps other personal data such as marital status, number of children, and so on. The pseudocode for part of this program might look like this:

Write "Do you have any children? (Y or N)"
Input Response
If Response = "Y" Then
    Write "How many?"
    Input NumberChildren
End If
Write "Questionnaire is complete. Thank you."

The first two lines of this program segment ask employees to state whether or not they have any children. If they respond "yes," the next question is how many; if they respond "no," there is no point in asking them how many—this question is skipped. To accomplish this, we use the If-Then structure:

If Response = "Y" Then
    Write "How many?"
    Input NumberChildren
End If

If the test condition (**Response** = "Y") is true, the Then clause—the statements between If and End If—are executed. If the Response is anything but "Y", the condition is false, and the Then clause is skipped; the next statement executed is the last Write statement in this program segment. (The flowchart on the left of Figure 1 illustrates the logic here.)

The If-Then-Else Structure   The If-Then-Else, or dual-alternative, structure has the general form:

If *test condition* Then
　　statement
　　statement
　　　•
　　　•
　　　•
　　statement
Else
　　statement
　　statement
　　　•
　　　•
　　　•
　　statement
End If

The action of the If-Then-Else structure

In this structure

- If the test condition *is* true, then the block of statements between the If-Then statement and the word Else (the *Then clause*) is executed.

- If the test condition is false, then the block of statements between Else and End If (the *Else clause*) is executed.

In either case, execution then proceeds to the program statement following End If.

EXAMPLE 2   As an example of an If-Then-Else structure, suppose part of a program is to input the costs incurred and revenue earned from producing and selling a certain product, and then display the resulting profit or loss. To do this, we need statements that:

- Compute the difference between revenue and costs.

- Describe this quantity as a *profit* if revenues are greater then costs (that is, if the difference is positive) and as a *loss* if revenues are not greater than costs (if the difference is not positive).

The following pseudocode does the job:

```
Write "Enter total costs and revenue:"
Input Cost, Revenue
Set Amount = Revenue – Cost
If Amount > 0 Then
    Set Profit = Amount
    Write "The profit is $", Profit
Else
    Set Loss = –Amount
    Write "The loss is $", Loss
End If
```

The first two statements in this program segment prompt for and input the costs and revenue for the product. We then compute the difference between these quantities (Amount), which will be a profit if positive and a loss otherwise. Now, the condition, **Amount > 0**, in the If statement is evaluated and

- If this condition is true, the Then clause

```
Set Profit = Amount
Write "The profit is $", Profit
```

is executed, which displays the amount of profit.

- If this condition is false, the Else clause

```
Set Loss = –Amount
Write "The loss is $", Loss
```

is executed. Here, Loss is set equal to the negative of Amount (so Loss is a positive number) and then this figure is displayed.

For example:

If the input values are	If the input values are
Cost = 3000 Revenue = 4000	Cost = 5000 Revenue = 2000
then, Amount = 1000 and the output is:	then, Amount = –3000 and the output is:
`The profit is $1000`	`The loss is $3000`

Style Pointer

Format an If Structure for Easy Readability   To make it easier to read the pseudocode or code for an If-Then or If-Then-Else structure, indent the statements that make up the Then and Else clauses. Moreover, in the program code, precede the structure with a step comment that explains its purpose.

Self-Test 4.1

1. Name the three types of selection structures.

2. What is the output of code corresponding to the following pseudo-code if

    a. Amount = 5?   b. Amount = –1?

    ```
    If Amount > 0 Then
        Write Amount
    End If
    Write Amount
    ```

3. What is the output of code corresponding to the following pseudo-code if

    a. Amount = 5?   b. Amount = –1?

    ```
    If Amount > 0 Then
        Write Amount
    Else
        Set Amount = –Amount
        Write Amount
    End If
    ```

4. For the following pseudocode:

    ```
    If Number > 0 Then
        Write "Yes"
    End If
    If Number = 0 Then
        Write "No"
    End If
    If Number < 0 Then
        Write "No"
    End If
    ```

    a. What is the output of the corresponding code if Number = 10? If Number = –10?

    b. Write a single If-Then-Else structure that has the same effect as the given pseudocode.

4.2   *Relational and Logical Operators*

As you have seen in Section 4.1, decision making involves testing a condition. To help construct these conditions, we use *relational* and *logical* operators. In Chapter 3, we introduced relational operators. In this section, we will review this subject and then discuss logical operators.

Relational Operators Revisited

In Section 4.1, we gave examples of selection structures, which included conditions such as **Response** = "Y" and **Amount** > 0. The *equal* (=) and *greater than* (>) symbols that appear in these conditions are known as **relational operators.** There are six standard relational operators; they, and their programming symbols, are:

Equal, =	Not equal, <>
Less than, <	Less than or equal, <=
Greater than, >	Greater than or equal, >=

All six operators can be applied to either numeric or character-based data. For the time being, we will only use the *equal* and *not equal* operators with characters; in Section 5.2, we will return to this topic and discuss it in greater generality. The next two examples illustrate the use of relational operators.

EXAMPLE 3   Let Num1 = 3, Num2 = –1, Char1 = "H", and Char2 = "K". Then all of the following expressions are true.

a.   Num1 <> Num2   b.   Num1 >= Num2
c.   Char1 <> Char2   d.   Char1 <> "h"

EXAMPLE 4   The program segment below on the right was obtained from the one on the left by reversing its test condition and its Then and Else clauses. The resulting pseudocode has the same effect as the original.

If Num >= 0 Then	If Num < 0 Then
Write Num	Set PosNum = –Num
Else	Write PosNum
Set PosNum = –Num	Else
Write PosNum	Write Num
End If	End If

Logical Operators

Logical operators are used to create more complicated (*compound*) conditions from given *simple* conditions. This is illustrated in the next few examples, which introduce the most important logical operators: Or, And, and Not.

EXAMPLE 5

The Or
operator

The following two program segments are equivalent. They both display the message OK if the number input is either less than 5 or greater than 10. The segment on the right uses the logical operator Or to help perform this task.

```
Input X
If X < 5 Then
      Write "OK"
End If
If X > 10 Then
      Write "OK"
End If
```

```
Input X
If (X < 5) Or (X > 10) Then
      Write "OK"
End If
```

In the second program segment, the compound condition (X < 5) Or (X > 10) is true if and only if *either* simple condition, X < 5 or X > 10, is true. It is false if *both* simple conditions are false.

The And
operator

The And operator also creates a compound condition from two simple ones. Here, however, the compound condition is true if and only if *both* simple conditions are true. For example, the expression (A > B) And (Response = "Y") is true if A is greater than B *and* Response is equal to "Y". If A is not greater than B or Response is not equal to "Y", then the compound condition is false.

The Not
operator

The Not operator, unlike Or and And, acts upon a single given condition. The resulting condition formed by using Not is true if and only if the given condition is false. For example, Not (A < 6) is true if A is not less than 6; it is false if A is less than 6. (Thus, Not (A < 6) is equivalent to the condition A >= 6.)

EXAMPLE 6

Suppose X = 1. Is each of the following expressions true or false?

a. $(2 * X + 1 = 3)$ And $(X > 2)$
b. Not $((X / 2) = 0)$

In part *a*, the first simple condition is true, but the second is false (X is not greater than 2). Hence, the compound And condition is false.

In part *b*, since X/2 = 1/2, X/2 is not equal to 0. Thus, the condition X/2 = 0 is false, and the given condition is true.

Truth tables for Or, And, and Not   The action of the operators Or, And, and Not can be indicated by the use of *truth tables*. Let X and Y represent simple conditions. Then for the truth values of X and Y given on each line at the left of the following table, the resulting truth values of X Or Y, X And Y, and Not X are as listed on the right.

X	Y	X Or Y	X And Y	Not X
true	true	true	true	false
true	false	true	false	false
false	true	true	false	true
false	false	false	false	true

Hierarchy of Operations

In a given condition, there may be arithmetic, relational, and logical operators. If parentheses are present, we perform the operations within parentheses first. In the absence of parentheses, the arithmetic operations are done first (in their usual order), then any relational operation, and finally, Not, And, and Or, in that order. This hierarchy of operations is summarized in Table 1.

TABLE 1
Hierarchy of Operations

Type	Operator	Order Performed
Arithmetic	$\wedge$ *, / +, −	First
Relational	=, <>, <, <=, >, >=	
Logical	Not And Or	Last

EXAMPLE 7   Let Q = 3 and let R = 5. Is the following expression true or false?

Not Q > 3 Or R < 3 And Q − R < 0

Keeping in mind the hierarchy of operations (in particular, the fact that among logical operators, Not is performed first, And is second, and Or is last), let us insert parentheses to explicitly show the order in which the operations are to be performed:

(Not(Q > 3)) Or ((R < 3) And ((Q − R) < 0))

We evaluate the simple conditions first and find that Q > 3 is false, R < 3 is false, and (Q − R) < 0 is true. Then, by substituting these values (true or false) into the given expression and performing the logical operations, we arrive at the answer. We can show this is by means of an "evaluation chart":

(Not(Q > 3)) Or ((R < 3) And ((Q − R) < 0))
(Not(false)) Or ((false) And (true))
    (true)   Or   (false)
              true

Thus, the given relational expression is true.

The next example* demonstrates one common occurrence of logical operators in programming.

EXAMPLE 8   Suppose we want to ensure that a number input by the user is between 1 and 4 (including both 1 and 4). The following program segment could be used to validate this data.

Write "Enter a number between 1 and 4 (inclusive):"
Input Number
While (Number < 1) Or (Number > 4)
    Write "The number must be between 1 and 4."
    Write "Please reenter it: "
    Input Number
End While

Suppose that in response to the first input prompt, the user enters an acceptable number, one lying between 1 and 4. Then, both simple conditions in the While statement (**Number < 1** and **Number > 4**) are

---

*This example makes use of material covered in Chapter 3.

false. Thus, the compound condition created by the Or operator is false. So, in this case, the data validation While loop is skipped.

On the other hand, if the user enters a number that is out of the allowable range, at least one of the simple conditions in the While statement will be true, making the compound Or condition true. Thus, in this case, the loop is entered and the user is requested to input a valid number.

Programming Pointer Some programming languages allow variables to be of logical (sometimes called *boolean*) type. Such a variable may only take one of two values, *true* or *false*. For example, in Pascal, we can declare a variable, say Answer, to be of boolean type and then use it in a statement anywhere that a value of true or false is valid, such as:

```
if Answer then Write('Congratulations!')
```

Self-Test 4.2

1. Replace the blank by the word *arithmetic, relational,* or *logical.*

   a. <= is a(n) _____ operator.
   b. + is a(n) _____ operator.
   c. Or is a(n) _____ operator.

2. Determine whether each of the following expressions is true or false.

   a. 8 <= 8   b. 8 <> 8
   c. "E" = "E"   d. "E" <> "E"

3. Let X = 1 and let Y = 2. Determine whether each of the following expressions is true or false.

   a. X >= X Or Y >= X   b. X > X And Y > X
   c. X > Y Or X > 0 And Y < 0 d. Not(Not X = 0 And Not Y = 0)

4. Write a program segment that inputs a number Num and displays the word *Correct* if it is not the case that Num is both greater than 0 and less than 100.

4.3 Selecting from Several Alternatives

The If-Then-Else (dual-alternative) structure selects, based upon the value of its test condition, one of two alternative blocks of statements. Sometimes, however, a program must handle decisions having more than two options. In such a case, we use a *multiple-alternative* selection structure. As you will see, this structure can be implemented in several different ways. To contrast the different methods, we will use each of them to solve the following problem, which involves a selection structure with four alternatives.

The *Rating* *Assignment* Problem Suppose that we are developing a program to compute and display ratings of various products, and need a program segment that translates a numerical score (represented by an integer from 1 to 10) into a letter "grade" according to the following rules:

- If the score is 10, the rating is "A".
- If the score is 8 or 9, the rating is "B".
- If the score is 6 or 7, the rating is "C".
- If the score is below 6, the rating is "D".

Using **If** *Structures*

We can implement a multiple-alternative structure using several applications of If-Then or If-Then-Else statements. The simplest technique makes use of a sequence of If-Then statements in which each test condition corresponds to one of the alternatives. Example 9 illustrates this technique.

EXAMPLE 9 The following program segment uses a sequence of If-Then structures to solve the Rating Assignment problem described above. (The variable Rating used here is of character type.)

```
If Score = 10 Then
    Set Rating = "A"
End If
If (Score = 8) Or (Score = 9) Then
    Set Rating = "B"
End If
If (Score = 6) Or (Score = 7) Then
    Set Rating = "C"
End If
If (Score >= 1) And (Score <= 5) Then
    Set Rating = "D"
End If
```

This technique is very straightforward and involves pseudocode (and corresponding program code) that is easy to understand. However, it is inefficient—regardless of the value of Score, the program must evaluate all four test conditions. Figure 3 contains a flowchart showing the flow of execution in this example.

Another way to implement a multiple-alternative structure is to *nest* If-Then-Else structures. This technique is illustrated in Example 10.

EXAMPLE 10   This program segment uses nested If-Then-Else structures to solve the Rating Assignment problem. Although the resulting code will be more efficient than that for Example 9, it will also be more difficult to follow. The flowchart in Figure 4 should help you to untangle the flow of execution in this pseudocode.

> If Score = 10 Then
>   Set Rating = "A"
> Else
>   If (Score = 8) Or (Score = 9) Then
>   Set Rating = "B"
>   Else

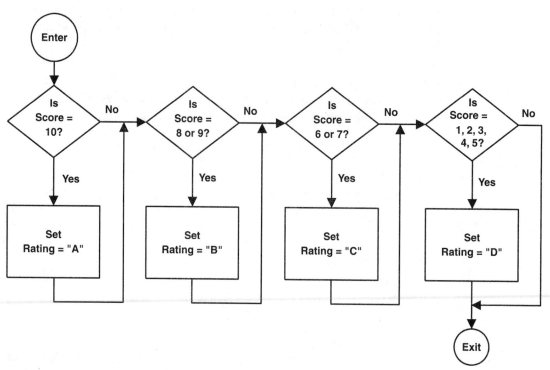

FIGURE 3   Flowchart for Example 9

> If (Score = 6) Or (Score = 7) Then
>> Set Rating = "C"
> Else
>> Set Rating = "D"
> End If
> End If
> End If

As an example of how this pseudocode works, suppose the variable Score is equal to 8. Since Score is not 10, the first Else clause is executed

FIGURE 4

Flowchart for Example 10

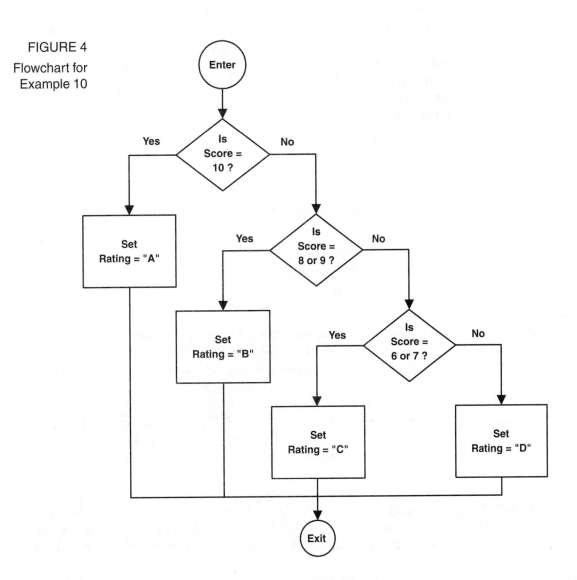

and the test condition (Score = 8) Or (Score = 9) is evaluated and found to be true. Thus, the Then clause of this particular structure is executed, Rating is set equal to "B", the corresponding Else clause is skipped, and execution of all If-Then-Else structures is complete. Notice that, unlike the technique used in Example 9, this program does not always have to evaluate *all* test conditions to accomplish the rating assignment.

Using **Case-***type Statements*

So far, we have demonstrated two ways, both using If structures, to create a multiple-alternative selection structure. To make it easier to code multiple-alternative structures, many programming languages contain a statement, usually called *Case* or *Switch,* specifically designed for this purpose. This statement contains a single *test expression* that determines which block of code is to be executed. A typical Case-type statement looks like this:

> Select Case Of *test expression*
>   Case *list of values 1 :*
>   *block of statements 1*
>   Case *list of values 2 :*
>   *block of statements 2*
>
>   .
>   .
>   .
>
>   Case *list of values n :*
>   *block of statements n*
> End Case

The action of the Case statement
Here's how this statement works: The test expression is evaluated and its value is compared to those in the first Case list. If there is a match, the first block of statements is executed and the structure is exited. If there is no match in the first list, the value of the test expression is compared to the second list of values. If there is a match here, the second block of statements is executed and the structure is exited. This process continues until either a match for the test expression value is found or End Case is encountered. In the latter situation, no action is taken and the structure is exited.

EXAMPLE 11
To illustrate the use of a Case statement, let us return to the Rating Assignment problem, which is stated at the beginning of this section. Here is a third solution. (The first two are given in Examples 9 and 10.)

```
Select Case Of Score
      Case 10 :
            Set Rating = "A"
      Case 8, 9 :
            Set Rating = "B"
      Case 6, 7 :
            Set Rating = "C"
      Case 1-5 :
            Set Rating = "D"
End Case
```

When this Case statement is executed, Score is evaluated and the Case lists are examined. If a constant equal to Score is found in one of the lists, the corresponding statement is executed. (The notation "1–5" denotes the range of numbers from 1 to 5.) See Figure 5 for a flowchart for this example.

FIGURE 5

Flowchart for
Example 11

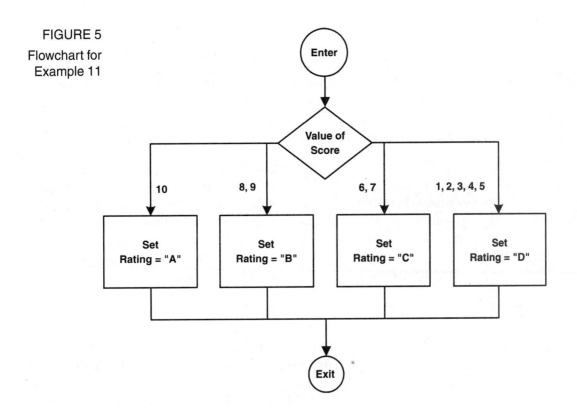

Self-Test 4.3

In Exercises 1–3, construct a multiple-alternative structure (using the indicated method) that displays "Low" if X is equal to 0, "Medium" if X is equal to 1 or 2, or "High" if X is greater than 2 but less than or equal to 10. (Assume that X is an integer.)

1. Use a sequence of If-Then statements.

2. Use nested If-Then-Else statements.

3. Use a Case statement.

4. Suppose Choice is a variable of character type. Give pseudocode for a multiple-alternative structure that calls modules

   - YesAction if Choice is "y" or "Y"
   - NoAction if Choice is "n" or "N"

   or, if Choice is any other character, displays the message:
   ```
   Signing off
   Goodbye
   ```

4.4   Applications of Selection Structures

In this section we will discuss two important applications of selection structures: defensive programming and menu-driven programming.

Defensive Programming

Defensive programming involves the inclusion of statements within a program to check, during execution, for improper data. The program segment that catches and reports an error of this sort is called an *error trap*. In this section, we will show how to prevent two common "illegal operations"—division by 0 and taking the square root of a negative number. (Section 3.3 presents another aspect of defensive programming —*data validation*, checking that input data are in the proper range.)

Avoiding a Potential Division by Zero   If a division operation is performed during execution of a program and the number being divided by (the *divisor*) is 0, execution will halt and an error message will be displayed. (We say, in such a situation, that the program has *crashed*.) The following example illustrates how to program defensively against this type of error with the aid of an If-Then-Else selection structure.

EXAMPLE
12

The *reciprocal* of a number x is given by $1/x$. For example, the reciprocal of –3 is $1/(-3) = -1/3$. Every number, except 0, has a reciprocal. We say that the reciprocal of 0 *is not defined* (because there is no real number equal to $1/0$). The following program segment displays the reciprocal of the number entered by the user unless that number is 0, in which case it displays an appropriate message.

```
Write "Enter a number."
Write "This program will display its reciprocal."
Input Num
If Num <> 0 Then
        Set Reciprocal = 1 / Num
        Write "The reciprocal of Num is ", Reciprocal
Else
        Write "The reciprocal of 0 is not defined."
End If
```

In this program segment, the Else clause handles the potential division by zero. By anticipating this illegal operation, we prevent the resulting program crash.

Dealing with Square Roots   In some applications, it is necessary to find the square root of a number. For this reason, most programming languages contain a "built-in" function that computes square roots. A typical square root function has the form

The Sqrt
function

Sqrt (*numeric expression*)

where *numeric expression* may be any number, variable, or arithmetic expression whose value is *nonnegative* (greater than or equal to 0). The square root function may be used anywhere in a program that a numeric constant is valid. When this function is encountered, the program finds the value of *numeric expression* and then calculates its square root. For example, the statements

```
Set Num1 = 7
Set Num2 = Sqrt(Num1 + 2)
Write Num2
```

will display the number 3 (the square root of 9).

Since the square root of a negative number is not a real number, taking such a square root is not defined—it is an "illegal operation." The next example illustrates how to guard against a program crash when using the Sqrt function.

EXAMPLE 13   This program segment inputs a number N. If N is nonnegative, it computes and displays its square root; if N is negative, it displays a message indicating that the square root is not defined.

```
Write "Enter a number."
Write "This program will display its square root."
Input N
If N >= 0 Then
    Write "The square root of ", N, " is ", Sqrt(N)
Else
    Write "The square root of ", N
    Write "is not defined."
End If
```

In the If-Then-Else structure, the Then clause displays the square root of the input number N if this operation is valid. If N < 0, the Else clause reports the fact that taking the square root in this case is an illegal operation.

Programming Pointer   When your program contains selection structures, it is important to make enough test runs so that all blocks, or branches, of the structures are executed. For example, to test the code corresponding to Example 13, we must run the program at least twice: once inputting a positive value for N to test the Then clause and a second time with a negative value for N to test the Else clause.

Style Pointer   **Program Defensively**   Include error-trapping structures in your programs to catch and report the following kinds of errors:

1. Division by 0

2. A negative argument for the square root function

3. Input data that is out of the allowable range (see Section 3.3)

Any one of these errors may cause your program to crash.

Menu-driven Programs

A major goal when writing programs is to make them *user-friendly*—to ensure that they are easy to use. For complex programs in which the user is presented with many options, listing these options in *menus* enhances user-friendliness. Programs that present their options in this fashion, instead of by requiring their users to memorize commands, are said to be **menu-driven.**

In a typical menu-driven program, the first screen that a user sees displays the **main menu,** a list of the program's major functions. For example, in a program that manages the inventory of a business, the main menu might look like this:

```
        The Legendary Lawn Mower Company
                Inventory Control

Leave the program ................. Enter 0
Add an item to the list ........... Enter 1
Delete an item from the list ...... Enter 2
Change an item on the list ........ Enter 3
```

In program design terms, the items displayed on the main menu usually correspond to separate modules. Selecting one of the main menu choices either leads the user to another more detailed *submenu* (corresponding to additional submodules), or directly into the specified task. As shown in the following example, a multiple-alternative structure is used to branch to the appropriate module once the user has selected an option.

EXAMPLE 14 The inventory control menu given above can be implemented by the following pseudocode:

```
Write "    The Legendary Lawn Mower Company"
Write "         Inventory Control"
Write
Write "Leave the program .......... Enter 0"
Write "Add an item to the list ........ Enter 1"
Write "Delete an item from the list .... Enter 2"
Write "Change an item on the list ..... Enter 3"
Write
Write "    Selection ---> "
Input Choice
Select Case Of Choice
    Case 0:
        Write "Goodbye"
    Case 1:
        Call AddItem Module
    Case 2:
        Call DeleteItem Module
    Case 3:
        Call ChangeItem Module
End Case
```

After the menu is displayed, this program segment prompts for and inputs the user's choice of options. Then, the multiple-alternative (Case) structure takes the appropriate action.

Enhancing the Menu Display Pseudocode The pseudocode of Example 14 can be improved in several ways:

- The statements that prompt for and input the user's choice should be placed in a data validation loop (see Section 3.3) that ensures that the number entered is an integer from 0 to 3:

```
Repeat
    Write
    Write "       Selection ---> "
    Input Choice
Until (Choice = 0) Or (Choice = 1) Or
    (Choice = 2) Or (Choice = 3)
```

- The entire program segment of Example 14 should be placed in a loop so that after a particular task (AddItem, DeleteItem, or ChangeItem) is completed, the menu is redisplayed and the user can select another option. To be more specific, the revised pseudocode has the form:

```
Repeat
    Write "     The Legendary Lawn Mower Company"
    Write "          Inventory Control"
    Write
    Write "Leave the program . . . . . . . . Enter 0"
        •
        •
        •
    End Case
Until Choice = 0
```

Now, users can carry out several tasks in a single program run.

Self-Test 4.4

1. If A = 4, find the value of the following:

    a. Sqrt (A)   b. Sqrt (2 * A + 1)

2. Rewrite the following code using defensive programming techniques:

```
Set C = Sqrt(A) / B
Write C
```

3. The formula for the sum, S, of the first N terms of a certain series is

$$S = (1 - R)^N / (1 - R)$$

where R is a given number.

   a. For what value of R does division by 0 occur?
   b. Write a program segment, which includes data validation, that computes and displays S (assuming that R and N have already been input).

4. Determine whether each of the following statements is true or false.

   a. A menu displays various program options for the user.
   b. Menu-driven programs are considered more user-friendly than programs that require the memorization of commands.

5. Write a program segment that displays a menu with the user options "order hamburger," "order hotdog," "order tuna salad," and then inputs the user selection.

4.5 *Focus on Problem Solving*

In this section, we will develop a program that makes use of selection structures and menus to compute the cost of a new car purchased with various options.

A New Car Price Calculator

Universal Motors makes new cars. They compute the purchase price of their autos by taking the base price of the vehicle, adding in various costs for different kinds of options, and then adding shipping and dealer charges. The shipping and dealer charges are fixed for each vehicle at $500 and $175, respectively, but regardless of the particular model, the buyer can select the following options: type of engine, type of interior trim, and type of radio. (The various choices for each option and the associated prices are listed in Table 2 on the following page.)

Universal Motors would like a program that allows them to input the base price of a vehicle and the desired options from the user, and which would then display the selling price of that vehicle.

TABLE 2

Options Available for Universal Motors' Vehicles

Engine	Purchase Code	Price
6 cylinder	S	$150
8 cylinder	E	$475
Diesel	D	$750
Interior Trim	Purchase Code	Price
Vinyl	V	$50
Cloth	C	$225
Leather	L	$800
Radio	Purchase Code	Price
AM/FM/Cassette	C	$300
AM/FM/CD	P	$400

Problem Analysis   This problem has very clearly defined input and output. The input consists of the base price (BasePrice), the engine choice (EngineChoice), the interior trim choice (TrimChoice), and the radio choice (RadioChoice). After the user has entered each choice of option, the program must determine the corresponding cost of that option: EngineCost, TrimCost, and RadioCost.

The only item output is the selling price (SellingPrice) of the vehicle. To determine this quantity, the program must also know the (fixed) value of the shipping and dealer charges (ShippingCharge and DealerCharge). Then, the computation is simple:

$$\text{SellingPrice} = \text{BasePrice} + \text{EngineCost} + \text{TrimCost} + \text{RadioCost} + \text{ShippingCharge} + \text{DealerCharge}$$

Program Design   Roughly speaking, our program must:

1. Input the base price

2. Process the various option choices to compute additional costs

3. Total all the costs

4. Display the final selling price

We will input the base price in the main module and then transfer control to several submodules, one for each available option. Within each submodule, a menu will be displayed allowing the user to enter a choice for that option (see Table 2). The submodule will then use this selection to determine the corresponding option cost. After all option selections are made, another module will compute the total cost and display the results. Thus, the main module will contain four submodules:

- Compute Engine Cost
- Compute Interior Trim Cost
- Compute Radio Cost
- Display Selling Price

The hierarchy chart in Figure 6 shows the program modules and their relationship to one another. We now describe each of the modules in more detail.

Main Module   This module displays a welcome message, gets the base price, and then calls the other modules. Its pseudocode is:

```
Display a welcome message
Prompt for and input the vehicle's base price:
    Write "Enter the base price:"
    Input BasePrice
Call Compute Engine Cost
Call Compute Interior Trim Cost
Call Compute Radio Cost
Call Display Selling Price
End Program
```

Compute Engine Cost Module   This module displays a menu to allow the user to specify the type of engine desired and then determines the cost of this engine option. Its pseudocode is:

FIGURE 6

Hierarchy Chart for *A New Car Price Calculator*

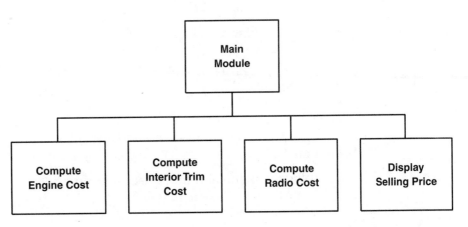

Display the menu and input user selection:
    Write "S - 6 cylinder engine"
    Write "E - 8 cylinder engine"
    Write "D - Diesel engine"
    Write "Selection?"
    Input EngineChoice

Determine the cost of the selected option:
    Select Case Of EngineChoice
        Case "S":
            Set EngineCost = 150
        Case "E":
            Set EngineCost = 475
        Case "D":
            Set EngineCost = 750
    End Case

Compute Interior Trim Cost Module   This module displays a menu to allow the user to specify the type of interior trim desired and then determines the cost of this trim option.

Display the menu and input user selection:
    Write "V - Vinyl interior trim"
    Write "C - Cloth interior trim"
    Write "L - Leather interior trim"
    Write "Selection?"
    Input TrimChoice

Determine the cost of the selected option:
    Select Case Of TrimChoice
        Case "V":
            Set TrimCost = 50
        Case "C":
            Set TrimCost = 225
        Case "L":
            Set TrimCost = 800
    End Case

Compute Radio Cost Module   This module displays a menu to allow the user to specify the type of radio desired and then determines the cost of this option.

Display the menu and input user selection:
    Write "C - Cassette player"

Write "P - Compact disc player"
Write "Selection?"
Input RadioChoice

Determine the cost of the selected option:
   If RadioChoice = "C" Then
      Set RadioCost = 300
   Else
      Set RadioCost = 400
   End If

Display Selling Price Module   This module computes and displays the selling price of the vehicle with the selected options.

Set ShippingCharge = 500
Set DealerCharge = 175
Set SellingPrice = BasePrice + EngineCost + TrimCost +
     RadioCost + ShippingCharge + DealerCharge
Write "The total selling price for your vehicle is"
Write SellingPrice

Improving the New Car Price Calculator Program   Using loops, which are covered in Chapter 3, we can improve this program by adding flexibility in the overall processing scheme and doing some data validation. To be more specific:

- We can allow the user to compute the costs for more than one car by placing the main module in a loop, as follows:

    Display a welcome message
    Repeat
       Prompt for and input BasePrice
       Call Compute Engine Cost
       Call Compute Interior Trim Cost
       Call Compute Radio Cost
       Call Display Selling Price
       Write "Continue? (Y/N)"
       Input Response
    Until Response = "N"
    End Program

- In the three option cost modules, we can employ data validation (see Section 3.3) to check if an incorrect letter code has been input. For example, in the Compute Radio Cost module, the user is supposed to enter "C" or "P". Here, the prompt and input statements could be placed in a loop to validate this data, like this:

> Repeat
>   Write "Selection?"
>   Input RadioChoice
> Until (RadioChoice = "C") Or (RadioChoice = "P")

Program Code In writing the program code, we make a few additional enhancements to the program:

- We include header and step comments for each module.

- We use the programming language's "clear screen" statement to remove all current text from the screen prior to displaying the welcome message and the various option menus.

Program Test Test runs of the program should use various base prices and option combinations to ensure that the calculations and purchase codes in the Case and If statements work properly. If you are using data validation techniques (see the TIP in the Program Design section), test runs should check for codes not on the list of acceptable choices.

Self-Test 4.5

These exercises refer to the New Car Price Calculator problem in this section.

1. Replace the Case statements in the Compute Engine Cost and Compute Trim Cost modules with If statements.

2. Replace the BasePrice input statement in the main module by a module that allows the user to choose among three car models, each with a different base price. The user will input the model designation "X", "Y", or "Z", and the program will determine the corresponding base price—$20,000, $25,000, or $28,000, respectively.

Chapter Review and Exercises

Key Terms

Selection (decision) structure	Test condition
Single-alternative structure	If-Then structure
Dual-alternative structure	If-Then-Else structure
Multiple-alternative structure	Relational operator
Logical operator	Defensive programming
Menu-driven program	Main menu

Chapter Summary

In this chapter, we have discussed the following topics:

1. The single-alternative selection structure:

    - Contains a single block of statements to be either executed or skipped.

    - Is implemented by an If-Then statement.

2. The dual-alternative selection structure:

    - Contains two blocks of statements, one of which is to be executed while the other is to be skipped.

    - Is implemented by an If-Then-Else statement.

3. The multiple-alternative selection structure:

    - Contains more than two blocks of statements, one of which is to be executed while the others are to be skipped.

    - Is implemented by a sequence of If-Then statements, nested If-Then-Else statements, or a Case-type statement.

4. Relational and logical operators:

    - The six relational operators are: equal (=), not equal (<>), less than (<), less than or equal (<=), greater than (>), and greater than or equal (>=).

    - The logical operators covered in the text are: Not, And, and Or.

    - The order of operations in the absence of parentheses is: arithmetic operations are done first (in their usual order), then relational operations, and finally, Not, And, and Or, in that order.

5. Defensive programming—anticipating and preventing errors that might result from using improper data. For example:
   - Avoiding division by 0 and taking the square root of a negative number
   - Ensuring that input data are in the proper range (Chapter 3)

6. Menu-driven programs:
   - Present options for the user in the form of menus.
   - Use a multiple-alternative structure to handle the user's option selection.

7. The built-in Sqrt function:
   - Is of the form Sqrt (*numeric expression*), where *numeric expression* has a nonnegative value.
   - May be used anywhere in a program that a numeric constant is valid.

Review Exercises

1. List the programming symbols for the six relational operators.

2. List three types of logical operators used in programming.

3. If Response = "Y", determine whether each of the following expressions is true or false.
   - a. Response = "y"   b. Response <> "N"

4. If X = 0, determine whether each of the following expressions is true or false.
   - a. X >= 0   b. 2 * X + 1 <> 1

5. If X = 0 and Response = "Y", determine whether each of the following expressions is true or false.
   - a. (X = 1) Or (Response = "Y")
   - b. (X = 1) And (Response = "Y")
   - c. Not (X = 0)

6. If Num1 = 1 and Num2 = 2, determine whether each of the following expressions is true or false.
   - a. (Num1 = 1) Or (Num2 = 2) And (Num1 = Num2)
   - b. ((Num1 = 1) Or (Num2 = 2)) And (Num1 = Num2)
   - c. Not (Num1 = 1) And Not (Num2 = 2)
   - d. Not (Num1 = 1) Or Not (Num2 = 2)

7. Write expressions equivalent to the following without using the Not operator:

   a. Not (N > 0)   b. Not ((N >= 0) And (N <= 5))

8. Write expressions equivalent to the following using a single *relational* operator:

   a. (X > 1) And (X > 5)   b. (X = 1) Or (X > 1)

9. Fill in the blank: A single-alternative structure is also known as a(n) _____ structure.

10. Fill in the blank: A dual-alternative structure is also known as a(n) _____ structure.

11. A multiple-alternative structure cannot be implemented by using

    a. A single If-Then statement.
    b. Several If-Then statements.
    c. Several If-Then-Else statements.
    d. A single Case-type statement.

12. The term *defensive programming* refers to

    a. Ensuring that input data are in the proper range.
    b. Ensuring that a division by 0 does not take place.
    c. Ensuring that the square root operation is valid.
    d. Techniques that include all the above points.

13. True or false: A menu-driven program requires the user to memorize a list of commands to select options offered by a program.

14. True or false: In a menu-driven program, the options on the main menu usually correspond to separate program modules.

15. Write a program segment that inputs Num; then displays "Yes" if Num is equal to 1 or 2.

16. Write a program segment that inputs Num; then displays "Yes" if Num = 1 and displays "No" if Num = 2.

17. Draw a flowchart that corresponds to Exercise 15.

18. Draw a flowchart that corresponds to Exercise 16.

19. Write a program segment that inputs Num; then displays "Yes" if Num = 1 and displays "No" otherwise.

20. Write a program segment that inputs Num; then displays "Yes" if Num = 1, displays "No" if Num = 2, and displays "Maybe" if Num = 3. Implement this program segment by
    a. A sequence of If-Then statements.
    b. Nested If-Then-Else statements.
    c. A Case-type statement.

21. Write a program segment that inputs a number X and
    • Displays the reciprocal of its square root, 1/Sqrt(X), if X > 0.
    • Displays "Error: Division by zero", if X = 0.
    • Displays "Error: Square root of negative number", if X < 0.

22. Rewrite the following statements using proper defensive programming techniques:
    Set Num3 = Sqrt(Num1) / Num2
    Write Num3

23. Which type of selection structure does the flowchart in Figure 7 represent?

24. Write pseudocode that uses If-Then statements to implement the flowchart in Figure 7. (Assume that Score is an integer between 1 and 10 inclusively.)

FIGURE 7
Flowchart for
Exercises
23–26

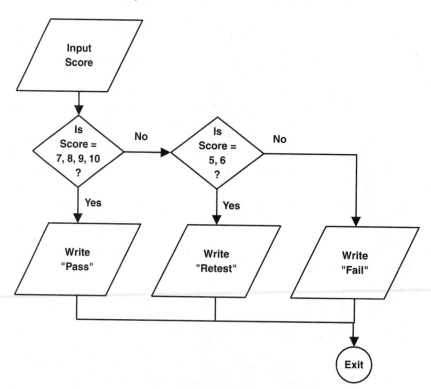

25. Write pseudocode that uses nested If-Then-Else statements to implement the flowchart in Figure 7. (Assume that Score is an integer between 1 and 10 inclusively.)

26. Write pseudocode that uses a Case-type statement to achieve the same action as that indicated by the flowchart in Figure 7. (Assume that Score is an integer between 1 and 10 inclusively.)

27. What is displayed when code corresponding to the following program segment is run?

```
Set X = 5
If X > 0 Then
     Write X
End If
If Not ((X = 0) Or (X < 0)) Then
     Write "Not"
End If
If (X ^ 2 >= 0) And (2 * X – 1) <> 0 Then
     Write "And"
End If
```

28. What is displayed when code corresponding to the following program segment is run?

```
Set Y = 1
If Sqrt(Y – 1) = 0 Then
     Write "YES"
Else
     Write "NO"
End If
```

29. What is displayed when code corresponding to the following program segment is run and the input is:

a. –1   b. 0   c. 1

```
Input Num
If Num < 0 Then
     Write "1"
Else
     If Num = 0 Then
          Write "2"
     Else
          Write "3"
     End If
End If
Write "DONE"
```

30. What is displayed when code corresponding to the following program segment is run and the input is:

    a. −1   b. 0   c. 1

    ```
    Set Num1 = 1
    Input Num2
    Select Case Of Num2
        Case: −1
            Write "A"
        Case: 0
            Write "B"
        Case: Num1
            Write "C"
    End Case
    ```

31. This program segment is supposed to display HELLO if Grade = "A" and display GOODBYE otherwise. Correct the logic error so that it works correctly.

    ```
    If Grade <> "A" Then
        Write "HELLO"
    Else
        Write "GOODBYE"
    End If
    ```

32. This program segment is supposed to display NEGATIVE if Num is less than 0, SMALL if Num lies between 0 and 5 (inclusive), and LARGE if Num is greater than 5. Correct the logic error so that this pseudocode works correctly.

    ```
    If Num < 0 Then
        Write "NEGATIVE"
    Else
        If Num > 5 Then
            Write "SMALL"
        Else
            Write "LARGE"
        End If
    End If
    ```

Programming Problems

For each of the following problems, use the top-down modular approach and pseudocode to design a suitable program to solve it. Where appropriate, use defensive programming techniques.

A. Input a number entered by the user and display "Positive" if it's greater than zero, "Negative" if it's less than zero, and "Neither positive nor negative" if it's equal to zero.

B. Develop a menu-driven program that inputs two numbers and, at the user's option, finds their sum, difference, product, or quotient.

C. Input a number X and find the area (A) of each of the following:
   - A square with side X, $A = X^2$
   - A circle with radius X, $A = 3.14 * X^2$
   - An equilateral triangle with side X, $A = (Sqrt(3)/4) * X^2$

   Note that, since X represents a dimension, we require that $X > 0$.

D. Develop a menu-driven program that inputs a number X and, at the user's option, finds the area of a square with side X, the area of a circle with radius X, *or* the area of an equilateral triangle with side X. (See Problem C.)

E. The equation $Ax^2 + B = 0$ has
   - Two solutions, $X1 = Sqrt(-B/A)$ and $X2 = - Sqrt(-B/A)$, if $B/A < 0$.
   - One solution, $X = 0$, if $B/A = 0$.
   - No real number solutions if $B/A > 0$.

   Input the coefficients, A and B, for this equation. If $A = 0$, terminate the program; otherwise, solve the equation.

F. Compute the income tax due (in a certain state) on a taxable income entered by the user, according to the following table:

TAXABLE INCOME		TAX DUE
From	To	
$0	$50,000	$0 + 5% of amount over $0
$50,000	$100,000	$2,500 + 7% of amount over $50,000
$100,000	. . . .	$6,000 + 9% of amount over $100,000

The solutions to the following problems require the use of repetition structures (which are covered in Chapter 3).

G. Find and display the largest of a list of numbers entered by the user and terminated by –9999.

H. For a list of numbers entered by the user and terminated by 0, find the sum of the positive numbers and the sum of the negative numbers.

Data Files in the Everyday World

You probably write down information you need to remember on little scraps of paper all the time, and that's good enough for a lot of things. If you try to run a business that way, however, you'll probably soon find yourself in trouble. Why? Well, for one thing, you'll have an awful time locating the data you need to pay bills, employees, and suppliers—lose that little piece of envelope on which you wrote a reminder, and someone may go unpaid. That's why offices have filing cabinets full of files. By keeping large amounts of data organized and stored in a uniform manner, it's easy to locate and process the paperwork. For example, there might be a drawer labeled "Payroll," with folders for each month of the year. Inside each folder may be copies of employees' time sheets or other pay records. Another drawer might contain folders for purchase orders and billing records, and so on. Even if a company is fully computerized, the same kinds of folders and files would exist, but in electronic form on a disk drive inside a company computer.

Regardless of the contents of a file, the information within it needs some structure to make processing it predictable and easy. For example, a simple employee file, whether on paper or disk, might contain the following record of information for each employee:

> File number
> Employee name
> Employee number
> Address
> Department
> Hire date
> Pay rate

If the collection of these records is filed in alphabetical order, then any person with access to the filing cabinet can easily and quickly find the record for a particular worker. Once the appropriate record is located, that person can, for example, use it for a report, modify it, or throw it away ("delete it"). On the other hand, sometimes the entire file needs to be processed. For example, when paychecks must be disbursed, everyone gets one, so one simply pulls out the entire file and processes all records sequentially, beginning with the first and stopping after the last.

There are other ways to organize a file system to save time and effort, but the important thing to remember is that just having a large quantity of related data is useless unless it is organized properly, so that you can get to the information you need in short order.

5

More on Data Types; Data Files

OVERVIEW Programming languages allow you to input, manipulate, and output various kinds of data, or **data types.** In Section 1.4, we introduced numeric and character data. In this chapter, we will explore these data types in more detail and then discuss the *string* data type. We will also introduce the important concept of data files and discuss the use of sequential files for data input. To be more specific, you will learn

1. About the integer and real (floating point) data types [Section 5.1].

2. About functions that can be used to test for integer values and to generate random numbers [5.1].

3. About the ASCII coding for character data and how it can be used to order the standard characters used in programming [5.2].

4. About the string data type, and how to order and concatenate strings [5.2].

5. About types of data files [5.3].

6. To create, write data to, and read data from a sequential file [5.3].

7. To delete, modify, and insert records into a sequential file [5.4].

8. To use the control break processing technique in certain programming situations [5.5].

5.1 Numeric Data

We have been using numeric data extensively throughout the first four chapters. In Chapter 1, we introduced the basic arithmetic operations and in subsequent chapters, we described how to sum a list of numbers and how to use relational and logical operators with numeric data. In this section, we will discuss two types of numeric data and introduce the concept of random numbers.

Types of Numeric Data

In the preceding chapters, we have not tried to distinguish between types of numbers. Most programming languages, however, provide at least two types of numeric data: *integers* and *real* (or *floating point*) numbers.

The Integer Data Type   An **integer** is a positive, negative, or zero whole number. For example, 430, –17, and 0 are integers. Because they are relatively simple numbers, integers take up relatively little storage space in the computer's memory.

Programming Pointer

In most programming languages, a variable can be **declared** (defined) to be of integer type by placing the proper statement at the beginning of the program or program module. For example, in Pascal, to declare the variable Number to be of integer type, we use the statement:

Number : integer

In some languages, a variable can simultaneously be declared of integer type and assigned an initial value. For example, to declare Number to be an integer and assign it a value of 50:

- In C++, we use the statement

    int Number = 50

- In BASIC, we use the statement

    LET Number = 50

In the latter case, BASIC declares Number to be an integer because the numeral 50 does not include a decimal point. In either case, the computer then allocates the amount of memory needed to store an integer, assigns the name Number to that storage location, and sets its contents equal to 50.

The five arithmetic operators (+, –, *, /, ^) may all be applied to integers. The result of adding, subtracting, or multiplying a pair of integers is another integer. Likewise, the result of taking a positive integer power of an integer is an integer. However, dividing one integer by another may result in a non-integer value. For example,

$$5 + 2, 5 - 2, 5 * 2, \text{ and } 5 \wedge 2$$

are all integers, but 5/2 is not *normally* an integer. (The next Programming Pointer explains why we use the word "normally" here.)

Programming Pointer

When the operator "/" is applied to two integers, the result may or may not be an integer, depending on the programming language. For example, suppose that Num1 and Num2 have been declared to be integers and assigned the values 11 and 4, respectively. Then:

- In BASIC and Pascal, the result of computing Num1/Num2 is the real number 2.75.

- In C++ and Java, Num1/Num2 is the integer 2. In these languages, the result of the dividing 11 by 4, 2.75, is *truncated* to the integer 2—its fractional part, .75, is discarded.

In this text, we take the former approach, so that 11/4 = 2.75.

The Real Data Type   In programming, a **real** (or **floating point**) number is, roughly speaking, any number that is not an integer.

Programming Pointer

In most programming languages, a variable is *declared* (defined) to be of real (or floating point) type by using the proper statement at the beginning of a program or program module. For example, to declare the variable Number to be of type real in C++ and Pascal, respectively, we use the statements:

    float Number
    real : Number

In either case, the computer then allocates the amount of memory needed to store the real variable Number. Typically, this is twice as much memory as needed for an integer variable.

In this text, we will usually not explicitly declare variables in our pseudocode. However, when we do, we will use statements like:

    Declare Number As Real
    Declare Counter As Integer

Notice that a real variable may in fact have an integer value. For example, in the Programming Pointer above, the real variable Number might have the value 50.0. It is sometimes useful in programming (see Example 2) to be able to determine whether or not a certain real variable has an integer value. This is accomplished in various different ways, depending on the programming language. In this text, we will determine whether or not a variable or arithmetic expression has an integer value with the aid of a function of the form:

The Int   Int (X)
function
Here, X is a number, variable, or expression with a real value, but Int(X) is an integer; it is the integer obtained by discarding the fractional part, if any, of the value of X.

EXAMPLE 1   Suppose that Num1 = 15.25, Num2 = 0, and Num3 = –4.5. Then:

$$Int(Num1) = 15$$
$$Int(Num2) = 0$$
$$Int(Num3) = -4$$
$$Int(Num1 + Num3 + 1) = 11 \ \text{(because Num1 + Num3 + 1 = 11.75)}$$

The Int function may appear anywhere in a program that an integer variable is valid. The next example demonstrates some uses of this function.

EXAMPLE 2   This program segment checks that the number N entered by the user is an integer, then displays a table of the squares of all integers from 1 to N. In this table, to improve readability, the program causes a line to be skipped after every three rows.

```
Repeat
      Write "Enter a positive integer:"
      Input N
Until (N > 0) And (Int(N) = N)
For Count = 1 Step 1 To N
      Write Count, Count ^ 2
      If Int(Count/3) = Count/3 Then
            Write
      End If
End For
```

As you can see, the Int function is used in two places in this program:

- In the data validation Repeat...Until loop, the condition Int(N) = N is true if and only if N is an integer.

- In the If-Then statement, the condition Int(Count/3) = Count/3 is true if Count/3 is an integer; that is, when Count = 3, 6, 9, and so on. In this case, the Then clause displays a blank line of output.

Scientific
and
exponential
notation

In applications, we sometimes encounter very large or very small real numbers, such as 1,502,000,000 or 0.00000571. These numbers can be written in a more manageable form using *scientific notation*. Here, a number is represented as a value between 1 and 10 multiplied by the appropriate power of 10. For example:

$$1,502,000,000 = 1.502 \times 10^9$$
$$0.00000571 = 5.71 \times 10^{-6}$$

The computer equivalent of scientific notation is known as **exponential notation.** In programming, instead of writing "10 to a power," we use the letter E followed by the given power. For example:

1.502×10^9 is written as 1.502E9
5.71×10^{-6} is written as 5.71E-6

If a number is displayed in exponential notation, you can convert it into ordinary notation by simply moving the decimal point the number of places indicated by the integer following E. If this integer is positive, move the decimal point to the right; if it is negative, move the decimal point to the left. For example:

- Given 1.67E-4, we write down 1.67 and move the decimal point four places to the left (filling in three zeros before the 1 to make this possible), which yields .000167.

- To convert 4.2E6, we move the decimal point six places to the right (filling in five zeros to the right of 2), which yields 4200000 or, as it is usually written, 4,200,000.

Random Numbers

Random numbers, those whose values form an unpredictable sequence, have many interesting applications in programming. One of their major uses is to provide an element of chance in computer games. They also have important, more serious uses, such as simulating situations or processes in business, mathematics, engineering, and other disciplines.

Most programming languages contain a function that is used to generate a sequence of random numbers, although the name of this function and the way it works varies from language to language. To illustrate the use of random numbers, we will define a function Random of the form

The Random
function

Random(N)

where N has a positive integer value. When the program encounters the expression Random(N), which may appear anywhere that an integer variable is valid, it generates a random *integer* in the range from 1 to N (inclusive). For example:

- Random(2) has a value that is either 1 or 2, and each of these numbers is equally likely to occur. This instance of the function can be used to simulate the flipping of a coin; a result of 1 is "heads," 2 is "tails."

- Random(6) has a value that is either 1, 2, 3, 4, 5, or 6, and each of these numbers is equally likely to occur. This instance of the function can be used to simulate the rolling of a *die* (one of a pair of dice).

If you want to generate random numbers in some range that does not start with 1, just "shift" the output of this function by adding an integer to it. For example,

Random(3) + 5 has a value that is either 6, 7, or 8.
Random(2) – 1 has a value that is either 0 or 1.

EXAMPLE 3   Suppose a pair of dice is rolled and its sum is recorded. For example, if the first die comes up 3 and the second comes up 6, we record the value 9. Is it more likely that the sum will be 5 or 8?

We can answer this question by simulating this "experiment" with a program that uses random numbers. For each roll of the dice, we need to generate two random numbers—one for each die—in the range from 1 to 6. We then add these numbers and keep track of the number of times the sum is 5 or 8. If we "roll the dice" (generate pairs of random numbers) thousands of times, the sum (5 or 8) with the larger count is presumably the one that is more likely to occur. Here's a program that carries out this plan.

```
Set FiveCount = 0
Set EightCount = 0
For K = 1 Step 1 To 1000
     Set Die1 = Random(6)
     Set Die2 = Random(6)
     Set Sum = Die1 + Die2
     If Sum = 5 Then
          Set FiveCount = FiveCount + 1
     End If
```

```
        If Sum = 8 Then
                Set EightCount = EightCount + 1
        End If
End For
Write "Number of times sum was 5: ", FiveCount
Write "Number of times sum was 8: ", EightCount
```

Programming Pointer

Random numbers are often produced by means of a mathematical algorithm which, given a starting number called the *seed,* generates a sequence of seemingly unpredictable numbers. However, by virtue of the fact that these numbers are produced by an algorithm, each number in the sequence determines the next. Thus, the numbers generated in this way are not really unpredictable, although they *are* all equally likely to occur. Such numbers are called *pseudorandom,* but for all practical purposes they are just as useful as those that are truly random.

When a function that generates random numbers in this way is encountered in a program, the computer (unless instructed otherwise) always uses the *same seed* to generate the pseudorandom numbers. This means that the same sequence of numbers will be produced each time a program is executed. This is useful for debugging purposes, but after a program is functioning correctly, the program must force the computer to use a different seed on each run so that the random numbers produced will indeed be unpredictable. This is usually accomplished by placing a statement at the beginning of the program or program module that changes the seed in an unpredictable way from run to run.

Self-Test 5.1

1. If X = 2.31, what is the value of Y in:
   a. Set Y = Int(X)
   b. If Int(X/2) = X/2 Then
          Set Y = 0
      Else
          Set Y = 1
      End If

2. Convert each of the following numbers, given in exponential nota-tion, into ordinary notation:
   a. –3.45E+4   b. 1.23E–5

3. Give the range of the random numbers generated by the following statements:
   a. Random(4)   b. Random(2) + 3

4. Write a program segment that displays 100 random integers be-tween 10 and 20 (inclusive).

5.2 Character-based Data

In this section, we will discuss two types of non-numeric data: characters and strings.

The ASCII Code

In Chapter 1, we loosely defined a *character* as any symbol (for example a letter, digit, punctuation mark, or blank space) that can be typed at the keyboard. To be more precise, a **character** is any symbol that is recognized as valid by the programming language you are using. Consequently, what constitutes a character varies from language to language. Nevertheless, most programming languages recognize a common core of about 100 basic characters (including all those that can be typed at the keyboard).

All data, including characters, are stored in the computer's memory as numbers (in *binary form*—as a sequence of ones and zeros). Thus, a programming language must have a scheme for associating each character with a number. The standard correspondence for a basic set of 128 characters is given by the **ASCII code.** (ASCII, pronounced "askey," stands for **A**merican **S**tandard **C**ode for **I**nformation **I**nterchange.)

Under this coding scheme, each character is associated with a number from 0 to 127. For example, the capital (uppercase) letters have ASCII codes from 65 ("A") to 90 ("Z"), the digits have codes from 48 ("0") to 57 ("9"), and the ASCII code for the *blank* (the character resulting from pressing the keyboard's spacebar) is 32. Table 1 lists the characters corresponding to ASCII codes from 32 to 127; codes 0 to 31 represent special symbols or actions, such as sounding a beep (ASCII 7) or issuing a "carriage return" (ASCII 13), and are not shown here.

The ordering of characters

In Section 4.2, we showed how to use the relational operators *equal to* (=) and *not equal to* (<>) with character data. The four other relational operators can also be applied to characters. To do so, we define an *ordering* for characters based on the numerical order of their ASCII codes. For example, "*" < "3" because the ASCII codes for these characters are, respectively, 42 and 51, and 42 < 51. Similarly, "8" < "h" and "A" > " " (blank). Notice that:

TABLE 1	Code	Character	Code	Character	Code	Character
The ASCII Codes from 32 to 127	32	[blank]	64	@	96	`
	33	!	65	A	97	a
	34	"	66	B	98	b
	35	#	67	C	99	c
	36	$	68	D	100	d
	37	%	69	E	101	e
	38	&	70	F	102	f
	39	'	71	G	103	g
	40	(	72	H	104	h
	41	)	73	I	105	i
	42	*	74	J	106	j
	43	+	75	K	107	k
	44	,	76	L	108	l
	45	-	77	M	109	m
	46	.	78	N	110	n
	47	/	79	O	111	o
	48	0	80	P	112	p
	49	1	81	Q	113	q
	50	2	82	R	114	r
	51	3	83	S	115	s
	52	4	84	T	116	t
	53	5	85	U	117	u
	54	6	86	V	118	v
	55	7	87	W	119	w
	56	8	88	X	120	x
	57	9	89	Y	121	y
	58	:	90	Z	122	z
	59	;	91	[	123	{
	60	<	92	\	124		
	61	=	93	]	125	}
	62	>	94	^	126	~
	63	?	95	_	127	[delete]

- Letters are in alphabetical order and all uppercase letters precede all lowercase letters.

- Digits (viewed as characters) retain their natural order ("1" < "2," "2" < "3," etc.).

- The blank precedes all digits and letters.

Programming Pointer

You may have noticed that whenever we refer to a specific character, we enclose it in quotation marks. For example, as in the condition:

Response = "Y"

This follows the standard practice in most programming languages. A few languages, notably Pascal, use "single-quotes" for this purpose; for example:

Response = 'Y'

EXAMPLE 4   All of the following conditions are *true*:

a. "a" > "B"   b. "1" <= "}"   c. "1" >= ")"

Character Strings

A **character string** (or more simply, a **string**) is a sequence of characters. In most programming languages, strings are enclosed in quotation marks. We have followed this practice in this text; as in, for example:

Write "Enter a number greater than 0"

A single character is also considered to be a string. In fact, a string may not contain *any* characters; in this case, it's called the *null string* and is denoted by two consecutive quotation marks, "".

The *length* of a string is simply the number of characters in it. For example, the string "B$? 12" has length 6 (remember that the blank between the ? and 1 is a character). Also, a character, such as "Y," has length 1 and the null string has length 0.

Programming Pointer

Some programming languages, such as BASIC and particular variants of Pascal and C++, contain a *string* data type. In these languages, we can declare (define) variables to be of string type in an appropriate statement at the beginning of the program or program module. In other languages, strings are constructed as *arrays* of characters (see Section 6.3). In this text, to explicitly declare a string variable, we will use a statement such as:

Declare Name As String

Using relational operators with strings

In some programming situations, it is useful to be able to apply relational operators (=, <>, <, <=, >, and >=) to character strings. For example, in a program that contains a list of names, we may want to search for a certain name in the list or perhaps sort all names in alphabetical order. This leads to statements of the form

> If Name = "Bob Jones" Then

or

> If Name1 < Name2 Then

where Name, Name1, and Name2 are variables of string type.

Equating strings

We say that two given strings, String1 and String2, are *equal* (String1 = String2) if they have the same length and the same characters in the same order. Otherwise, the given strings are *not equal* (String1 <> String2).

The ordering of strings

To use the relational operators <, <=, >, >= with strings, we place an ordering on strings with the help of the ASCII code. To determine which of two unequal strings comes first, use the following procedure:

1. Scan the strings from left to right, stopping at the first position for which the corresponding characters differ or when one of the strings ends.

2. If two corresponding characters differ before either string ends, the ordering of these two characters determines the ordering of the given strings.

3. If one string ends before any pair of corresponding characters differ, then the shorter string precedes the longer one.

EXAMPLE 5

Is each of the following expressions true or false?

a. "Word" <> "word" b. "Ann" = "Ann "
c. "*?/!" < "*?,3" d. "Ann" <= "Anne"

- In part *a*, the two strings do not consist of the same characters; the first contains "W" which is a different character from "w". Hence, the strings are not equal, and this expression is true.

- In part *b*, again the strings do not consist of the same characters (they're not even the same length); the second contains a blank, the first does not. Hence, this expression is false.

- For part *c*, the first pair of characters that differ occurs in the third position. Since "/" has ASCII code 47 and "," has code 44, the first string is *greater than* the second. Therefore, this expression is false.

- For part *d,* the first string ends before any pair of characters differ. Hence, the first string is *less than* the second, and this expression is true.

Character strings may be entered by the user at an input prompt (normally, it is not necessary to type the surrounding quotation marks) and string variables may be displayed by a program. The next example illustrates these points, and also provides a simple application of the < operator applied to strings.

EXAMPLE 6   This program segment inputs two names and displays them in alphabetical order.

> Write "Enter two names, separated by commas."
> Input Name1, Name2
> Write "The two names, in alphabetical order:"
> If Name1 < Name2 Then
> > Write Name1
> > Write Name2
> Else
> > Write Name2
> > Write Name1
> End If

In this program segment, Name1 and Name2 must be declared as string variables. After they are assigned values by the Input statement, the If-Then-Else structure ensures that they are displayed in alphabetical order.

Beware of strings of digits   A character string may consist solely of digits, say "123," in which case it looks like a number. However, 123 is not the same as "123"; the first is a numeric constant, the second is a string constant. (The first is stored in memory by storing the binary equivalent of 123; the second, by successively storing the ASCII codes for "1," "2," and "3.") Moreover, since we have no mechanism for comparing numbers and strings, if Num is a numeric variable, statements like

> If Num = "123" Then

make no sense and, if used in a program, will lead to an error message.

There is another, more subtle, problem in comparing strings of digits. Following the procedure given above for ordering strings, we see that "123" < "25" and "24.0" > "24" are true statements (check for yourself!), even though neither inequality may seem reasonable.

Concatenation of Strings In Section 1.5, we introduced five basic *arithmetic* operators: addition, subtraction, multiplication, division, and exponentiation. Each of these operators acts on two given numbers to produce a numeric result. Many programming languages include at least one *string* operator, **concatenation,** which takes two strings and joins them together to produce a string result. The symbol often used to concatenate two strings is the plus sign, +. For example, if String1 = "Part" and String2 = "Time", then the statement

    Set NewString = String1 + String2

assigns the string "PartTime" to the string variable NewString.

EXAMPLE 7 This program segment inputs a first and last name from the user and uses the concatenation operator to create a string of the form *Last, First.* It then displays this string.

    Write "Enter the person's first name: "
    Input FirstName
    Write "Enter the person's last name: "
    Input LastName
    Set FullName = LastName + ", " + FirstName
    Write FullName

For example, if FirstName = "Sam" and LastName = "Smith", then FullName = "Smith, Sam".

Self-Test 5.2

1. Is each of the following statements true or false?
    a. Two characters are *equal* only if their ASCII codes are equal.
    b. A single character is considered a string.
    c. If one string is longer than another, then the second must be greater than the first.
2. Is each of the following expressions true or false?
    a. "m" <= "M"   b. "*" > "?"
3. Is each of the following expressions true or false?
    a. "John" < "Jon"   b. "????" <= "??"
4. Write a program segment that inputs two names and displays the one that comes first under alphabetical order.

5. Suppose S is a string variable with S = "Step". What would be displayed if code corresponding to the following program segment were run?

Set T = S + "-by-" + S
Write T

5.3 An Introduction to Files

So far in this text, we have assumed that all input to a program would be entered by the user from the keyboard and that all output from a program would be displayed on the screen or perhaps by a printer. (In the pseudocode, we have used the Input and Write statements to represent these operations.) In the remainder of this chapter, we will discuss data files, which provide another means of supplying input and accepting output.

File Basics

A **file** is a collection of information that has been assigned a name and stored on a disk, separately from the program that created it. Files may contain programs, in which case they are called *program files*, or they may contain data to be used by programs, which are *data files*. The information in a data file is often broken into groups of related data called **records.** For example, in a file that contains an airline's reservations, each reservation, consisting of date, flight number, passenger name, etc., would make up a record.

Input provided by the user (for example, by using a keyboard or mouse) while the program is running is called **interactive input;** input to a program from a data file is called **batch processing.** Although, as you have already seen in many examples, interactive input can be very useful, batch processing (using data files) has some advantages too. They are:

- Data files are usually superior for input of large amounts of data.

- Data files can circumvent the need to reenter data in certain programming situations.

- Data files can be used by more than one program.

- Data files can store the *output* of a program for future review or for input to another program.

All files are divided into two general types:

1. **Text files** are files that consist solely of ASCII characters (see Section 5.2). Examples of text files include certain operating system files, simple word processing files, some program files, and specialized files produced by certain applications.

2. **Binary files** contain, in addition to ASCII characters, symbols that are not ASCII. Nowadays, most operating system files, program files, and data files produced by applications are binary files.

Text files have one big advantage over binary files—their simplicity. To be more specific:

- Text files are easier to create, whether from within the programming language software (as demonstrated later in this section) or by typing their contents directly into a text editor.

- Text files can, without using any special software, be displayed on the screen or printed on a printer.

- Text files are universal in nature. Virtually every computer system can correctly interpret the contents of a text file (again, without any special software).

For example, every e-mail system can create, transmit, receive, and display text files; on the other hand, one system cannot necessarily receive or display messages transmitted in binary form by another system.

Data files can also be divided into two other categories:

- **Sequential files** contain records that must be processed in the order in which they were created. They are accessed in the same way as music on a cassette tape. For example, to print the 50th record in a sequential file, we must first read ("scan") the 49 that precede it.

- **Direct access files** (sometimes called *random files*) have the property that each record can be accessed independently of the rest. Locating their data is analogous to finding tracks on a compact disc.

Either type of file can be used to solve a given problem. A sequential file is generally the better choice if you have to frequently display and/or modify the entire file (as with a file that contains a teacher's grades). A direct access file, on the other hand, is more efficient if you have lots of data to store but expect to change or display small amounts of it at a time (as with a program to manage airline reservations).

In the remainder of this chapter, we will employ sequential text files to illustrate how files are used in programming.

Creating and Reading Sequential Files

We will now discuss two fundamental operations on data files—creating and reading the contents of a file.

Creating a Sequential File   Developing a program segment that creates a sequential file involves three basic steps:

1. The file must be *opened*; for this file, we must specify

   - An *external name*—the name under which the file will be saved to disk. (The name you choose must conform to rules specified by your computer's operating system.)

   - An *internal name*—the name by which the file will be known in the program code. (This name must conform to the rules for variable names specified by the programming language.)

   - The file *mode*, which states the purpose for which you want to open the file—typically, either Output mode for writing (creating) data in the file or Input mode for reading (accessing) the contents of an existing file.

2. Data must be *written* to the file, creating its contents.

3. The file must be *closed*, terminating the process, saving the file's contents to disk, and breaking the connection between the internal and external names. Closing a file also places a special symbol, known as an *end-of-file marker*, at the end of the file.

The Open, Write, and Close statements — The statements used to carry out these steps vary considerably depending on the programming language used to implement them. To show how the process works, we will use the following generic (pseudocode) statements.

- To open a file:

    Open *"external name"* For *mode* As *internal name*

    For example, to create a file which we will call GRADES on disk and NewFile within the program, use:

    Open "GRADES" For Output As NewFile

- To write a record (a line) of data to a file, we will use a Write statement, just as if we were displaying this information on the screen, but precede the data by the name of the file to which we are writing:

Write *internal name, data*

For example, if the file's internal name is NewFile, to add the name "John Doe" and his test score, 85, to the file, use:

Write NewFile, "John Doe", 85

This statement creates a file record with two **fields**—the first containing the name, the second the score. It also places an *end-of-line marker*, a special ASCII symbol, after this data to separate it from the next record.

- To close a file:

    Close *internal name*

For example, to close the file NewFile, use:

Close NewFile

The next example illustrates how these statements are used to create a sequential file.

EXAMPLE 8   This program segment creates a file called GRADES containing records with two fields each; the first field is the student's name (a string variable, Student) and the second, his or her test score (an integer variable, Score).

```
Open "GRADES" For Output As NewFile
Write "Enter the student's name and test score."
Write "Enter 0 for both when done."
Input Student, Score
While Student <> "0"
     Write NewFile, Student, Score
     Write "Enter the student's name and test score."
     Write "Enter 0 for both when done."
     Input Student, Score
End While
Close NewFile
```

In this program segment, the statement

Open "GRADES" For Output As NewFile

assigns the internal name NewFile to a file that will appear on disk as GRADES and prepares it for Output (to be created). First, the user inputs the initial student and score, and then the program enters the While loop. Within this loop, the statement

Write NewFile, Student, Score

transmits the input data to the file GRADES. This input data/write record process continues until the user enters 0 for the student name, causing an exit from the loop. Finally, the statement

Close NewFile

closes the file, ending the Output mode and the association of the names NewFile and GRADES.

To see the effect of this program segment, suppose that the user input is

```
Jones, 86
Martin, 73
Smith, 84
0, 0
```

After execution, a file named GRADES would have been created on disk, containing the following data:

"Jones",86<CR>"Martin",73<CR>"Smith",84<CR><EOF>

Here, <CR> represents an end-of-line marker generated after each Write statement is executed and <EOF> is an end-of-file marker placed there when the file GRADES is closed.

Programming Pointer If a file is opened for Output, and a file of that name already exists in the same disk folder, all data in the existing file will be lost! Although this is sometimes useful when modifying a file, it could be catastrophic if done accidentally.

Reading the Contents of a File Once a file has been created, we can input (or *read*) data contained within it into a program. To do so, we need

- To open the file. We will use the same type of statement to perform this operation as was used in creating a file, but take the mode to be *Input*:

    Open *"external name"* For Input As *internal name*

    For example, to open the file GRADES, stored on disk, and assign it the internal (program) name GradeFile so that we can access its contents, use:

    Open "GRADES" for Input As GradeFile

- To assign the data in the file records to program variables. We do this by means of a Read statement of the form:

The Read statement

Read *internal name, variable1, variable2, ...*

For example, given a file with internal name GradeFile, to read the next record in this file, assigning the string data in its first field to the string variable Name and the integer data in its second field to the integer variable Score, use the statement:

Read GradeFile, Name, Score

After a Read statement is executed, the *file pointer*, which indicates the current file position, moves to the beginning of the next record.

To read all the records in a file into a program, we place a Read statement within a loop; on successive passes through this loop, the contents of successive records are input into program variables. To terminate the input process and force an exit from the loop, most programming languages contain an "end-of-file" (EOF) function. We will take this function to be of the form:

EOF (*internal name*)

The EOF function

The EOF function, which may appear in the test condition of any loop or selection structure, has the value *true* if the end of the file *internal name* has been reached; that is, if the file pointer is located at the end-of-file marker. (Recall that this marker, which we denote by <EOF>, was automatically placed at the end of the file when that file was created.) Otherwise, the value of this function is *false*.

EXAMPLE 9

This program segment displays the contents of the file GRADES created in Example 8, which has records of the form

student name, test score

```
Open "GRADES" For Input As GradeFile
While Not EOF (GradeFile)
    Read GradeFile, Name, Score
    Write Name, " ", Score
End While
Close GradeFile
```

In this program segment, the Open statement prepares the file GRADES for Input, allowing the transfer of data from the file to the program to take place, and assigns it the internal name GradeFile. Then, the While loop is entered. The condition

Not EOF (GradeFile)

is true if we have *not* reached the end-of-file marker for GRADES. On the first pass through the loop, this condition will be true unless the file is *empty* (does not contain any data). Within the loop, the statement

Read GradeFile, Name, Score

reads the next two data items (fields) from the file and assigns them to the variables Name and Score, respectively. These values are displayed on the screen by the Write statement; then the loop is reentered if more data remain in the file or exited if the end of the file has been reached.

If the file GRADES contained the data input in Example 8,

```
"Jones",86<CR>"Martin",73<CR>"Smith",84<CR><EOF>
```

then the (screen) output of this program segment would be:

```
Jones   86
Martin  73
Smith   84
```

Self-Test 5.3

1. a. What is a text file?
    b. What advantage does it have over a non-text (binary) file?

2. What is the difference between a sequential file and a direct access file?

3. Write a program that displays the contents of an existing file named EMPLOYEE containing a list of employee names (in records with a single field of string type).

4. Write a program that creates the EMPLOYEE file of Problem 3.

5.4   Modifying a Sequential File

In this section, we will continue the discussion of sequential files that was begun in Section 5.3. We will describe three basic file operations: deleting, changing, and inserting records within an existing sequential file. To carry out any of these operations requires that the entire file be *rewritten*—every record in it must be read (and modified if so desired), temporarily stored somewhere else, and, after all records have been processed, written back to the given file. A standard way of doing this makes use of a second file, called a *scratch file*, to temporarily store the contents of the given file. Using this technique, the file modification process proceeds as follows:

The general file modification process

1. Open the given file for Input and the scratch file for Output.

2. Input data concerning the change from the user.

3. Read records from the given file and write them to the scratch file until you reach the one to be modified.

4. Make the change: write a new or modified record to the scratch file, or in the case of a deletion, do *not* write the specified record to the scratch file.

5. Read the rest of the records from the given file and write them to the scratch file.

6. Close both files.

7. Replace the contents of the given file with that of the scratch file.

The flowchart in Figure 1 (on the next page) provides a pictorial representation of this process.

The next few examples show how this general process can be applied to the specific operations of deleting, inserting, and changing records. In these examples, we assume that the file GRADES exists on disk with records of the form:

student name, test score

(See Example 8 in Section 5.3.)

Deleting Records

The following example illustrates how to delete a record from a sequential file.

EXAMPLE 10

In this program segment, we create a file called SCRATCH that is identical to GRADES except for a record that has been deleted at the request of the user. The basic idea is simple:

FIGURE 1

Flowchart for the General File Modification Process

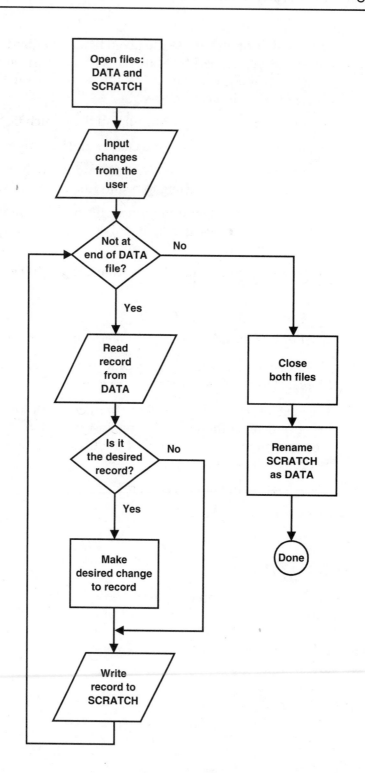

- Successively, read records from GRADES.

- If the current record is *not* the one to be deleted, write it to SCRATCH; if it *is* the one to be deleted, do not write it to SCRATCH.

Here is detailed pseudocode to carry out this plan:

```
Open "GRADES" For Input As GivenFile
Open "SCRATCH" For Output As TempFile
Write "Enter name of student to be deleted:"
Input DeleteName
While Not EOF (GivenFile)
    Read GivenFile, Student, Score
    If Student <> DeleteName Then
        Write TempFile, Student, Score
    End If
End While
Close GivenFile, TempFile
```

In this program segment, the While loop reads all records, one at a time, from the file GRADES (with internal name GivenFile) and writes each of them, except for the record specified for deletion, onto the file SCRATCH (with internal name TempFile). At the end of execution, SCRATCH is identical to GRADES, except for the deleted record. For example, suppose that prior to execution GRADES contains

```
"Jones",86<CR>"Smith",94<CR>"Martin",73<CR><EOF>
```

and the user inputs the name Martin. Then, after execution, SCRATCH would contain:

```
"Jones",86<CR>"Smith",94<CR><EOF>
```

The file GRADES does not change during the execution of the program segment in Example 10. To restore GRADES as the name of the *updated* (modified) file, we can copy the records in the SCRATCH file to GRADES. The following example shows how to carry out this operation.

EXAMPLE 11 This pseudocode makes a copy, called GRADES, of the file SCRATCH.

```
Open "GRADES" For Output As TargetFile
Open "SCRATCH" For Input As SourceFile
While Not EOF (SourceFile)
    Read SourceFile, Student, Score
```

> Write TargetFile, Student, Score
> End While
> Close SourceFile, TargetFile

Recall that opening a file for Output erases all data in that file. Thus, after the Open statement, for all practical purposes, the file GRADES (known to the program as TargetFile) is empty. The While loop then reads each record from SCRATCH (internal name SourceFile) and writes it to GRADES, effectively creating it as a copy of SCRATCH.

Programming Pointer

As you can see in Example 11, it is not difficult to write a program that copies one sequential file onto another. Some programming languages, however, provide a much more efficient way of accomplishing this—by using a pair of statements that *delete* the file GRADES from disk and *rename* the file SCRATCH as GRADES. (The deletion must take place first because to rename a file, the operating system requires that no file with the new name be present in that disk folder.) For example, in BASIC, the statements would look like this:

```
KILL "GRADES"
NAME "SCRATCH" AS "GRADES"
```

Both files must be closed prior to execution of these statements, and after the renaming, only the GRADES file will appear in the disk directory.

Changing Records

The following example shows how to change one of the data fields in a specified record of a sequential file.

EXAMPLE 12

This program segment modifies a specified record in the GRADES file; it allows the user to replace a given student's test score by a new one. Again, the basic idea is simple:

- Successively, read records from the GRADES file.

- If the current record is the desired one, write the new record to a scratch file. Otherwise, write the current record to the scratch file.

- Copy the scratch file to the GRADES file.

Here is detailed pseudocode to carry out this plan:

> Open "GRADES" For Input As GivenFile
> Open "SCRATCH" For Output As TempFile
> Write "Enter the name of the student:"

```
Input NewName
Write "Enter new test score:"
Input NewScore
While Not EOF (GivenFile)
      Read GivenFile, Student, Score
      If Student = NewName Then
            Write TempFile, Student, NewScore
      Else
            Write TempFile, Student, Score
      End If
End While
Close GivenFile, TempFile
Copy the file SCRATCH onto the file GRADES
```

Here, the While loop copies all records from GRADES onto SCRATCH except for the one to be modified. The latter is replaced (due to the If-Then-Else statement) by the one containing the input data. Thus, if prior to execution, GRADES contains

```
"Jones",86<CR>"Post",71<CR>"Smith",94<CR><EOF>
```

and the user enters the name Smith and the score 96, then after execution, the GRADES file will contain

```
"Jones",86<CR>"Post",71<CR>"Smith",96<CR><EOF>
```

Inserting Records

Inserting a record into a specified location in a sequential file is, surprisingly, the most complex of the three file modification operations. The next example shows how to do the job.

EXAMPLE 13

Suppose that the contents of the file GRADES, records of the form

student name, test score

are in alphabetical order according to student name. Also suppose that we want to insert a record—NewName, NewScore—specified by the user into this file at the appropriate place (retaining alphabetical order). Since this operation is somewhat difficult to accomplish in a sequential file, we will first give a general idea of how it's done—a rough pseudocode solution:

1. Open the GRADES file and a scratch file.

2. Input the NewName and NewScore from the user.

3. Read records (Student, Score) from GRADES and write them to the scratch file until the desired location is reached.

4. Write the new record (NewName, NewScore) to the scratch file.

5. Read the rest of the records in GRADES and write them to the scratch file.

Although this plan is fairly straightforward, there are a couple of somewhat tricky points that need to be considered before refining it:

- The first issue we will consider is, in step 3, how do we know when we've reached the proper location in the GRADES file? Since the Student names in GRADES are in alphabetical order, as we read records from this file, the value of the string variable Student is increasing. So, when we reach the first record for which

    NewName < Student

  we know that the new record must be inserted just *before* the current one. Thus, we rewrite step 3 as:

  3. Read records from GRADES and write them to the scratch file until NewName < Student

- The second issue is: What if the condition NewName < Student never occurs? In this case, the new record must be added to the end of the file. (The opposite might also be true: NewName < Student for *all* names in the file GRADES. In this case, the new record must be placed at the beginning of the file.)

Taking these points into account, we arrive at the refined pseudocode for the record insertion operation:

```
Open "GRADES" For Input As GivenFile
Open "SCRATCH" For Output As TempFile
Write "Enter name of and score for new student:"
Input NewName, NewScore
Repeat
      Read GivenFile, Student, Score
      If NewName < Student Then
            Write TempFile, NewName, NewScore
      End If
      Write TempFile, Student, Score
Until (NewName < Student) Or (EOF(GivenFile))
```

```
If Student < NewName Then
    Write TempFile, NewName, NewScore
End If
While Not(EOF(GivenFile))
    Read GivenFile, Student, Score
    Write TempFile, Student, Score
End While
Close GivenFile, TempFile
Copy SCRATCH onto GRADES
```

The Repeat...Until loop reads records from the GRADES file and writes them onto the scratch file until *either*

- The current record name (Student) follows, under alphabetical order, the input name (NewName), which means that the new record has been inserted.

or
- The end of the GRADES file is reached.

If the latter condition (end-of-file) occurs first, then the loop has been exited without inserting the new record. In this case, the If-Then structure that follows the Repeat...Until loop will insert the new record at the end of the scratch file. On the other hand, if the loop is exited due to the former condition (because the new record has been inserted), the If-Then condition will be false, and its Then clause skipped. Then, the While loop reads the rest of the records (if any) from GRADES and writes them to SCRATCH. Finally, the updated SCRATCH file is copied back to GRADES.

If prior to execution of this program segment, GRADES contains

```
"Jones",86<CR>"Smith",94<CR><EOF>
```

and the user inputs the name "Martin" and the score 71, then after execution GRADES would contain the data

```
"Jones",86<CR>"Martin",71<CR>"Smith",94<CR><EOF>
```

Programming Pointer Some programming languages, such as C++, make it easy to insert new records at the *end* of an existing file. All that need be done in this case is to:

1. Open the desired file in "append mode."
2. Input data from the user.
3. Write that data to the file.

The new record is automatically added (appended) to the end of the file.

Self-Test 5.4

In Problems 1–3, assume that a file PAYROLL exists with records of the form

employee number (Number), name (Name), rate of pay (Rate)

and is arranged in order of increasing employee number. Write a program segment that performs each of the following operations:

1. It deletes a record with employee number 138.

2. It changes the rate of pay of employee 456 to 7.89.

3. It inserts the record

    ```
    167,"C.Jones",8.50
    ```

    into the appropriate place in the file to maintain its order.

5.5 Focus on Problem Solving

In this section, we will present a programming problem and, in the course of solving it:

-   We will review some of the material in this chapter. The program will make use of a sequential data file and several different kinds of data types.

-   We will introduce a common programming technique, called *control break processing*, that is used to handle problems like the one presented here.

Control Break Processing

Harvey's Hardware Sales Report problem

Harvey's Hardware Company has three locations in Los Angeles, and at each location there are several salespeople. Harvey wants to produce a combined monthly sales report for the three stores. The program that creates this report would read a data file called SALESDATA containing records with the following fields:

store, salesperson, sales

Here, *store* is 1, 2, or 3, *salesperson* gives the name of a salesperson in that store, and *sales* is the monthly sales, in dollars, for that salesperson. All records for store 1 appear first, then those for store 2, and finally those for store 3. The last record in the file has a 0 in the store column to indicate the end of the data file.

The computer-generated sales report should include for each store

- The store number.
- A list of the salespeople at that store and the monthly sales for each of them.
- The total monthly sales for that store (which is actually a *subtotal* for the total sales for the three stores).

The total sales for the three stores should appear at the bottom of the report (on the "bottom line," so to speak).

Problem Analysis   As usual, we begin our program development by examining the required output, as outlined in the problem specifications. The output for this problem is a sales report, most of which consists of a table with the headings:

```
Store       Salesperson       Sales
```

In this table, we will list all salespeople for store 1, then those for store 2, and finally those for store 3. Thus, in the store column of this table, the beginning entries will all be 1, the middle entries will all be 2, and the remaining entries will all be 3. After listing all salespeople in a given store, the subtotal consisting of all sales for that store will be displayed. Finally, after the subtotal for store 3 is displayed, the grand total of all sales for the three stores will be displayed. A typical report of this kind is shown in Figure 2 on the next page.

The *input* variables needed for this program correspond to the fields in each record of the file SALESDATA. They are: Store (integer), Salesperson (string), and Sales (real). The *output* variables are:

- Subtotal—the total monthly sales for each store (real)
- Total—the grand total of the three subtotals (real)

Control break processing

To proceed from the given input (the data in the file) to the desired output (a report listing sales for each store and the total sales for all three stores), we use a technique called **control break processing.** This technique gets its name from the way the procedure is carried out: A data file is processed until a "control variable," representing a field in that file, changes value or reaches a preassigned level. This causes a "break" in the processing to take place, allowing an action (usually a computation) to be carried out. Processing then resumes until another control break occurs, again initiating an action. This procedure typically continues until the end of the file is reached.

In this program, the control variable is the store number (Store) and the "action" is the computation of a subtotal. To be more specific, the program will process records (in a loop) until the store number changes. At that point, control is transferred to a module that computes the sales subtotal. Then, file processing continues (control transfers back to the loop) until a control break occurs again. The entire process terminates when the end of the file is reached.

Program Design   As indicated in the Problem Analysis section, the heart of this program is a module that reads file records, writes them to the report, and sums the sales for a particular store until a control break takes place (that is, until the store number changes). At this point, another module is called to display the store subtotals and, if the last store has just been processed, the grand total of sales for all stores.

The remaining tasks are small ones: displaying a welcome message, opening the data file, initializing variables, and displaying the report headings. Thus, our program will consist of the following modules:

FIGURE 2

A Typical
Sales
Report

```
             Harvey's Hardware Company
                Monthly Sales Report

   Store          Salesperson              Sales
     1       T. Arnold                     4444.44
     1       J. Baker                      5555.55
     1       C. Connerly                   6666.66
             Total sales for store 1:     16666.65


     2       T. Dashell                    7777.77
     2       E. Everly                     8888.88
             Total sales for store 2:     16666.65


     3       B. Franklin                   9999.99
     3       L. Gomez                      1111.11
     3       W. Houston                    2222.22
             Total sales for store 3:     13333.32

        Total sales for all stores:       46666.62
```

1. Main Module—calls its submodules into action

2. Welcome Message module—displays a welcome message

3. Setup module—performs "housekeeping" tasks such as displaying the table title and headings, opening the data file, and initializing variables

4. Process Records module—reads and displays file records, and sums sales for each store

5. Display Totals module—displays the store subtotals and the grand total for all stores

Modules 2, 3, and 4 are called from the Main module. Module 5 is called from the Process Records module when a control break occurs. This division of the programming tasks leads to the hierarchy chart shown in Figure 3.

We now supply pseudocode for each module.

Main module

> Call Welcome Message module
> Call Setup Module
> Call Process Records module
> End Program

FIGURE 3

Hierarchy Chart for the *Harvey's Hardware* Problem

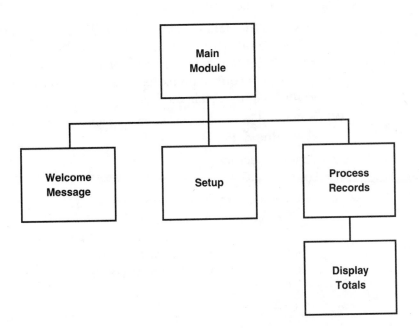

Welcome Message module   Displays a welcome message for the program (presenting the program title, identifying the programmer and other program data, and providing a brief explanation of what the program does)

Setup module   This module

- Displays a title and headings for the sales report.
- Opens the SALESDATA file and reads its first record.
- Initializes certain program variables.

More detailed pseudocode for this module is:

Write "Harvey's Hardware Company"
Write "   Monthly Sales"
Write
Write "Store number", "Salesperson", "Sales"
Open "SALESDATA" For Input As DataFile
Read DataFile, Store, Salesperson, Sales
Set PreviousStore = Store   [The variable PreviousStore will
         enable us to determine when the control variable Store has
         changed, which will initiate the action of computing totals]
Set Total = 0
Set Subtotal = 0

Process Records module   This module loops through all the records in the SALESDATA file, and

- Displays the data in each record to the report on the screen.
- Adds the sales for each salesperson to the store's subtotal.
- Reads a new record, checks to see if the store number has changed (that is, if a control break has occurred), and if so, transfers control to the Display Totals module.

When the end of the file has been reached (when Store = 0), the loop is exited and the data file is closed.

To be more specific:

While Store <> 0
         Write Store, Salesperson, Sales
         Set Subtotal = Subtotal + Sales
         Read DataFile, Store, Salesperson, Sales
         If Store <> PreviousStore Then
              Call Display Totals module
         End If

End While
Close DataFile

Display Totals module   This module is called when a control break occurs. It displays the total sales for each store, and if the last store has been processed (if the end of the file has been reached), it also displays the grand total of sales for all stores. If the last store has not yet been processed, this module resets Subtotal to 0 and sets the current store variable, PreviousStore, to the new store number.

```
Write "Total sales for store ", PreviousStore, ": ", Subtotal
Write
Set Total = Total + Subtotal
If Store = 0 Then
        Write "Total sales for all stores: ", Total
Else
        Set PreviousStore = Store
        Set Subtotal = 0
End If
```

Program Code   The program code is now written using the design as a guide. At this stage, header comments and step comments (see Section 2.3) are inserted into each module, providing internal documentation for the program. Here are a couple of other points concerning the coding that are specific to this program:

- Both the welcome message and the sales report should be displayed on a blank screen. Recall that this is accomplished by using the programming language's "clear screen" statement.

- To produce a professional-looking sales report, similar to the one shown in Figure 2, we will need to *format* the output—ensure that the data in the report lines up in columns and that the dollar amounts align on their decimal points. This can be accomplished using the programming language's special print formatting statements.

Program Test   This program can be adequately tested by creating a data file, SALESDATA, that contains the data in Figure 2, shown earlier in this section. This file can be created either by using the technique described in Section 5.3 or by typing its content in a text editor and saving it under the name SALESDATA.

Self-Test 5.5

All of the following problems refer to the Harvey's Hardware Sales Report program developed in this section.

1. Add appropriate statements to the Setup module to input (from the user) the month and year for which sales are being totaled.

2. Add an additional statement or two to the Setup module that displays (under the report title) the month and year input in Problem 1.

3. What are the first and last values assigned to the variable PreviousStore during a run of this program with the data shown in Figure 2?

4. What changes, if any, would have to be made to the Process Records module to accommodate sales from additional stores?

Chapter Review and Exercises

Key Terms

Data type
Real (floating point) data type
Random numbers
ASCII code
String
File
Interactive input
Text file
Sequential file
Field (in file record)

Integer data type
Exponential notation
Character
Character string
Concatenation
Record (in file)
Batch processing
Binary file
Direct access file
Control-break processing

Chapter Summary

In this chapter, we have discussed the following topics.

1. The integer and real (floating point) data types:
   - Declaring integer and real variables
   - Exponential notation
   - Determining if a real number has an integer value—the Int function, Int(X)

2. Generating and using random numbers—the Random function, Random(N)

3. The ASCII code:
   - Ordering characters by their ASCII codes
   - Ordering strings by the characters that they contain

4. The concatenation operator (+) for joining strings

5. Types of files:
   - Text files—consist entirely of ASCII characters
   - Binary files—may contain non-ASCII symbols
   - Sequential files—records must be read in the order in which they appear
   - Direct access files—any record can be read independently of the others

6. Creating a sequential file:
   - Open the file for output—the Open statement
   - Write data to the file, creating records—the Write statement
   - Close the file—the Close statement

7. Reading the contents of a sequential file:
   - Open the file for input—the Open statement
   - Assign data in a record to program variables—the Read statement
   - Close the file—the Close statement

8. Modifying a sequential file:
   - The general procedure for deleting, changing, or inserting a file record:
     a. Open the given file for input and a scratch file for output
     b. Input data concerning the change from the user
     c. Read records from the given file and write them to the scratch file until you reach the one to be modified
     d. Make the change to this record
     e. Read the rest of the records from the given file and write them to the scratch file
     f. Close both files
     g. Replace the original contents of the given file with that of the scratch file
   - Specific procedures for deleting, changing, and inserting a specified record

9. Control-break processing—using a control variable to periodically break out of a loop and perform an action

Review Exercises

1. Fill in the blank: The two basic types of numeric data are _____ data and _____ data.

2. Fill in the blank: In most programming languages, integer variables must be _____ , or defined, prior to their use.

3. Fill in the blank: The real data type is also known as the _____ data type.

4. Suppose that Num1 = 15 and Num2 = 12 are both of integer type. Give the two possible values (depending on the programming language in use) of Num1/Num2.

Exercises 5–8 make use of the Int function defined in Section 5.1.

5. Give the value of each of the following expressions:

    a. Int (5)   b. Int (4.7)

6. Let Num1 = 2 and Num2 = 3.2. Give the value of each of the following expressions:

    a. Int (Num2 – Num1)   b. Int (Sqrt (Num1))

7. What is the output of code corresponding to the following pseudo-code?

        Set N = 3
        If N/3 = Int(N/3) Then
            Write "Yes"
        Else
            Write "No"
        End If

8. Write a program segment that inputs numbers from the user until the number entered is a positive integer.

Exercises 9–12 make use of the Random function defined in Section 5.1.

9. Give the range of possible integers produced by the following expressions:

    a. Random(5)   b. Random(5) + 3

10. Write an expression that produces random numbers in each of the following ranges:

    a. 1, 2, 3, 4, 5, 6   b. 0, 1

11. Write a program segment that simulates flipping a coin 25 times by generating 25 random integers, each of which is either 1 or 2.

12. Write a program segment that simulates rolling a die 50 times by generating 50 random integers in the range 1 to 6.

13. True or false: The ASCII coding scheme associates a number between 0 and 127 with every lowercase and uppercase letter.

14. True or false: If Char1 and Char2 are characters, then Char1 = Char2 if and only if their ASCII codes are the same.

15. If Char1 = "/" and Char2 = "?", which of the following expressions are true?

    a. Char1 < Char2   b. Char1 <= Char2
    c. Char1 > Char2   d. Char1 >= Char2

16. Determine whether each of the following expressions is true or false:

    a. "**?" < "***"   b. "** " < "***"

17. If Name = "John", determine whether each of the following expressions is true or false.

    a. Name > " John"   b. Name >= "JOHN"

18. If Name1 = "John" and Name2 = "Smith", what string results from each of the following operations:

    a. Name1 + Name2   b. Name2 + ", " + Name1

19. In Exercise 18a, what is the length of the resulting string?

20. If Char1 and Char2 are characters, is Char1 + Char2 a character? If not, what is it?

21. Fill in the blank: A _____ is a collection of data that has been given a name and stored on disk.

22. Fill in the blank: Data files are often made up of records, which consist of one or more items called _____.

23. Fill in the blank: A _____ file consists solely of ASCII characters.

24. Fill in the blank: A _____ file may contain non-ASCII characters.

25. Fill in the blank: To access the fifth record in a _____ file, we must first read the first four records.

26. Fill in the blank: To access the fifth record in a _____ file, we need not also read the first four records.

27. Determine if each of the following statements is true or false.

   a. A data file can be used by more than one program.
   b. A data file can store a program's output for future use.

28. Determine if each of the following statements is true or false.

   a. If a file is opened for Output, and a file of that name already exists in that disk folder, then all data on the latter is erased.
   b. The statement

      Write DataFile, Number

      transmits the value of Number to the file with internal name DataFile.

29. Determine if each of the following statements is true or false.

   a. When a file is opened for Input, data can be written from the program to that file.
   b. When a sequential file is closed, the connection between the internal and external names is terminated.

30. Determine if each of the following statements is true or false.

   a. If a single record is to be changed in a sequential file, the entire file must be rewritten.
   b. A file cannot be renamed UPDATE if another file named UPDATE already exists in the same disk folder.

In Exercises 31–35, give the contents of the file UPDATE after each program segment is executed. Assume that the content of the file ORIGINAL at the beginning of each program segment is

"A",25<CR>"C",20<CR>"E",15<CR><EOF>

and that the following statements precede each program segment:

Open "ORIGINAL" For Input As GivenFile
Open "UPDATE" For Output As TempFile

31. Read GivenFile, Item, Number
    Write TempFile, Item, Number
    Close GivenFile, TempFile

32. While Not EOF(GivenFile)
    Read GivenFile, Item, Number
    Write TempFile, Item, Number
    End While
    Close GivenFile, TempFile

33. While Not EOF(GivenFile)
    Read GivenFile, Item, Number
    If Item <> "C" Then
    Write TempFile, Item, Number
    End If
    End While
    Close GivenFile, TempFile

34. Set InputItem = "D"
    Set InputNumber = 90
    While Not EOF(GivenFile)
    Read GivenFile, Item, Number
    If InputItem < Item Then
    Write TempFile, InputItem, InputNumber
    End If
    End While
    Close GivenFile, TempFile

35. Set InputItem = "C"
    Set InputNumber = 75
    While Not EOF(GivenFile)
    Read GivenFile, Item, Number
    If InputItem = Item Then
    Write TempFile, InputItem, InputNumber
    Else
    Write TempFile, Item, Number
    End If
    End While
    Close GivenFile, TempFile

36. In the program segment of Exercise 35

    a. Give two possible data types for the variable Item.
    b. Give two possible data types for the variable Number.

37. Fill in the blank: In the technique of _____, we transfer control from a loop and perform an action whenever the value of a specified variable changes or reaches a predetermined level.

38. Fill in the blank: The "specified variable" of Exercise 37 is called the _____ variable for the process.

Programming Problems

For each of the following problems, use the top-down modular approach and pseudocode to design a suitable program to solve it. List, prior to the pseudocode, each variable used in your program and whether it is of type integer, real, character, or string.

A. Input a positive integer, N, from the user. Then display the integers from 1 to N and, next to each integer, its square root. Your program should ensure that the number entered by the user is a positive integer and should skip a line after displaying every five integers and their square roots.

B. Simulate the process of dealing cards from a 52-card deck by generating 1000 random integers in the range 1 to 52. Suppose that numbers 1 to 13 represent *clubs,* 14 to 26 represent *diamonds,* 27 to 39 represent *hearts,* and 40 to 52 represent *spades.* Display the number of times each suit occurred in the 1000 "deals."

C. Generate a random integer in the range 1 to 100 and have the user try to guess the number. After each guess, display one of the following messages, as appropriate: "Your guess is too high!", "Your guess is too low!", or "Congratulations, you guessed it!" Terminate the program if the user guesses the number; otherwise, allow the user another guess.

D. A list of names is contained in the data file NAMES (one name per record, beginning with the second record). The first record gives the number, N, of names in the file. From this list of names, randomly select a first-, second-, and third-place prize winner. (*Hint:* Generate three *different* random numbers in the range 1 to N and, for each of these random numbers, display the corresponding file record.)

E. Input names of students from the user, terminated by ZZZ, and create a data file GRADES with records of the form:

      student (string), test1 (integer), test2 (integer), test3 (integer)

In this file, all test scores should be set equal to 0.

F. At the option of the user, display the entire contents of the file GRADES created in Problem *E* or just the record of a specified student. In either case, for each student displayed, also display his or her total test score.

Arrays in the Everyday World

By now, you are aware of the importance of instruction lists in your daily life. Chances are that you also use another kind of list—not one of *actions*, but one for *items* that are grouped together. Here is a common example:

Shopping List
1. Milk
2. Bread
3. Eggs
4. Butter

Or, if you've ever done a home improvement project, you might have developed a:

Tools Required List
1. Hammer
2. Saw
3. Screwdriver

If you write individual items on separate pieces of paper here and there, you might get them confused, and end up going to the grocery store for a saw. A list prevents that from happening, by presenting a convenient method of organizing and separating your data.

Sometimes a single list isn't powerful enough for a given purpose. In this case, we use a *table*—a collection of related lists—like the following:

Phone Book:

A. Name List	B. Address List	C. Phone List
1. Ellen Cole	1. 341 Totem Dr.	1. 212-555-2368
2. Joe Jones	2. 96 Elm Dr.	2. 212-555-0982
3. Fred Smith	3. 1412 Main St.	3. 212-555-1212

Notice that this table contains three separate (vertical) lists that are all related horizontally. For example, to call someone, you would scan down the Name List for the appropriate name, then look across that line to the Phone List to get the corresponding phone number. Could anything be more convenient? Thanks to a little organization and structure, you can easily find what you're looking for, even if the individual lists are hundreds of items long.

Who uses lists and tables? Virtually everyone, from farmers (weather tables) to accountants (ledgers) to sports fans (player statistics). Here are a couple of computer-related examples: If you use a spreadsheet program, you're using an electronic table; and if you write a computer program involving a lot of data that "goes together," you might organize it as a list or table called an *array*.

6

Arrays:
Lists and Tables

OVERVIEW   Although the value of a variable may change during execution of a program, in all our programs so far, a single value has been associated with each variable name at any given time. In this chapter, we will discuss the concept of an **array**—a collection of variables of the same type, all of which are referenced by the same name. We will discuss both one-dimensional arrays (lists) and two-dimensional arrays (tables), concentrating on the former. This chapter describes how to set up arrays and how to use them to accomplish various tasks. To be more specific, you will learn

1. About declaring arrays and how to access the data in a one-dimensional array [Section 6.1].

2. To manipulate parallel arrays [6.1].

3. To search an array for a specified element and to sort an array into a specified order [6.2].

4. To represent character strings as arrays [6.3].

5. To use arrays to manipulate sequential files [6.3].

6. About declaring and using two-dimensional arrays [6.4].

6.1   One-dimensional Arrays

A **one-dimensional array** is a list of related data of the same type (numbers, characters, etc.) referred to by a single variable name. In this section, we will discuss how to set up and manipulate these arrays, and present several advantages of their use.

Array Basics

Since an array stores many data values under the same variable name, we must have some way of referring to the individual variables (or **elements**) contained within it. To do so, programming languages follow the array name by a number enclosed in parentheses or brackets to indicate a particular element. For example, suppose that an array called Scores contains the final exam scores for a certain class. Then, to refer to the third score in this list (that is, to refer to the third element of the array Scores), we use the expression Scores[3]. We read this expression as "Scores sub 3," and the value 3 is called the *subscript* for this array element.

An array element like Scores[3] is treated by the program as a single (or *simple*) variable, and may be used in input, assignment, and output statements in the usual way. Thus, to display the value of the third student's final exam score, we use the statement:

Write Scores[3]

Or, to input the final exam scores of a class of 25 students, we could use the loop

```
For K = 1 Step 1 To 25
    Write "Enter score:"
    Input Scores[K]
End For
```

In this program segment

- On the first pass through the loop, the input prompt ("Enter score:") is displayed and the Input statement pauses execution, allowing the user to enter the first test score. This value is then assigned, since K = 1, to the first element, Scores[1], of the array Scores.

- On the second pass through the loop, the next value input is assigned to Scores[2], the second element of Scores.

- On the third pass through the loop, the value input is assigned to Scores[3].

And so on.

Programming Pointer

Arrays are stored in a computer's memory in a sequence of *consecutive* storage locations, one location for each array element. (The name of the array acts as the address for the first element and, because the array elements are stored consecutively, the subscript for a particular element defines the location of that element.) Thus, the computer must know, prior to the first use of an array, how many storage locations to set aside (or *allocate*) for that array. In program code, this is done by *declaring* (defining) the array in a statement at the beginning of the program or program module in which it is used. This declaration statement varies from language to language. Here's how an array named A, consisting of a maximum of 10 integer values, would be declared in several popular programming languages:

Declaring arrays

- In C++, the statement

    int A[10]

  allocates 10 locations referred to as A[0], A[1], ..., A[9].

- In Pascal, the statement

    A = array[1..10] of integer

  allocates 10 locations referred to as A[1], A[2], ..., A[10].

- In Visual Basic, the statement

    DIM A(1 TO 10)

  allocates 10 locations referred to as A(1), A(2), ..., A(10).

In this text, we will use the pseudocode

    Declare A[10]

to allocate 10 locations referred to as A[1], A[2], ..., A[10]. In memory, this array would occupy ten consecutive storage locations and, assuming that the elements have been assigned the values 1, 4, 9, 16, ..., the array can be pictured as follows:

Address	A[1]	A[2]	A[3]	A[4]	A[5]	A[6]	A[7]	A[8]	A[9]	A[10]
Contents	1	4	9	16	25	36	49	64	81	100

The following example illustrates the declaration and use of an array.

EXAMPLE 1   This program uses arrays to find the average monthly rainfall for the year 2000 in a certain city once the user has entered the rainfall for each month. After computing the average, the program displays the list of monthly rainfalls and their average.

```
Declare Rain[12]
Set Sum = 0
For K = 1 Step 1 To 12
    Write "Enter rainfall for month ", K
    Input Rain[K]
    Set Sum = Sum + Rain[K]
End For
Set Average = Sum / 12
For K = 1 Step 1 To 12
    Write "Rainfall for Month ", K, " is ", Rain[K]
End For
Write "The average monthly rainfall is ", Average
```

In this program, the first For loop inputs the 12 rainfall figures (one for each month) into the array Rain and adds their values. Then, after the average is computed, the second For loop displays the input data and the last Write statement displays their average.

Parallel Arrays

In programming, we often use **parallel arrays,** arrays of the same size in which elements with the same subscript are related. For example, suppose we wanted to modify the program of Example 1 to find the average monthly rainfall *and* snowfall. If we store the snowfall figures for each month in an array Snow, then Rain and Snow would be parallel arrays—for each K, Rain[K] and Snow[K] are related data items; they both refer to the same month. The next example further illustrates this idea.

EXAMPLE 2   This program segment inputs the names of salespersons and their total sales for the month into two parallel arrays (Names and Sales) and determines which salesperson has the greatest sales (Max).

```
Declare Names[100], Sales[100]
Set Max = 0
Set K = 1
Write "Enter a salesperson's name and monthly sales."
Write "Enter *, 0  when done."
Input Names[K], Sales[K]
```

```
While Names[K] <> "*"
    If Sales[K] > Max Then
        Set Index = K
        Set Max = Sales[Index]
    End If
    Set K = K + 1
    Write "Enter name and sales (enter  *, 0  when done)"
    Input Names[K], Sales[K]
End While
Write "Maximum sales for the month: ", Max
Write "Salesperson: ", Names[Index]
```

In this program segment, we do not use a For loop to input the data because the number of salespersons may vary from run to run. We do, however, still need a counter (K) to serve as a subscript for the array element currently being processed. The determination of the maximum sales is done by the If-Then structure within the While loop. When a "new" maximum sales figure is found, the array element at which this occurs (Index) is recorded and Max is set equal to this new maximum value. After looping through all salespersons, we display the largest sales figure and the name of the salesperson who achieved it. (See Figure 1, on the next page, for a pictorial description of the logic used to solve this problem.)

Programming Pointer

In Example 2, each element of the array Names is a string of characters and each element of Sales is a number. (We say that "Names is an array of strings" and "Sales is an array of numbers.") In writing pseudocode, we will not normally state the *type* (for example, numbers or strings) of the array we are using. In writing program code, however, the array type must be given in the declaration statement because a different amount of memory has to be allocated for each data type.

Some Advantages of Using Arrays

We will close this section by describing some of the benefits of using arrays. As you have already seen, arrays can reduce the number of variable names needed in a program—we can use a single array instead of a collection of simple variables to store related data. Arrays can also help create more efficient programs. Once data are entered into an array, they can be processed many times without having to be input again. The next example illustrates this point.

FIGURE 1
Flowchart for
Example 2

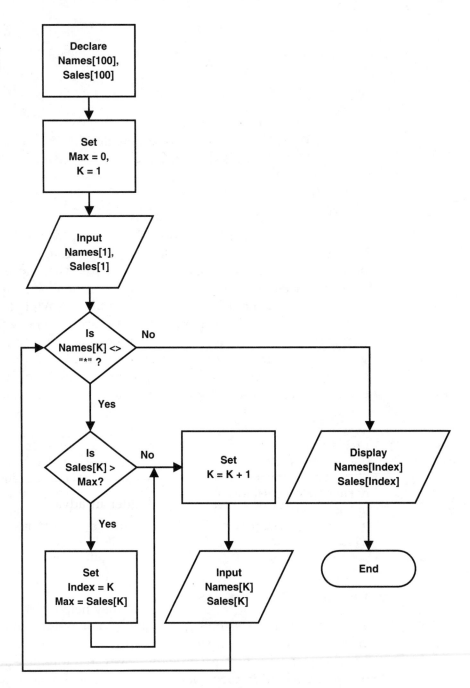

EXAMPLE 3   Suppose we want to average a set of numbers input by the user and
              then determine how many of them are above the average. Without ar-
              rays, we would have to enter the numbers, find their average, and then

enter them again to determine how many exceed the average. However, using arrays, we need not reenter input, as demonstrated in the following program.

```
Declare X[100]
Set Sum = 0
Set Count1 = 0
Write "Enter a number (or 0 to quit): "
Input Num
While Num <> 0
    Set Count1 = Count1 + 1
    Set X[Count1] = Num
    Set Sum = Sum + Num
    Write "Enter another number or 0 to quit: "
    Input Num
End While
Set Average = Sum/Count1
Set Count2 = 0
For K = 1 Step 1 To Count1
    If X[K] > Average Then
        Set Count2 = Count2 + 1
    End If
End For
Write "The average is:", Average
Write "The number of items above the average is: ", Count2
```

In the While loop, which inputs the numbers, the Count1 variable serves as a subscript for the array X and also counts the number of items input. Since we do not know the latter in advance, we must use a sentinel-controlled loop here. However, when it's time to determine the number of items above the average (Count2), we *do* know how many items have been input. Hence, a For loop can be used now with a limit value of Count1.

Another benefit of using arrays is that they help create programs that can be used with greater generality. When we use simple variables, their number is fixed. However, because we do not have to use *all* the elements that were allocated to an array when it was declared, arrays give us more flexibility, as illustrated in the next example.

EXAMPLE 4   Suppose we want to input a list of names and display them in reverse order. This is easy to do using arrays, even if the number of names to be input is unknown at the time the program is written.

```
Declare Names[100]
Set Count = 0
Write "Enter a name. (Enter * to quit.)"
Input TempName
While TempName <> "*"
    Set Count = Count + 1
    Set Names[Count] = TempName
    Write "Enter a name. (Enter * to quit.)"
    Input TempName
End While
For K = Count Step –1 To 1
    Write Names[K]
End For
```

This program simply inputs a list of names into an array and then displays the elements of that array in reverse order by "stepping backward" through a For loop whose control variable (K) is also the array subscript. (The purpose of the variable TempName is to temporarily hold the data entered by the user. If that data is really a name—not the sentinel value "*"—then the While loop is entered and that data is assigned to the next array element.)

Self-Test 6.1

In Exercises 1 and 2, what is displayed when code corresponding to the given pseudocode is executed? In Exercise 2, assume that Letter is an array of characters and that the characters input are F, R, O, D, O.

1. Declare A[12]
    Set A[2] = 10
    For K = 1 Step 1 To 3
        Set A[2 * K + 2] = K
        Write A[2 * K]
    End For

2. Declare Letter[5]
    For J = 1 Step 1 To 5
        Input Letter[J]
    End For
    For J = 1 Step 2 To 5
        Write Letter[J]
    End For

3. The following program segment is supposed to find the average of the numbers input. It contains one error. Find and correct it.

```
Declare A[100]
Set Sum = 0
For K = 1 Step 1 To 10
    Input X[K]
    Set Sum = Sum + X[K]
End For
Set Average = Sum/10
```

4. Write a program segment that inputs 20 numbers and displays them in reverse order.

5. State two advantages of using arrays, when possible, instead of a collection of simple (unsubscripted) variables.

6.2 Searching and Sorting Arrays

The need to **search** a one-dimensional array (or list) to locate a given item or to **sort** it in a specified order occurs relatively frequently in programming. Consequently, there are many algorithms available to perform each of these tasks. In this section, we will present simple techniques for searching and sorting a list.

The Serial Search Technique

Suppose you have just arrived at the airport to meet an incoming passenger. You know her flight number but not the arrival time or gate, so you consult the posted flight information which is given in the following tabular form:

Flight	Origin	Time	Gate
43	Kansas City	4:15 pm	5
21	St. Louis	5:05 pm	4
35	Dubuque	5:30 pm	7
•	•	•	•
•	•	•	•
•	•	•	•

To find the arrival time and gate of your friend's flight, you scan down the leftmost column of this table until you locate her flight number and then move across that row to read the corresponding time and gate in the last two columns.

In carrying out this process, you have performed a *table lookup*. In data processing terminology, the item you were seeking (your friend's flight number) is called the *search key*, the list of all such items makes up the *table keys*, and, in general, the data in the table are called the *table values*. The way in which you looked for the desired flight number, checking them in the order listed, makes this a **serial search.**

Basic steps in a serial search

In writing a program to perform a serial search to find a given search key, we have to:

1. *Load the table*—input the data in the table, usually from a file (see Section 5.3), into parallel arrays, one for each column of the table.

2. *Search the array that contains the table keys*—compare the search key to the elements of this array, one by one, until a match occurs (or the end of the array is reached).

3. *Display the search key and corresponding table values* or, if the search key is not found in the array, display a message to this effect.

Use a Flag to Indicate a Successful Search   In step 2 of the search procedure described above, we loop through the array of table keys to see if any element is identical to the given search key. Either

- The search will be successful—the item we are seeking (the search key) will match one of the table keys.

or

- The search will fail—no match will occur.

When we exit the loop and carry out step 3 of the procedure, we must know which of these two possibilities has occurred so that the appropriate message can be displayed. An elegant way to indicate whether or not the search was successful is to use a variable known as a flag.

A **flag** is a variable that takes on one of two values, typically 0 and 1, and is used to indicate whether or not a certain action has taken place. Usually, a value of 0 indicates that the action has *not* occurred; a value of 1 indicates that it *has* occurred. In a serial search, we set the flag equal to 0 prior to the search (prior to entering the search loop) and, if a match does occur within the loop, we change the flag's value to 1. Thus, when we exit the loop, the value of the flag can be used to verify the success or failure of the search and to display the proper message.

Pseudocode for a serial search

If a list of table keys is contained in an array (KeyData) with N elements, the pseudocode for performing a serial search for an item called Key is as follows.

Set the subscript (Index) of the current table key equal to 0

Set a flag (Found) equal to 0
While (Found = 0) And (Index < N)
    Increment Index by 1: Set Index = Index + 1
    If KeyData[Index] = Key Then
        Set Found = 1
    End If
End While
If Found = 1 Then
    Display the array elements with subscript = Index
Else
    Display a message that the search was unsuccessful
End If

In this pseudocode, the variable Index is used within the loop to hold the current array subscript; the variable Found is a flag that indicates whether or not the search has been successful. (We could have used a For loop with counter Index running from 1 to N, but the While loop allows us to exit as soon as a match is found.) Upon exit from the While loop, a value of 1 for Found indicates that the search was successful—Key has been found among the table keys—and Index gives its location (subscript) in KeyData. If the value of Found is 0 upon loop exit, the search Key was not found and we display this fact. The flowchart in Figure 2 (on the next page) pictures the logic used in a serial search.

The next example provides a particular instance of the serial search technique.

EXAMPLE 5   This program segment displays the test score for a particular student when the student's identification number is input by the user. To do so, it searches an array, IDNumbers, of identification numbers for the ID number input (IDKey), and

- Displays the corresponding student name and test score contained in two parallel arrays, Names and Scores, if the number IDKey *is* found in the array IDNumbers.

or

- Displays an appropriate message if the IDKey *is not* found in the array IDNumbers.

We assume that the arrays IDNumbers, Names, and Scores have already been declared and loaded with the necessary data (from a file or files) and that the number of elements in each of these parallel arrays is N.

Write "Enter a student ID number: "

FIGURE 2
Serial
Search of
the Array
KeyData for
Element *Key*

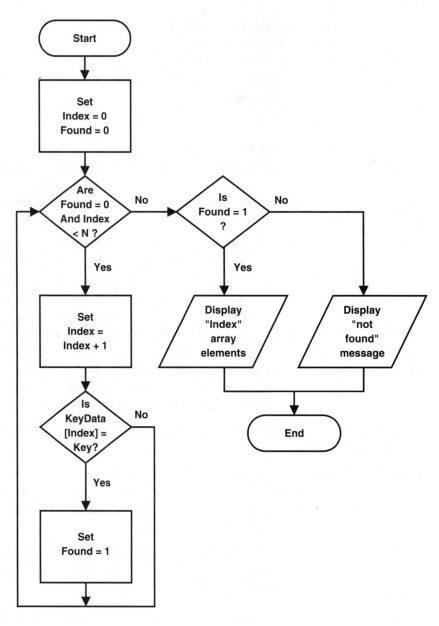

Input IDKey
Set Index = 0
Set Found = 0
While (Found = 0) And (Index < N)
     Set Index = Index + 1

```
            If IDNumbers[Index] = IDKey Then
                  Set Found = 1
            End If
      End While
      If Found = 0 Then
            Write "STUDENT ID NOT FOUND"
      Else
            Write "ID Number: ", IDKey
            Write "Student name: ", Names[Index]
            Write "Test score: ", Scores[Index]
      End If
```

The first two statements of this program segment prompt for and input the ID number for the student we are seeking. The remaining statements search for this ID number and display the appropriate message depending on whether or not it's found. (Compare this part of the program segment to the general pseudocode given earlier in this section.)

The Bubble Sort Technique

In sorting data, we arrange it in some prescribed order. For numbers, the "prescribed order" would be either *ascending* (from smallest to largest) or *descending* (from largest to smallest); for names it would usually be *alphabetical*.

As long as the number of items to be sorted is relatively small (say, fewer than 100), the **bubble sort** algorithm provides a reasonably quick and simple way of doing it. To apply this technique, we make several sweeps (or *passes*) through the data, and on each pass

- We compare all adjacent pairs of data items.

and

- We interchange the data in an adjacent pair if they are not already in the proper order.

We continue making passes until no interchanges are necessary in an entire pass, which indicates that the data are now sorted.

To illustrate the bubble sort, let us first do a simple example by hand. Figure 3 demonstrates the process for a data set consisting of the numbers 9, 13, 5, 8, 6. In each pass, we show the data at the start of the pass on the left and the results of the four comparisons in the next four columns. If an interchange takes place, the arrows cross, indicating which items have been swapped.

FIGURE 3

Bubble Sort of the Numbers 9, 13, 5, 8, 6

First Pass

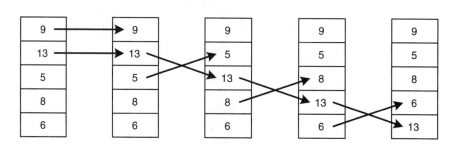

Second Pass

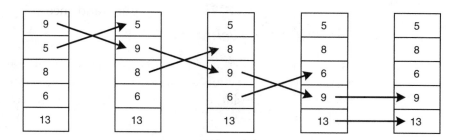

Third Pass

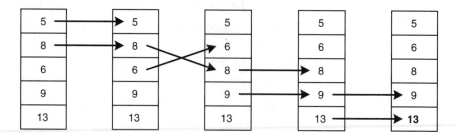

Fourth Pass

No interchanges take place; the numbers are sorted.

The bubble sort gets its name from the fact that, as you can see in Figure 3, the larger numbers "sink" to the bottom (the end) of the list and the smaller ones "bubble" to the top. After the first pass, the largest number will be at the bottom of the list; after the second pass, the second largest will be next to last; and so on. Thus, in sorting N items, it will take *at most* N – 1 passes through the list to sort them (and one additional pass to determine that they are sorted).

Pseudocode for the bubble sort

The bubble sort of an array A of N numbers in ascending order is described in pseudocode as follows (a flowchart is given in Figure 4 on the next page):

> While the array A is not sorted
> > For K = 1 Step 1 To N – 1
> > > If A[K] > A[K + 1] Then
> > > > Interchange A[K] and A[K + 1]
> > > End If
> > End For
> End While

This pseudocode is somewhat vague (and needs to be refined) regarding two issues:

1. To interchange array elements A[K] and A[K + 1], we temporarily copy one of them to another location and then swap their values:

   > Set Temp = A[K]
   > Set A[K] = A[K + 1]
   > Set A[K + 1] = Temp

   (Try it out; execute these statements with A[K] = 3 and A[K + 1] = 5.) Notice that we *cannot* swap the values using the pair of statements:

   > Set A[K] = A[K + 1]
   > Set A[K + 1] = A[K]

   This pair of statements sets both elements equal to the original value of A[K + 1]!

2. To determine when the list is sorted, we borrow a trick from the serial search algorithm given earlier in this section—we use a flag. In the bubble sort algorithm, a flag value of 0 indicates that during the latest pass, an interchange *did* take place. We therefore initialize the flag to 0, and continue to reenter the While loop as long as its value remains 0. Once inside the loop, we set the flag equal to 1 and change it back to 0 if an interchange takes place. If no interchange

takes place (meaning the data are sorted), the flag remains 1 and the loop is exited.

FIGURE 4

Bubble Sort of the Array A in Ascending Order

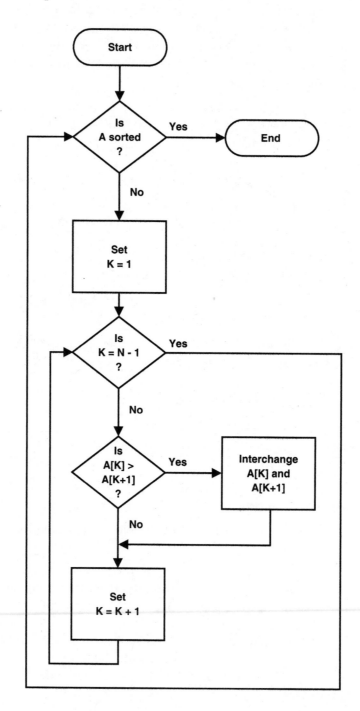

The next example gives detailed pseudocode for a typical bubble sort.

EXAMPLE 6   This program segment implements the bubble sort procedure described above. It inputs numbers from the user, sorts them in ascending order, and then displays the results.

```
Declare A[100]
Write "Enter a number; enter –9999 when done: "
Input Num
Set Count = 0
While Num <> –9999
    Set Count = Count + 1
    Set A[Count] = Num
    Write "Enter a number; enter –9999 when done: "
    Input Num
End While
Set Flag = 0
While Flag = 0
    Set Flag = 1
    For K = 1 Step 1 To Count – 1
        If A[K] > A[K + 1] Then
            Set Temp = A[K]
            Set A[K] = A[K + 1]
            Set A[K + 1] = Temp
            Set Flag = 0
        End If
    End For
End While
Write "Sorted list ..."
For K = 1 Step 1 To Count
    Write A[K]
End For
```

The first While loop accomplishes two things: It inputs and counts the numbers entered by the user. (Due to the Declare statement, this program segment can sort up to 100 numbers.) The next While loop implements the general bubble sort procedure given above. Finally, the For loop at the end of the program segment displays the sorted list.

Other sorts We can use the pseudocode presented in Example 6, with little or no modification, to perform a couple of related sorting tasks.

- Identical pseudocode can be used to sort names in alphabetical order; of course, in this case, the array A must be declared to be an array of character strings (see Section 5.2).
- Virtually the same pseudocode can also be used to sort numbers in *descending* order. The only modification needed here is to change the first line of the If statement to read:

    If A[K] < A[K + 1] Then

Self-Test 6.2

1. Choose one answer. The serial search

    a. Requires that the list of table keys be arranged in order.
    b. Cannot be used if the list of table keys is ordered.
    c. Can be used with a list of characters.
    d. Can only be used with a list of numbers.

2. Write a program that searches an array, Client, consisting of 100 names for the name "Smith". If this name is found, the program should display "FOUND"; if not, it should display "NOT FOUND".

3. How many interchanges take place in sorting the numbers 3, 2, 1 in ascending order using a bubble sort?

4. Write a program that sorts an array, Client, of 100 names in alphabetical order using the bubble sort method.

6.3   Other Uses of Arrays*

In the first two sections of this chapter, we have described some examples of, and algorithms used with, one-dimensional arrays. In this section, we will return to two topics introduced in Chapter 5—character strings and files—and discuss their connection to arrays.

Strings as Arrays of Characters

In Section 5.2, we introduced character strings (or more simply, *strings*) as one of the basic data types, and discussed to some extent how to

---

*This section makes use of some material from Chapter 5.

input, process, and output them. Many programming languages do not contain a string data type; instead, strings are implemented as arrays whose elements are characters. Even in programming languages that *do* contain this data type, strings can also be formed as arrays of characters. In this section, we will consider strings from this point of view.

Style Pointer

Specifying Array Data Types   In our pseudocode, we have used a Declare statement to declare a variable to be an array and to define the size of that array. For example,

Declare Sales[100], Names[100]

declares two arrays of 100 elements each. In writing pseudocode (unlike program code), it is not necessary to specify the data type of the array elements, especially if the variable name implies their type; for example, Sales is an array of numbers, Names is an array of strings. However, to avoid confusion, especially if we want to define an array to be a string of characters, it is a good idea to use declaration statements like

Declare Sales[100] Of Integers
Declare Names[100] Of Strings
Declare FullName[25] Of Characters

In the last case, we are defining the variable FullName to be a string of (at most) 25 characters.

Whether we consider strings as a built-in data type or as arrays of characters, we can still perform basic operations on them as described in Section 5.2. The next example illustrates this point.

EXAMPLE 7   This program inputs two strings from the user, *concatenates* them (joins them together), and displays the result.

Declare String1[25] Of Characters
Declare String2[25] Of Characters
Declare String3[50] Of Characters
Write "Enter two strings, separated by commas. "
Input String1, String2
Set String3 = String1 + String2
Write String3

In this pseudocode, notice that String1, String2, and String3 are defined as arrays of characters, but when they are used in the program, the array brackets do not appear; for example, we write

Input String1, String2
not   Input String1[25], String2[25].

This usage is typical of actual programming languages and also conforms to our previous way of referencing strings (in Chapter 5), when they were considered as a built-in data type.

After the two strings have been input, the statement

Set String3 = String1 + String2

concatenates them (joins them together, see Section 5.2) and the Write statement displays the result. For example, if code corresponding to this pseudocode is run and the user enters the strings "Part" and "Time", the program's output would be PartTime.

String Length vs. Array Size   Recall (from Section 5.2) that the *length* of a string is the number of characters it contains. For example, the array String3 of Example 6 has 50 elements. When "PartTime" is assigned to String3, however, only the first eight array elements are used, so the length of the string "PartTime" is 8.

In some algorithms (see below), it is useful to know the length of a string that has been assigned to a given array of characters. For this purpose, programming languages contain a "length function," which we will write as:

The Length function

Length(*string*)

The Length function may be used in a program wherever a numeric constant is valid. For example, when code corresponding to the following pseudocode is run

Declare Str[10]
Set Str = "Hello"
Write Length(Str)

the output will be the number 5 (the length of the string "Hello").

Programming Pointer   Recall that when an array is declared, the number specified in the declaration statement determines the number of storage locations in the computer's memory allocated to that array. If the array represents a string (that is, it is an array of characters), then each storage location consists of one *byte* (see Section 1.2) of memory. When a string is assigned to this array, the beginning elements of the array are filled with the characters that make up the string (actually, they are filled with ASCII codes — see Section 5.2), a special symbol is placed in the next storage location, and the rest of the array elements remain "blank" (unassigned). For example, a string Str declared as an array of 10 characters and assigned the value "Hello" can be pictured to look like this in memory:

Address	Str[1]	Str[2]	Str[3]	Str[4]	Str[5]	Str[6]	Str[7]	Str[8]	Str[9]	Str[10]
Contents	"H"	"E"	"L"	"L"	"O"	•				

Here, the symbol • represents the character that is automatically placed at the end of the assigned string. Thus, to determine the length of the string contained in Str, the computer simply counts the storage locations (bytes) associated with the variable Str until the terminator symbol • is reached.

The next example illustrates how strings can be manipulated by manipulating the arrays in which they are contained.

EXAMPLE 8   This program segment inputs a person's full name (with first name first) from the user, stores the initials of that person as characters, and displays the name in the form:

LastName, FirstName

This pseudocode uses three strings, one to store the input name (FullName) and one each for the first and last names (FirstName and LastName). It also makes use of two character variables to store the initials (FirstInitial, LastInitial). The trick to determining which part of the input string is the first name and which part is the last name is to locate the blank space between them.

```
Declare FullName[30] Of Characters
Declare FirstName[15] Of Characters
Declare LastName[15] Of Characters
Write "Enter a name with first name first: "
Input FullName
Set Count = 1
While FullName[Count] <> " "
    Set FirstName[Count] = FullName[Count]
    Set Count = Count + 1
End While
Set FirstInitial = FullName[1]
Set LastInitial = FullName[Count+1]
For K = Count + 1 Step 1 To Length(FullName)
    Set LastName[K] = FullName[K]
End For
Write LastName + ", " + FirstName
```

After the person's full name is input, the counter-controlled While loop assigns characters in FullName to FirstName until the blank between the first and last names is encountered. At this point, the value of Count is one more than the length of FirstName, and (since the blank is character number Count) the first character in LastName is numbered Count + 1. Thus, the two assignment statements that follow the While loop correctly store the person's initials, and the For loop copies the correct part of FullName to LastName. Finally, the Write statement, with the help of the concatenation operator +, displays the person's name, last name first.

Using Arrays in File Maintenance

In Section 5.4, we described how to perform certain operations on (or how to *maintain*) an existing sequential file. Due to the way in which a sequential file must be accessed, these techniques required the use of a "scratch file" to temporarily hold the contents of the modified file.

Instead of using a scratch file in the modification process, it is sometimes preferable to *load* (input) the given file into arrays in the computer's internal memory. This technique is *possible* if the file is small enough to fit into available memory. It is *desirable* (due to the relatively high speed of internal memory) if there are a large number of changes to be made to the file—for example, if it must be sorted. The general procedure is as follows:

The general procedure

1. Open the given file for Input (to be read from).

2. Read the file records into parallel arrays, one array for each field.

3. Close the file (so that it can later be opened for output).

4. Make the desired modifications to the arrays.

5. Open the file for Output.

6. Write the contents of the arrays (the modified data) to the given file.

7. Close this file.

The next example illustrates this process.

EXAMPLE 9   This program segment allows the user to add a second test score for each student in a file called GRADES, which currently has records of the form:

student name (string), test 1 score (integer)

We will load these records into two parallel arrays, Student (an array of strings) and Test1 (an array of integers), then input the scores for the second test into a third (parallel) array Test2 and write all this data back to the file GRADES, in which each record will now have three fields:

student name, test 1 score, test 2 score

```
Declare Student[100], Test1[100], Test2[100]
Open "GRADES" For Input As DataFile
Set Count = 0
While Not EOF(DataFile)
     Set Count = Count + 1
     Read DataFile, Student[Count], Test1[Count]
End While
Close DataFile
Open "GRADES" For Output As DataFile
For K = 1 Step 1 To Count
     Write "Enter Test 2 score for ", Student[K]
     Input Test2[K]
     Write DataFile, Student[K], Test1[K], Test2[K]
End For
Close DataFile
```

Since our modified records will have three fields each, we declare three arrays to hold their values. The While loop loads the existing records (two fields each) into the appropriate arrays and also counts the number (Count) of records. Finally, the For loop inputs the modifications (the new test scores) from the user and writes the modified records to the file GRADES. (Notice that, as is usually required by the programming language, the file is closed and reopened for Output after it has been loaded into memory and before it can be rewritten.)

If prior to execution of this program segment, GRADES contains

```
"Jones",86<CR>"Post",71<CR>"Smith",96<CR><EOF>
```

and the user enters scores of 83, 79, and 88 for the three students in the file, then after execution, GRADES will contain

```
"Jones",86,83<CR>"Post",71,79<CR>"Smith",96,88<CR><EOF>
```

Self-Test 6.3

1. Is each of the following statements true or false?

   a. If a string variable Str has been declared to be an array of 25 characters, then the length of Str must be 25.

    b. To input a string from the user, we must know how many characters are in that string.

2. Suppose that a string variable, Name, has been declared as an array of characters and has been assigned a value. Write a program segment that displays the first and last characters of Name. [*Hint:* The Length function comes in handy here.]

3. Write a program segment that declares string variables String1 and String2 to be arrays of 25 characters, inputs a value for String1 from the user, and copies this value into String2.

4. Assume that a file PAYROLL exists with records of the form

      employee number (Number), name (Name), rate of pay (Rate)

and is ordered by increasing employee number. Write a program segment that loads this file into parallel arrays and

- Deletes the record with employee number 138.
- Changes the rate of pay of employee 456 to 7.89.

6.4 *Two-dimensional Arrays*

In the arrays you have seen so far, the value of an element (say, a student ID number) has depended upon a *single* factor (in this case, the student being processed). It is sometimes convenient to use arrays whose elements are determined by *two* factors such as the score of a particular student on a particular test or the sales of a certain salesperson in a certain month. In these cases, we use *two-dimensional arrays*.

An Introduction to Two-dimensional Arrays

A **two-dimensional array** is a collection of elements of the same type stored in consecutive memory locations, all of which are referenced by the same variable name using two subscripts. For example, A[2, 3] is an element of a two-dimensional array named A. The next example illustrates one use of two-dimensional arrays.

EXAMPLE 10   Suppose we want to input the scores of 30 students on 5 tests into a program. We can set up a single two-dimensional array named Scores to hold all these test results. The first subscript of Scores references a particular student; the second subscript references a particular test. For example, the array element Scores[9, 2] contains the score of the ninth student on the second test.

This situation may be easier to understand if you picture the array elements in a rectangular pattern of horizontal rows and vertical columns. The first row gives all test scores of the first student, the second row gives the scores of the second student, and so on. Similarly, the first column gives the scores of all students on the first test, the second column gives all scores on the second test, and so on (see Figure 5). The entry in the box at the intersection of a given row and column represents the value of the corresponding array element. For example (in Figure 5):

- Scores[2, 4], the score of Student 2 on Test 4, is 73.

- Scores[30, 2], the score of Student 30 on Test 2, is 76.

Declaring two-dimensional arrays

Like their one-dimensional counterparts, two-dimensional arrays must be declared before they are used. We will use a declaration statement for two-dimensional arrays that is similar to the one we've been using for one-dimensional arrays. For example, we will declare the array of Example 10 using the statement:

Declare Scores[30, 5]

This statement allocates 150 (30 × 5) consecutive storage locations in the computer's internal memory to hold the 150 elements of the array Scores.

The next example illustrates some basic points about using two-dimensional arrays.

FIGURE 5

The Array *Scores* of Example 10

	Test 1	Test 2	Test 3	Test 4	Test 5
Student 1	92	94	87	83	90
Student 2	78	86	64	73	84
Student 3	72	68	77	91	79
	·	·	·	·	·
	·	·	·	·	·
	·	·	·	·	·
Student 30	88	76	93	69	52

EXAMPLE 11

Consider the pseudocode:

    Declare A[10, 20], B[20]
    Set N = 5
    Set A[N, 10] = 6
    Set B[7] = A[5, 10]
    Write A[5, 2 * N], B[7]

Here, the Declare statement declares two arrays—the first is two-dimensional with 10 rows and 20 columns (200 elements) and the second is one-dimensional with 20 elements. Since N is 5:

- The first assignment statement sets A[5, 10] equal to 6.

- The second assignment statement sets B[7] equal to 6, the value of A[5, 10].

- The Write statement displays the value of A[5, 10] and B[7]; it displays 6 twice.

Using Two-dimensional Arrays

As you have seen, counter-controlled loops, especially the For variety, provide a valuable tool for manipulating one-dimensional arrays. In the two-dimensional case, nested For loops (see Section 3.4) are especially useful.

EXAMPLE 12

This program segment inputs data into a two-dimensional array, Scores, whose elements are test scores. The first subscript of Scores refers to the student being processed; the second subscript refers to the test being processed. For each of the 30 students, the user is to input five test scores. The pseudocode is as follows:

    Declare Scores[30, 5]
    For Student = 1 Step 1 To 30
        Write "Enter 5 test scores for student ", Student
        Write "After typing each score, press the Enter key"
        For Test = 1 Step 1 To 5
            Input Scores[Student, Test]
        End For (Test)
    End For (Student)

This pseudocode results in one input prompt for each student that instructs the user to enter the five scores for that student. For example, if code corresponding to this pseudocode is run, the following text will be displayed

```
Enter 5 test scores for student 1
After typing each score, press the Enter key
```

and then execution will pause for input. After the user enters the five scores, he or she will see:

```
Enter 5 test scores for student 2
After typing each score, press the Enter key
```

And so on.

EXAMPLE 13 Suppose that a two-dimensional array Scores has been declared and assigned data as described in Example 12. The following pseudocode allows the user to display the test scores of a student specified by the user.

> Write "Enter the number of a student, and"
> Write "his or her test scores will be displayed."
> Input Index
> For Test = 1 Step 1 To 5
>   Write Scores[Index, Test]
> End For

The pseudocode in Examples 12 and 13 is somewhat user-unfriendly because it requires the user to refer to students by number (student 1, student 2, etc.) rather than by name. We will now present a more comprehensive example that corrects this defect by using a second (parallel) one-dimensional array of names.

EXAMPLE 14 This program inputs the names and test scores for a class of students and then displays each name and that student's average test score. It uses a one-dimensional array, Names, whose elements are strings to hold the student names and a two-dimensional array, Scores, of numbers to hold the test scores.

We assume that there is a maximum of 30 students in the class, but that the exact number is unknown prior to running the program. Thus, we need a sentinel-controlled While loop to input the data. However, during the input process, we discover how many students are in the class, and henceforth, a For loop can be used to process and display the array elements.

Declare Names[30], Scores[30, 5]

```
Set Count = 0
Write "Enter a student's name; enter * when done."
Input StudentName
While StudentName <> "*"
    Set Count = Count + 1
    Set Names[Count] = StudentName
    Write "Enter 5 test scores for ", Names[Count]
    Write "After typing each score, press the Enter key."
    For Test = 1 Step 1 To 5
        Input Scores[Count, Test]
    End For
    Write "Enter a student's name; enter * when done."
    Input StudentName
End While
For K = 1 Step 1 To Count
    Set Sum = 0
    For J = 1 Step 1 To 5
        Set Sum = Sum + Scores[K, J]
    End For (J)
    Set Average = Sum / 5
    Write Names[K], Average
End For (K)
```

The While loop inputs the student names and test scores. Notice that:

- We use the variable Count to determine the number of students in the class. This variable will be used later in the program segment as the limit value for the For loop that computes each student's average.

- To avoid inputting the sentinel value, *, into the array Names, we temporarily assign each input string to the variable StudentName. If the value of StudentName is not "*", the While loop is entered and that string is assigned to the next element of Names.

After all data have been input, the For loop finds the average test score for each student (by summing the student's scores and dividing by five) and displays the student's name and average.

Higher-Dimensional Arrays Although they are not so often used, arrays with three or more subscripts are allowed in most programming languages. These *higher-dimensional arrays* can be used to store data that depend upon more than two factors (subscripts).

Self-Test 6.4

1. How many storage locations are allocated by each statement?

   a. Declare A[5, 10]   b. Declare Left[10], Right[10, 10]

2. A two-dimensional array Fog has two rows and four columns:

   ```
   5      10     15     20
   25     30     35     40
   ```

   a. What are the values of Fog[1, 2] and Fog[2, 3]?
   b. Which elements of Fog contain the numbers 15 and 25?

3. What is displayed when code corresponding to the following pseudocode is executed?

   ```
   Declare A[2, 3]
   For I = 1 Step 1 To 2
       For J = 1 Step 1 To 3
           Set A[I, J] = I + J
       End For (J)
   End For (I)
   Write A[1, 2], " ", A[2, 1], " ", A[2, 2]
   ```

4. How many times is the prompt in this pseudocode displayed?

   ```
   For I = 1 Step 1 To 5
       For J = 1 Step 1 To 12
           Write "Enter rainfall in state ", I, " in month " J
           Input Rain[I, J]
       End For (J)
   End For (I)
   ```

5. Write a program segment that determines the largest element, Max, of a two-dimensional array X of positive integers that has already been declared (with three rows and five columns) and input.

6.5   Focus on Problem Solving

In this section, we will apply the material we have discussed in this chapter to developing a program that prepares an *invoice*, a bill for items ordered. The program makes use of one-dimensional arrays and contains both search and sort routines.

An Invoice Preparation Program

The Legendary Lawnmower Company wants to have a program that will prepare invoices for parts ordered by its customers. The customer's name and the parts ordered (part numbers and quantities) will be input by the user. The program will then locate the part numbers in a file to determine their names and prices, and print an invoice. This invoice should contain the customer's name and, for each part ordered, the quantity, part number, part name, unit price, and total price. The parts ordered should be listed on the invoice in ascending part number order and the total amount due should be given at the bottom.

We will assume that the part numbers, names, and prices (the price list) are contained in a sequential file called PRICELIST, with records of the form:

> part number (integer), part name (string), part price (number)

Problem Analysis   The input for this program is of two types:

1. The price list for the lawn mower parts is read from the PRICELIST file. Its fields will be loaded into parallel arrays—

> Numbers, Names, and Prices

2. The following data are input from the user:

> The customer name—Customer
> The part numbers and quantities of all parts ordered—arrays
>   OrderNums and OrderAmts

The output for this program is the invoice. It will be in the form of a table with headings:

```
Quantity  Part Number  Part Name  Unit Price  Item Cost
```
Here:

- The entries in the Quantity, Part Number, Part Name, and Unit Price columns of the table are obtained from the data input into the OrderAmts, OrderNums, Names, and Prices arrays, respectively.

- The entries in the Item Cost column are obtained by multiplying the corresponding unit price by the quantity ordered; that is, by using the formula:

> ItemCost[K] = Prices[K] * OrderAmts[K]

The invoice also displays the total amount due for the parts order, AmountDue, which is the sum of all the ItemCost entries. A typical invoice is shown in Figure 6.

Program Design This program needs to perform three major tasks:

1. Input data—load the price list from the PRICELIST file into parallel arrays and input the customer's order from the user.

2. Sort the parts ordered.

3. Output the invoice.

The first task clearly contains two substantial subtasks—loading the price list data and inputting the parts order. Moreover, the third task requires that we search the price list for each of the ordered parts to determine its price. Thus, we arrive at the following modularization of this program. The main module calls three submodules:

1. The Input Data module, which calls the submodules:

   Load Price List module
   Input Parts Order module

2. The Sort Parts Order module

3. The Print Invoice module, which calls the submodule:

   Search for Part Number module

```
                          INVOICE
              THE  LEGENDARY  LAWNMOWER  COMPANY

Customer:  John  Robert  Smith

Quantity   Part Number    Part Name        Unit Price    Item Price
-------------------------------------------------------------------

   10        13254       Handle             $   15.65    $    156.50
             14000       ***   Invalid part number   ***
    5        15251       Starter (recoil)   $   24.80    $    124.00
    4        16577       Axle (small)       $    7.50    $     30.00
                                                         ----------
                                            TOTAL DUE ... $    310.50
```

FIGURE 6   A Sample Invoice

A hierarchy chart depicting this modularization is shown in Figure 7. Pseudocode describing each module is given below.

Main Module   The main module declares the arrays to be used in the program, displays a welcome message, and calls its submodules.

    Declare Numbers[100], Names[100], Prices[100]
    Declare OrderNums[50], OrderAmts[50]
    Display a welcome message
    Call Input Data module
    Call Sort Parts Order module
    Call Print Invoice module
    End Program

Input Data module   All this module does is to call its two submodules:

    Call Load Price List module
    Call Input Parts Order module

Load Price List module   This module reads the data in the sequential file PRICELIST and assigns it to three parallel arrays—Numbers, Names, and Prices. While reading the file, we use a counter

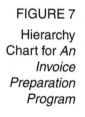

FIGURE 7

Hierarchy Chart for An Invoice Preparation Program

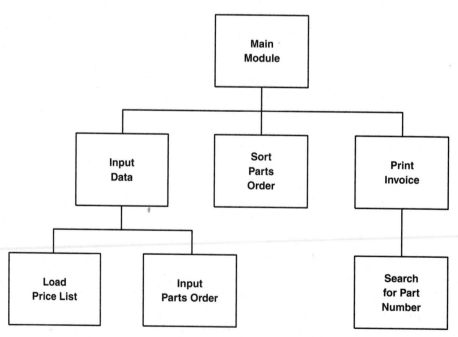

(ListCount) to count the number of records it contains. The counter not only serves as a subscript for the arrays, but also gives the number of elements in each array and can be used as the limit value in For loops that process these arrays.

```
Open "PRICELIST" For Input As DataFile
Set ListCount = 0
While Not EOF(DataFile)
      Set ListCount = ListCount + 1
      Read DataFile, Numbers[ListCount],
            Names[ListCount], Prices[ListCount]
End While
Close DataFile
```

Input Parts Order module   This module inputs the data about the parts order from the customer. This data consist of the customer name and the numbers and quantities of the parts to be ordered. The latter are input into the parallel arrays OrderNums and OrderAmts. This module also contains a counter (OrderCount) that acts as a subscript for the two arrays and determines the number of items in the order.

```
Prompt for and input the customer's name (Customer)
Set OrderCount = 0
Write "Enter part number, quantity desired."
Write "Enter  0, 0  when done."
Input Num, Amt
While Num <> 0
      Set OrderCount = OrderCount + 1
      Set OrderNums[OrderCount] = Num
      Set OrderAmts[OrderCount] = Amt
      Write "Enter part number, quantity desired."
      Write "Enter  0, 0  when done."
      Input Num, Amt
End While
```

Sort Parts Order module   This module uses the bubble sort method (see Section 6.2) to sort the list of ordered part numbers (the array OrderNums) in ascending order. It also reorders the parallel array OrderAmts in the same way so that the two arrays remain parallel.

```
Set Flag = 0
While Flag = 0
```

```
Set Flag = 1
For K = 1 Step 1 To OrderCount – 1
    If OrderNums[K] > OrderNums[K + 1] Then
        Set Temp = OrderNums[K]
        Set OrderNums[K] = OrderNums[K + 1]
        Set OrderNums[K + 1] = Temp
        Set Temp = OrderAmts[K]
        Set OrderAmts[K] = OrderAmts[K + 1]
        Set OrderAmts[K + 1] = Temp
        Set Flag = 0
    End If
End For
End While
```

Print Invoice module   This module displays the invoice. (See Figure 6 for a sample invoice.) This task entails displaying a title, customer name, headings, the list of all parts ordered, and the total amount due. For each part ordered:

- We must search the price list for the corresponding name and price.

- If the item is found, the quantity ordered, part number, part name, unit price, and total cost of that item are displayed on one line of the invoice.

- If the item is not found, the part number and an appropriate message is displayed on that line of the invoice.

The same loop that displays the above information also sums the total cost of the parts ordered (by summing the ItemPrice values) so that the amount due can be displayed at the bottom of the invoice.

```
Set AmountDue = 0
Display a title for the invoice
Write "Customer: ", Customer
Write "Quantity   Part Number   Part Name
    Unit Price   Item Price"
For K = 1 Step 1 To OrderCount
    Search the parts list for OrderNums[K]:
        Call the Search for Part Number module
            (Found = 1 indicates that the search is successful;
            Index is the subscript of the item found.)
    If Found = 1 Then
        Set ItemCost = OrderAmts[K] * Prices[Index]
```

```
        Write OrderAmts[K], OrderNums[K], Names[Index],
            Prices[Index], ItemCost
        Set AmountDue = AmountDue + ItemCost
    Else
        Write OrderNums[K], "Invalid Part Number"
    End If
End For
Write "TOTAL DUE . . . ", AmountDue
```

Search for Part Number module   This submodule performs a serial search (see Section 6.2) of the array Numbers for OrderNums[K]. If this number is found, it sets the variable Index equal to the current subscript and sets the variable Found equal to 1; otherwise, it sets Found equal to 0.

```
Set Index = 0
Set Found = 0
While (Found = 0) And (Index < ListCount)
    Set Index = Index + 1
    If Numbers[Index] = OrderNums[K] Then
        Set Found = 1
    End If
End While
```

Program Code   The program code is now written using the design as a guide. At this stage, header comments and step comments (see Section 2.3) are inserted into each module, providing internal documentation for the program. Here are a couple of other points concerning the coding that are specific to this program:

- Both the welcome message and the invoice should be displayed on a blank screen. Recall that this is accomplished by using the programming language's "clear screen" statement.

- To produce a professional-looking invoice, similar to the one shown in Figure 6, we will need to *format* the output—ensure that the data in the invoice lines up in columns and that the dollar amounts align on their decimal points. This can be accomplished using the programming language's special print formatting statements.

Program Test   This program can be adequately tested by creating a data file, PRICELIST, that contains the following records:

```
13254, "Handle", 15.65
14153, "Wheel (6 in.)", 5.95
14233, "Blade (20 in.)", 12.95
14528, "Engine (260 cc)", 97.50
14978, "Carburetor", 43.00
15251, "Starter (recoil)", 24.80
15560, "Adjusting knob", .95
16195, "Rear skirt", 14.95
16345, "Grass bag", 12.95
16577, "Axle (small)", 7.50
```

This file can be created either by using the technique described in Section 5.3 or by typing its content in a text editor and saving it under the name PRICELIST. Then, inputting the part numbers 13254, 14000, 15251, 16577 from the keyboard should produce an invoice similar to the one in Figure 6.

Self-Test 6.5

The following problems refer to the Invoice Preparation Program of this section.

1. Describe the contents of the invoice if the user enters 0,0 at the first input prompt in the Input Parts Order module.

2. Replace the outer pre-test loop in the Input Parts Order module by a post-test loop.

3. Write a Welcome Message module and rewrite the main module so that it consists solely of Declare and Call statements.

Chapter Review and Exercises

Key Terms

Array
Element (of an array)
Search an array
Serial search
Bubble sort

One-dimensional array
Parallel arrays
Sort an array
Flag
Two-dimensional array

Chapter Summary

In this chapter, we have discussed the following topics.

1. One-dimensional arrays:

   - Declaring one-dimensional arrays—the Declare statement
   - Using arrays and parallel arrays in input, processing, and output operations
   - Advantages of using arrays—reduce the number of program variables, create more efficient programs, create more general programs.

2. Searching and sorting a one-dimensional array:

   - The serial search—examine array elements in order, one-by-one, until the desired element is found.
   - The bubble sort—make passes through the array, comparing consecutive pairs of elements on each pass and interchanging them if they're not in the correct order.

3. Viewing strings as arrays of characters:

   - Declaring a string as an array with elements that are of character type
   - Finding the length of a string—the Length function
   - Locating and extracting substrings by examining the array in which the string is located

4. Loading file records into arrays.

5. Two-dimensional arrays:

   - Declaring two-dimensional arrays
   - Using two-dimensional arrays in input, processing, and output operations

Review Exercises

1. True or false: The elements of an array are stored in consecutive storage locations in the computer's internal memory.

2. True or false: An array may have some elements that are numbers and other elements that are strings.

3. True or false: A single declaration statement can declare an array of characters and a array of numbers.

4. True or false: If a declaration statement allocates 100 storage locations to an array, the program must assign values to all 100 elements.

In Exercises 5 and 6, what is the output of code corresponding to the following pseudocode?

5. Declare X[100]
   Set N = 4
   For K = 1 Step 1 To N
       Set X[K] = K ^ 2
   End For
   Write X[N/2]
   Write X[1], " ", X[N – 1]

6. Declare A[20], B[20]
   For K = 1 Step 1 To 3
       Set B[K] = K
   End For
   For K = 1 Step 1 To 3
       Set A[K] = B[4 – K]
       Write A[K], " ", B[K]
   End For

7. True or false: Before using the serial search method, you must sort the table keys in ascending order.

8. True or false: The bubble sort method cannot be used to arrange numeric data in descending order.

9. The following program segment is supposed to search an array A consisting of N elements for a value Key and set Found equal to 1 or 0, depending on whether or not Key is located. It contains two errors. Correct them.

   Set Index = 0
   Set Found = 0
   While (Found = 1) And (Index < N)
       Set Index = Index + 1
       If A[Index] = Key Then
           Set Found = 0
       End If
   End While

10. The following program segment is supposed to sort an array A consisting of N elements in ascending order. It contains two errors. Correct them.

    Set Flag = 0
    While Flag = 0
        Set Flag = 1
        For K = 1 Step 1 To Count – 1

If A[K] <= A[K + 1] Then
    Set Temp = A[K]
    Set A[K] = A[K + 1]
    Set A[K + 1] = Temp
    Set Flag = 1
End If
  End For
End While

Exercises 11–14 refer to the following pseudocode:

Declare Name[20] Of Characters
For K = 1 Step 1 To 8
    Set Name[K] = "A"
End For
Set Name[9] = " "
Set Name[10] = "B"

11. Fill in the blank: The Declare statement allocates _____ storage locations (bytes) to the array Name.

12. Fill in the blank: The length of the string Name is _____.

13. Write a single statement that displays the first and last characters in the string Name.

14. Write a program segment that displays the characters in Name except the blank.

In Exercises 15–18, assume that a file TEST has 25 records of the form:

score 1 (integer), score 2 (integer), score 3 (integer)

Suppose we want to load the TEST file records into arrays Score1, Score2, and Score3.

15. Write a declaration statement that declares these arrays.

16. Fill in the blank: Because they have the same size and corresponding elements contain related data, Score1, Score2, and Score3 are said to be _____ arrays.

17. Write a program segment that loads the TEST file into the arrays.

18. Write a program segment that displays the contents of the arrays of Exercise 17 on 25 lines, each containing three test scores.

19. True or false: One- and two-dimensional arrays may be declared in the same statement.

20. True or false: If we know that 100 elements have been allocated to the two-dimensional array A, then both subscripts of A must run from 1 to 10; that is, A must have 10 rows and 10 columns.

21. Write a program segment that declares a two-dimensional array X of numbers with five rows and columns and inputs 25 numbers into this array from the user.

22. Write a program segment that sums the elements in each row of the array X of Exercise 21 and displays these five numbers.

23. What is the output of code corresponding to the following pseudo-code?

```
Declare Q[10, 10]
For R = 1 Step 1 To 2
    For C = 1 Step 1 To 2
        If R = C Then
            Set Q[R, C] = 1
        Else
            Set Q[R, C] = 0
        End If
    End For (C)
End For (R)
For R = 1 Step 1 To 2
    For C = 1 Step 1 To 2
        Write Q[R, C]
    End For (C)
End For (R)
```

24. Suppose that the file DATA consists of the three records

```
"Huey",1,2
"Dewey",4,5
"Louie",7,8
```

What is the output of code corresponding to this pseudocode?

```
Declare String[10], T[10, 20]
Open "DATA" For Output As DataFile
For K = 1 Step 1 To 3
    Read DataFile, String[K]
    For J = 1 Step 1 To 2
        Read DataFile, T[K, J]
    End For (J)
End For (K)
For J = 1 Step 1 To 2
```

```
          For K = 1 Step 1 To 3
              If K = 1 Then
                      Write String[K], T[K, J]
              End If
          End For (K)
      End For (J)
      Close DataFile
```

Programming Problems

For each of the following problems, use the top-down modular approach and pseudocode to design a suitable program to solve it.

A. Input a list of positive numbers, terminated by 0, into an array Numbers. Then, display the array and the largest and smallest number in it.

B. The Eversoft Eraser Company has a list of its customers' names and telephone numbers in a file CUSTOMER with records such as:

"John Smith", 2135551212

Display this list in alphabetical order of last names. [*Hint:* Use the techniques of Section 6.3 to create arrays FirstName and LastName from the given data.]

C. Input a list of employee names and salaries, and determine the mean (average) salary as well as the number of salaries above and below the mean.

D. Input the selling prices of all homes in Botany Bay sold during the year 2000 and determine the median selling price. The *median* of a list of N numbers is

- The middle number of the *sorted* list, if N is odd.

- The average of the two middle numbers in the *sorted* list, if N is even.

[*Hint:* After inputting the prices into an array, sort that array.]

E. The Department of Motor Vehicles of the State of Euphoria has finally decided to computerize its list of licensed drivers. The program you write should make use of the existing file LICENSES with records of the form:

name of driver, driver license number, number of tickets

When a license number is input by the user, the corresponding name and number of tickets should be output by the program. [*Hint:* Load the LICENSES file into three parallel arrays and search one of these for the license number input.]

F. A *magic square* is a two-dimensional array of positive integers in which the number of rows equals the number of columns, and every row, every column, and the two diagonals add up to the same number. Input a two-dimensional array with four rows and four columns and determine if it is a magic square.

Subprograms in the Everyday World

As you know, a basic problem-solving strategy involves breaking a problem into modules and submodules, and solving each subproblem separately. In carrying out this technique, we often use the data generated by one module in another module. For example, suppose you want to send your mother a bouquet of flowers and, as luck would have it, you have just received the mail-order catalog for Ye Olde Flower Shop. So, the problem of how to get a gift of flowers to your mom has a simple solution:

1. Locate a suitable bouquet and the shop's phone number in the catalog.
2. Call Ye Olde Flower Shop.
3. Place your order.

In carrying out this solution to the problem, the data collected in step 1, the phone number and bouquet name, are used in steps 2 and 3, respectively. In the language of programming, we say that the phone number and bouquet name are *exported* from the "Locate Information" module and *imported by* the "Call Shop" and "Place Order" modules, respectively.

As another example of passing data among modules, consider the steps you take to file your federal income tax return. You have to:

1. Gather data about your income and (possibly) your expenses.
2. Fill out the forms.
3. Mail your return to the IRS.

In filling out the main form (Form 1040), you may discover that you also have to complete two other forms—Schedule A (deductions) and Schedule B (interest and dividends). So, a refinement of step 2 might look like this:

2. Fill out Form 1040.

    2a. Fill out Schedule A.
    2b. Fill out Schedule B.

Here, the Form 1040 module imports all data from Gather Data and exports

   a. The expense data (if necessary) to the Schedule A module, which imports these data and exports the total deductions to Form 1040.
   b. The interest and dividend income data (if necessary) to the Schedule B module, which imports these data and exports the total interest and total dividend income to Form 1040.

In the everyday world, you "transfer data from one module to another" by looking at it and writing it down. In programming, this action is accomplished, as you will see, by using *parameters* and *arguments*.

7

More on Program Modules and Subprograms

OVERVIEW In Chapter 2, we introduced the idea of modular programming—designing and coding a program as a set of interrelated modules. In subsequent chapters (mainly in the Focus on Problem Solving sections), we have used this technique to help simplify the design of relatively complicated programs. In this chapter, we will discuss more advanced aspects of this topic, including arguments and parameters, functions, and recursion. To be more specific, you will learn

1. To use a data flow diagram to indicate the data that are being transmitted among the program's modules   [Section 7.1].

2. To use arguments and parameters to pass data between modules [7.1].

3. About value and reference parameters [7.2].

4. About the scope of a variable [7.2].

5. About some functions commonly built into a programming language [7.3].

6. To create your own functions [7.3].

7. To create recursive functions to solve certain programming problems [7.4].

7.1 Data Flow Diagrams and Parameters

In this section, we will describe the means by which data are normally transmitted between program submodules, or **subprograms***. We will discuss subprogram parameters, which allow the program to transmit information between modules, and data flow diagrams, which keep track of the data transmitted to and from each subprogram.

Data Flow Diagrams

Most subprograms manipulate data. If a data item in the main program is needed in a certain subprogram, its value must be *passed to*, or **imported** by, that subprogram. Conversely, if a data item processed by a subprogram is needed in the main program, then it must be *returned to*, or **exported** to, that module. To illustrate these concepts, let us consider the following simple programming problem:

Sale Price Computation problem

A department store needs a program that will compute and display the sale price of a discounted item when the original price of that item and the percentage it is discounted are input.

Problem Analysis Our program will input the original price (OriginalPrice) of an item and the percentage it is to be discounted (DiscountRate), then compute the sale price (SalePrice) of the item and display this amount. To arrive at the sale price, we first compute the amount of the discount using the formula

AmountSaved = OriginalPrice * DiscountRate / 100

(we divide by 100 to convert from percent to a decimal) and then compute the sale price using

SalePrice = OriginalPrice – AmountSaved.

For example, if the price of an item (OriginalPrice) is \$200 and it is discounted 20% (DiscountRate = 20), then:

AmountSaved = 200 * 20 / 100 = \$40
SalePrice = 200 – 40 = \$160

---

* We will use the word *subprogram* to describe the code that implements a program submodule; later we will consider a specific type of subprogram— the *function*. Be aware that the words *subprogram* and *function* may have other meanings in particular programming languages.

Program Design   We will use a modular design for this program that consists of a main module and four submodules, constructed as follows:

> Main Module
>> Call WelcomeMessage module
>> Call InputData module
>> Call ComputeResults module
>> Call OutputResults module
> WelcomeMessage module
>> Display a brief description of the program
> InputData module
>> Input the original price, OriginalPrice
>> Input the percentage discounted, DiscountRate
> ComputeResults module
>> Set AmountSaved = OriginalPrice * DiscountRate / 100
>> Set SalePrice = OriginalPrice – AmountSaved
> OutputResults module
>> Write OriginalPrice, DiscountRate, SalePrice

In the Sale Price Computation program:

- The WelcomeMessage module does not import or export any data; that is, it has no data passed to it and does not return any data to the main module.

- The InputData module inputs data, OriginalPrice and DiscountRate, from the user and then sends (*exports* or *returns*) these values to the main module so that they can be used by another module.

- The ComputeResults module *imports* (*is passed*) the values of OriginalPrice and DiscountRate from the main module and exports the value of SalePrice to the main module. (The value of AmountSaved is neither imported by, nor exported from, the ComputeResults module.)

- The OutputResults module displays the values of OriginalPrice, DiscountRate, and SalePrice, so it needs to import these values from the main module. It does not export any data to another program module.

Data flow diagrams   When designing a program, we can keep track of the data passed among the various modules by using a **data flow diagram**, a hierarchy chart that shows the data imported by and exported from each program module. For example, the data flow diagram for the Sale Price

Computation program design is given in Figure 1. The arrows indicate the direction in which the data are passed.

IPO charts   Instead of data flow diagrams, some programmers prefer to use **IPO** (Input-Process-Output) **charts** to indicate the data imported and processed by, and exported from, each module. Here, for example, is an IPO chart for the ComputeResults module of the Sale Price Computation program.

Input	**Processing**	**Output**
OriginalPrice	Compute SalePrice	SalePrice
DiscountRate		

An Introduction to Arguments and Parameters

To pass data between a calling module and a submodule, programming languages make use of *parameters*. As an example, consider the OutputResults module in the Sale Price Computation problem, which imports and displays the values of OriginalPrice, DiscountRate, and SalePrice. At the time OutputResults is called, these variables have values that were assigned in other subprograms and then transmitted to the main program.

We will use the following pseudocode to call the OutputResults subprogram and, at the same time, pass the values of OriginalPrice, DiscountRate, and SalePrice to this subprogram:

FIGURE 1

The Data Flow Diagram for the Sale Price Computation Problem

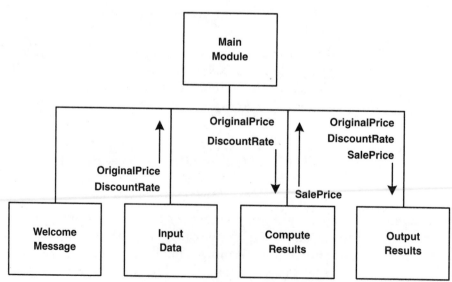

Call OutputResults (OriginalPrice, DiscountRate, SalePrice)

placing the relevant variable names in parentheses, separated by commas. This pseudocode transfers control to the OutputResults subprogram and simultaneously transmits the values of the indicated variables to this subprogram.

When we use this pseudocode for the Call statement, then the first line (the **header**) in the description of the OutputResults subprogram itself must contain a corresponding list of three variables, like this:

Subprogram OutputResults (OldPrice, Rate, NewPrice)

Notice that the names of the variables listed in the Call statement and the subprogram header need not be the same. However, they must agree in number (in this case, there are three of each) and corresponding variables must agree in type (integer, real, string, etc.). For example, if the second variable in the Call statement is of type integer, then the second variable in the subprogram header must be of type integer as well.

The items listed in parentheses in the Call statement are known as **arguments** (or sometimes *actual parameters*), whereas those appearing in the subprogram header are known as **parameters** (or sometimes, *formal parameters*). Arguments (appearing in the call) may be constants, variables, or more general expressions; parameters (appearing in the subprogram header) must be variables.

The Benefits of Using Arguments and Parameters   Using arguments and corresponding parameters to pass data among program modules is important to the modular programming process for the following reasons:

- It enhances the usefulness of subprograms. They can be designed and coded independently of the main program and even used in several different programs, if so desired. Only the structure of the subprogram is important; not the naming of its variables.

- It makes it easier for different programmers to design and code different subprograms. All the programmer of a particular subprogram need know is what kinds of variables are transmitted to or from that module; he or she need not be concerned about how these variables are named or used in the main program or another subprogram.

- It makes it easier to test and debug a subprogram independently of the main program.

When a subprogram is called, the current values of the arguments are assigned to the corresponding parameters, and this correspondence is made solely on the basis of the order of appearance in the two lists. For example, when the subprogram with header

Subprogram OutputResults (OldPrice, Rate, NewPrice)

is called by the statement

Call OutputResults (OriginalPrice, DiscountRate, SalePrice):

- The value of the first argument (OriginalPrice) is assigned to the first parameter (OldPrice).
- The value of the second argument (DiscountRate) is assigned to the second parameter (Rate).
- The value of the last argument (SalePrice) is assigned to the last parameter (NewPrice).

As a specific example, suppose that prior to the call to OutputResults, the values of OriginalPrice, DiscountRate, and SalePrice are, respectively, 200, 20, and 160. Then, after the call (within the OutputResults subprogram), the variables have these values:

OldPrice = 200
Rate = 20
NewPrice = 160

Pictorially, we can represent the way the values of the arguments in the call are transmitted to the parameters in the subprogram header as follows:

Call OutputResults (OriginalPrice, DiscountRate, SalePrice)

Subprogram OutputResults (OldPrice, Rate, NewPrice)

Argument and Corresponding Parameter Names   Be aware that we *need not* use different names for an argument and its corresponding parameter. For example, the header for the OutputResults subprogram could be:

Subprogram OutputResults (OriginalPrice, DiscountRate, SalePrice)

Regardless of the names used, be sure that you use the name listed in the subprogram header to refer to a given parameter when you write the statements in that subprogram description. For example, the pseudocode for the OutputResults subprogram (with parameters OldPrice, Rate, and NewPrice) is

Subprogram OutputResults (OldPrice, Rate, NewPrice)

Write "Original Price: ", OldPrice
Write "Rate of Discount: ", Rate, "%"
Write "Sale price: ", NewPrice
End Subprogram

On the other hand, the following pseudocode would work just as well:

Subprogram OutputResults (OriginalPrice, DiscountRate, SalePrice)
Write "Original Price: ", OriginalPrice
Write "Rate of Discount: ", DiscountRate, "%"
Write "Sale price: ", SalePrice
End Subprogram

Programming Pointer

Remember that the arguments that appear in a *call* to a subprogram may be constants, variables, or expressions. If variables appear in the call, in most programming languages they must be declared in the module that contains the Call statement. The parameters that appear in the *subprogram* itself, however, are declared in that subprogram's header. For example, in Pascal, the header for the OutputResults subprogram (in Pascal, it's called a *procedure*) would look like this:

procedure OutputResults (OldPrice:real, Rate:integer, NewPrice:real)

We will return to the Sale Price Computation program in Section 7.2, but before closing this section, we present a simple yet complete example that illustrates the use of subprogram parameters.

EXAMPLE 1   This program displays a sequence of asterisks (*****) before and after a message entered by the user. It contains one subprogram (named SurroundAndDisplay), which imports the input character string from the main program and displays that string enclosed within asterisks. In this pseudocode, we will explicitly declare the necessary program variables.

Main Program
    Declare Message As String
    Write "Enter a short message: "
    Input Message
    Call SurroundAndDisplay (Message)
    End Program
Subprogram SurroundAndDisplay (Words : string)
    Write "***** ", Words, " *****"
    End Subprogram

As usual, execution begins with the first statement in the main program. Thus, when code corresponding to this pseudocode is run, the user is prompted to enter a message, which is assigned to the variable Message. Then, the statement

Call SurroundAndDisplay (Message)

calls the subprogram, transferring control to it and assigning the value of the argument Message to the parameter Words. Thus, the subprogram's Write statement

Write "***** ", Words, " *****"

displays the value of Message preceded and followed by five asterisks. Control then returns to the next statement in the main program, and execution terminates.

Self-Test 7.1

1. Draw a data flow diagram for the following problem: A salesperson's commission is 15 percent of total sales. Input total sales and compute and display the commission.

2. Write a program that inputs a name and uses the subprogram
   Subprogram DisplayName (Name)
       Write Name
       End Subprogram
   to display the input name three times.

3. What is the output when code corresponding to the following pseudocode is run?
   Main Program
       Set Num1 = 1
       Set Num2 = 2
       Set Num3 = 3
       Call Display (Num3, Num2, Num1)
       End Program
   Subprogram Display (Num3, Num1, Num2)
       Write Num1, Num2, Num3
       End Subprogram

4. Suppose the subprogram header in Exercise 3 were changed to
   Subprogram Display (A, B, C)

   a. What changes (if any) should be made to the subprogram body (description)?
   b. What changes (if any) should be made to the main program?

7.2 More on Subprograms

In Section 7.1, we introduced the concepts of subprogram arguments and parameters. In this section, we will delve more deeply into this subject.

Value and Reference Parameters

In Section 7.1, we used arguments and parameters for the sole purpose of passing data from the main program to a subprogram. Here, we will consider the reverse process—exporting data from a subprogram to the main program. This occurs automatically when control is transferred to the main program at the end of the subprogram, but there is a subtle, but important, difference in the way various programming languages implement this action. We illustrate this difference in the next example.

EXAMPLE 2   Consider the pseudocode:

```
Main Program
    Set Num = 1
    Call ChangeValue (Num)
    Write Num
    End Program
Subprogram ChangeValue (Number)
    Set Number = 2
    End Subprogram
```

The output of code corresponding to this pseudocode will differ, depending on the programming language used. In *all* languages, the variable Num is set equal to 1 in the main program and this value is transmitted to the parameter Number of the subprogram when the latter is called. Then, the value of Number is changed to 2 in the subprogram and the subprogram ends. What happens next, however, depends on the language:

- In some programming languages (for example, Visual Basic), when control is returned to the main program, the *new* value of Number is assigned to the corresponding variable, Num, so the output in this case is 2.

- In other programming languages (for example, Pascal and C++), when control is returned to the main program, *unless otherwise indicated in the subprogram header*, changes to the parameter Number do not affect the corresponding variable, Num, in the main program. Hence, the output in this case is 1.

In this text, we will follow the lead of most programming languages and distinguish between two types of subprogram parameters:

- **Value parameters** have the property that changes to their values in the subprogram do *not* affect the value of the corresponding (argument) variables in the calling module. These parameters can only be used to import data into a subprogram.

- **Reference parameters** (also called *variable parameters*) have the property that changes in their values *do* affect the corresponding arguments in the calling module. They can be used to both import data into and export data from a subprogram.

Programming Pointer It may seem a little strange that changes to a subprogram parameter (such as Number in Example 2) might not change the corresponding variable (Num, in Example 2) in the main program. However, there is a good reason why many programming languages support value parameters—they enhance the independence of subprograms from the main program and each other, a key ingredient in the modular programming method. In particular, the use of value parameters prevents the code in one subprogram from inadvertently affecting the action of the main program or another subprogram through unwanted changes in its variables.

Distinguishing between value and reference parameters Every programming language that distinguishes between these two kinds of parameters has a way of indicating in the subprogram header whether a parameter is of value or reference type. In this text, we will place the symbols "As Ref" after the parameter name to indicate that it is of reference type (and changes to it *will* affect the corresponding argument in the calling module); if these words are omitted, then the parameter is of value type. For example, in the header

Subprogram Switch (Number1, Number2 As Ref)

Number1 is a value parameter and Number2 is a reference parameter. The next example further illustrates this usage.

EXAMPLE 3 Consider the following pseudocode:

Main Program
    Set Num1 = 1
    Set Num2 = 2
    Call Switch (Num1, Num2)
    Write Num1, " ", Num2
    End Program

```
Subprogram Switch (Number1, Number2 As Ref)
    Set Number1 = 2
    Set Number2 = 1
    End Subprogram
```

In this pseudocode, when control is transferred to the subprogram Switch, Num1 = 1 and Num2 = 2, so the parameter Number1 takes the value 1 and parameter Number2 takes the value 2. Then, in the subprogram, Number1 is assigned the value 2 and Number2 is assigned the value 1. Now, when control is returned to the main program, Num1 retains the value (namely, 1) it had when the subprogram was called because Number1 is a value parameter. On the other hand, Num2 changes to the current value of Number2 (which is 1) because Number2 is a reference parameter. Thus, the output of code corresponding to this pseudocode is:

1 1

To actually switch the values of Num1 and Num2, both Number1 and Number2 must be specified as reference parameters.

As a more complete example of the use of value and reference parameters, let us return to the Sale Price Computation problem described at the beginning of Section 7.1. For the sake of convenience, we repeat it here:

Sale Price Computation problem

A department store needs a program that will compute and display the sale price of a discounted item when the original price of that item and the percentage it is discounted are input.

Recall that:

- The InputData module inputs the pre-sale price and the percentage it is being discounted (OriginalPrice and DiscountRate) from the user. Since these quantities must be exported to the main program, they must be reference parameters.

- The ComputeResults module imports these quantities from the main program, computes the sale price (SalePrice) of the item, and exports the latter to the main program. Thus, OriginalPrice and DiscountRate are taken to be value parameters, while SalePrice is a reference parameter.

- Finally, the OutputResults module imports OriginalPrice, DiscountRate, and SalePrice from the main program and displays their values. All parameters here are value parameters; OutputResults does not export any data to the main program.

Here is the pseudocode for the entire program.

```
Main Program
    Declare OriginalPrice, SalePrice As Real
    Declare DiscountRate As Integer
    Call WelcomeMessage
    Call InputData(OriginalPrice, DiscountRate)
    Call ComputeResults(OriginalPrice, DiscountRate, SalePrice)
    Call OutputResults(OriginalPrice, DiscountRate, SalePrice)
    End Program
Subprogram WelcomeMessage
    Display a brief description of the program
    End Subprogram
Subprogram InputData(Price As Ref, Rate As Ref)
    Write "Enter the price of an item: "
    Input Price
    Write "Enter the percentage it is discounted: "
    Input Rate
    End Subprogram
Subprogram ComputeResults(OriginalPrice, DiscountRate,
        SalePrice As Ref)
    Declare AmountSaved As Real
    Set AmountSaved = OriginalPrice * DiscountRate / 100
    Set SalePrice = OriginalPrice – AmountSaved
    End Subprogram
Subprogram OutputResults(OldPrice, Rate, NewPrice)
    Write "Original Price:   ", OldPrice
    Write "Rate of Discount:   ", Rate, "%"
    Write "Sale price:   ", NewPrice
    End Subprogram
```

When code corresponding to this pseudocode is run, execution proceeds as follows:

1. The program starts and control transfers to the WelcomeMessage subprogram, which displays a welcome message and transfers control back to the main program.

2. Control transfers to the InputData subprogram. Since the InputData arguments are undefined (have not been assigned values), the parameters Price and Rate are initially undefined as well. However, they are assigned values by the Input statements and, since both are reference parameters, these values are exported to the main program and assigned to OriginalPrice and DiscountRate.

3. Control transfers to the ComputeResults subprogram, in which the value of SalePrice is computed and returned to the main program.

4. Control now transfers to the OutputResults subprogram. The values of OriginalPrice, DiscountRate, and SalePrice are assigned to OldPrice, Rate, and NewPrice, respectively, and displayed.

5. Control returns to the main program and execution terminates.

Programming Pointer When a subprogram is called, the kind of parameter, value or reference, determines the way in which memory is allocated for the value of that parameter.

- If the parameter is of value type, then:

    1. A new (temporary) storage location is set up in memory to hold the value of that parameter while the subprogram executes.

    2. The value of the corresponding argument is copied into this location.

    3. Whenever the value of the parameter is modified by the subprogram, only the contents of this temporary storage location are changed, so the corresponding argument is unaffected.

- If the parameter is of reference type, then:

    1. It is assigned the same storage location as the corresponding argument (which, in this case, must be a variable).

    2. Whenever the value of the parameter is modified by the subprogram, the contents of this common storage location are changed, so the value of the argument is modified as well.

The Scope of a Variable

When a variable is used (input, processed, or output) in a program module, we say that this variable has been *referenced* in that module. Sometimes, a variable that is declared in one program module cannot be referenced in another module; trying to do so will result in an *undefined variable* error message when the program is executed. The part of the program in which a given variable *can* be referenced is called the **scope** of that variable.

In many programming languages, the scope of a variable declared in a certain program module consists of that module together with all its submodules. We will follow this practice in this text. For example, in the Sale Price Computation program given above:

- The variables OriginalPrice, DiscountRate, and SalePrice are declared in the main program. Since all other program modules are subprograms of the main program, we will consider the scope of these variables to be the entire program; they can be referenced in any module.

- The variable AmountSaved is declared in the ComputeResults subprogram, so its scope is limited to this subprogram; it cannot be used in any other program module.

Global and local variables

Notice that, in this text, variables declared in the main program have a scope that is the entire program. Such variables are called **global variables**. (In some programming languages, a variable is global if it is declared outside of, or prior to, *all* program modules including the main program.) For example, in the Sale Price Computation program, the variables OriginalPrice, DiscountRate, and SalePrice are global variables. Variables that are declared in a particular subprogram, such as AmountSaved in the ComputeResults subprogram, are said to be *local* to that module. **Local variables** have the following properties:

- When the value of a local variable changes in a subprogram, the value of a variable with the same name outside that subprogram remains unchanged.

- When the value of a variable changes elsewhere in a program, a local variable with the same name retains its current value in its subprogram.

Sometimes, local and global variables come into conflict. For example, suppose a variable X is declared in the main program and another variable, also called X, is declared in a subprogram. (We say that X has a *multiple declaration* in the program.) Now, the X declared in the main program is a global variable and thus may be assigned a value in any subprogram. But the X declared in the subprogram is local to that subprogram, so changes to its value do not affect a variable with the same name outside the subprogram. To resolve this conflict, the *local declaration takes precedence*—the value of the main program X is not changed when the subprogram X is assigned a new value. The next example illustrates this situation.

EXAMPLE 4   Consider the pseudocode:

```
Main Program
    Declare X As Integer
    Set X = 1
    Call Sub
    Write X
    End Program
```

Subprogram Sub
    Declare X As Integer
    Set X = 2
    End Subprogram

The main program begins by assigning X the value 1, and then control is transferred to the subprogram. In the subprogram, X is a local variable, so the value assigned to it there does not affect the value of the main program's variable X, even though we consider the latter to be a global variable. Thus, when control is returned to the main program, the Write statement displays the number 1, the value of the main program variable X.

Programming Pointer The computer treats local variables in the same way as value parameters (discussed earlier in this section). Whenever a local variable is declared, even if it has the same name as a previously declared variable, it is allocated a new storage location in memory. Thus, in Example 4, from the computer's point of view, the main program X and the subprogram X are treated as two different variables, and changing one has no effect on the other.

Style Pointer **Use Parameters, Not Global Variables, to Pass Data among Modules** In many programming languages , it is possible to pass data among modules by making use of global variables. By its nature, a global variable can be imported by, or exported from, every program module. Nevertheless, it is considered poor programming practice to use global variables for this purpose because doing so diminishes the independence of program modules. The proper way to pass data among program modules is through the use of arguments and parameters, as described in Section 7.1 and earlier in this section.

Self-Test 7.2

The following program is used in Problems 1–4:

Main Program
    Declare X, Y, Z As Integer
    Set X = 1
    Set Y = 2
    Set Z = 3
        Call Display (Z, Y, X)
        Write X, Y, Z
        End Program
    Subprogram Display (Num1, Num2, Num3 As Ref)
        Write Num1, Num2, Num3

```
Set Num1 = 4
Set Num2 = 5
Set Num3 = 6
Write Num1, Num2, Num3
End Subprogram
```

1. What is the output of code corresponding to this pseudocode?

2. Suppose that all occurrences of Num1, Num2, and Num3 in this program were changed to X, Y, and Z, respectively. What is the output of code for the modified program?

3. Determine the output of code for the given program if its subprogram header were changed to:

   a. Subprogram Display (Num1, Num2, Num3)

   b. Subprogram Display (Num1 As Ref, Num2 As Ref, Num3 As Ref)

4. Identify the local and global variables in this program.

5. What is the output of code corresponding to the following pseudocode? (Assume that variables declared in the main program are global variables.)

   a.
   ```
   Main Program
       Declare X As Integer
       Set X = 0
       Call Simple
       Write X
       End Program
   Subprogram Simple
       Set X = 1
       End Subprogram
   ```

   b.
   ```
   Main Program
       Declare X As Integer
       Set X = 0
       Call Simple
       Write X
       End Program
   Subprogram Simple
       Declare X As Integer
       Set X = 1
       End Subprogram
   ```

7.3 Functions

A **function** is a special type of subprogram—one whose name can be assigned a value. In this section, we will discuss **built-in functions**, those that are supplied by the programming language, and **user-defined functions**, which are program modules created by the programmer.

Built-in Functions

Programming languages typically provide a wide assortment of built-in (or *library*) functions. The code for these functions is supplied in separate modules and need not be physically placed within your program. In this text, you have already seen several examples of built-in functions:

- Sqrt(X) computes the square root of the number X (Section 4.4).
- Int(X) computes the integer obtained by discarding the fractional part of the number X (Section 5.1).
- Random(N) computes a random number in the range 1 to N (Section 5.1).
- Length(S) computes the length of the string S (Section 5.2).
- EOF(F) determines whether or not the end of the sequential file F has been reached and takes on a value of *true* or *false* accordingly (Section 5.3).

Viewed as subprograms, built-in functions contain one or more parameters and *return* (export) at least one value. As with any subprogram, the arguments in the call to a built-in function may be constants, variables, or expressions of the appropriate type (as long as the corresponding parameters are of value type). However, built-in functions (including the ones listed above) differ from the subprograms discussed in Sections 7.1 and 7.2 in several ways:

1. The header and definition of (code for) a built-in function do not appear in the program that calls that function.
2. When a built-in function is called, the function name is assigned a value (of the type specified for that function).
3. A built-in function is called by using the function name anywhere in the program that a constant of its type is allowed.

For example, the Sqrt function is of type real—it is assigned a real (floating point) value when it is called. Sqrt may be used (called) anywhere in a program that a constant of type real is allowed. Thus, all the following are valid calls to the Sqrt function (assuming that the value of the argument is a nonnegative number):

- Set X = Sqrt(10)
- Write Sqrt(2 * Num + 1)
- Call Display(Sqrt(Num))

(Note that the last call is valid only if Display's parameter is of value type.)

A few more built-in functions

Here are a few more functions that are commonly built into a programming language. (Note that the name and form of the functions given here may differ from those used for similar functions in a particular programming language.)

- Abs(X) computes and returns the absolute value of a number X (the number obtained by ignoring the sign, if any, of X); it is of type real.

- Round(X) rounds X to the nearest whole number and returns that number; it is of type integer.

- Str(X) converts the number X into the corresponding string (sequence of ASCII codes) and returns that string; it is of type string.

- Val(S, N) converts the string S, if it represents a number, into a number of the appropriate type and sets N = 1; if S does not represent a number, it sets both Val and N equal to 0. Val is of type real and N must be a variable of numeric type.

EXAMPLE 5   The following examples show the result of applying the indicated function to the specified argument:

Abs(10) returns 10   Abs(−10) returns 10
Round(10.5) returns 11   Round(100 * 10.443)/100 returns 10.44
Str(31.5) returns "31.5"   Str(−100) returns "−100"
Val("31.5", N) returns the number 31.5, and N = 1
Val("abc", N) returns the number 0, and N = 0

Programming Pointer

Although the string "31.5" and the number 31.5 may look similar, from a programming point of view they are quite different:

- The number 31.5 is stored in memory as the binary equivalent of 31.5. Moreover, since it of numeric type, it can be added to, subtracted from, divided by, or multiplied by another number.

- The string "31.5" is stored in memory by placing the ASCII codes for "3", "1", ".", and "5" in consecutive storage locations (see Section 5.2). Since "31.5" is a string, we cannot perform arithmetic operations on it, but we can concatenate it with another string.

The next example gives an application of the Val and Str functions to defensive programming (see Section 4.4).

EXAMPLE 6   The following pseudocode prompts the user to enter an integer. It receives the input as a string, checks whether that string represents an integer, and repeats the prompt if it is not.

```
Declare InputString As String
Declare N, Number As Integer
Repeat
      Write "Enter an integer:"
      Input InputString
      Set Number = Val(InputString, N)
Until (N <> 0) And (Number = Int(Number))
```

The Repeat-Until loop *validates* the input string (see Section 3.3) with the aid of the Val and Int functions. If the string entered by the user *is* an integer, then both conditions in the Until statement are true and the loop is exited. If the input string is not a number, the first condition is false; if it is a number but not an integer, then the second condition is false. In either of these two cases, the loop is reentered and the user is again asked to input an integer.

Programming Pointer

Although you need not include the code for a built-in function in the program you are writing, the file that contains that code may have to be *linked* to your program in order for the latter to run. This is usually done by inserting a statement at the beginning of the program that tells the compiler where to locate the function's code and instructs the compiler to link that code to your program.

User-defined Functions

Programming languages also allow you to create your own function subprograms, which are called *user-defined functions**. In some languages (like C++), all subprograms are functions; in others (like Pascal), functions are one special type of subprogram. In this text, we consider both subprograms *and* functions.

The difference between a subprogram that is a function and one that is not (sometimes referred to as a *procedure*) is twofold:

1. A function's name may be assigned a value (of a specified type) in the code that defines it.

2. A function is called by placing its name (and desired arguments) anywhere in the program that a constant of the specified type is allowed.

---

* Here, the word *user* refers to the programmer (the user of the programming language), not the person executing the program.

Moreover, in this text, we will begin a function's header with the word Function (instead of Subprogram). The next example illustrates these points.

EXAMPLE 7   This program defines and calls a function Cube that imports a number X from the main program and returns its cube, X^3, to the main program, where it is displayed.

```
Main Program
    Declare Num As Real
    Set Num = Cube(10)
    Write Num
    End Program
Function Cube(X) As Real
    Set Cube = X^3
    End Function
```

The call to the function is made in the second statement of the main program:

```
Set Num = Cube(10)
```

When this statement is executed, control transfers to the function subprogram Cube and its parameter, X, is assigned the value 10. (Notice that the function header declares the function type—the type for Cube—as "real.") Then, the statement

```
Set Cube = X^3
```

assigns the value 1000 (10^3) to the name of the function. When the function ends, this value is returned to the main program, assigned to Num, and displayed.

Style Pointer

When to Use a Function   If the programming language you are using contains both functions and non-function subprograms, then either one may be used to implement a given program submodule. Which you use in a particular instance is a matter of style. Here is a guideline for deciding whether or not to use a function to implement a particular submodule: If the submodule in question computes and returns *a single value* to the calling module, then implement it with a function. Notice that the function in Example 7 satisfies this criterion.

To illustrate this style pointer, and to provide another example of the use of a user-defined function, let us reexamine the Sale Price Computation program given in Section 7.2. To facilitate our discussion, we will repeat the description and data flow diagram for this problem here.

Sale Price
Computation
problem
revisited

A department store needs a program that will compute and display the sale price of a discounted item when the original price of that item and the percentage it is discounted are input.

The data flow diagram (Figure 2) makes it clear that the only submodule that returns a single value to the main module is ComputeResults. Therefore, following the guideline stated in the Style Pointer above, we would use *subprograms* to implement the WelcomeMessage, InputData, and OutputResults modules (as in Sections 7.1 and 7.2), but use a *function* to implement the ComputeResults module. The pseudocode for the modified main program and ComputeResults subprogram (which, here, becomes the NewPrice function) is given below; the pseudocode for the other three modules is identical to that given in Section 7.2.

```
Main Program
        Declare OriginalPrice, SalePrice As Real
        Declare DiscountRate As Integer
        Call WelcomeMessage
        Call InputData(OriginalPrice, DiscountRate)
        Set SalePrice = NewPrice(OriginalPrice, DiscountRate)
        Call OutputResults(OriginalPrice, DiscountRate, SalePrice)
        End Program
```

FIGURE 2

Data Flow
Diagram for
the Sale
Price
Computation
Problem

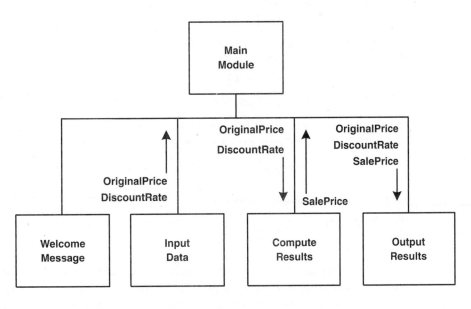

Function NewPrice(OriginalPrice, DiscountRate) As Real
    Declare AmountSaved As Real
    Set AmountSaved = OriginalPrice * DiscountRate / 100
    Set NewPrice = OriginalPrice – AmountSaved
End Function

Self-Test 7.3

1. Determine the value of each expression.

    a. Sqrt(4)   b. Int(3.9)

2. Determine the value of each expression.

    a. Abs(0)   b. Round(3.9)
    c. Str(0.1)   d. Val("–32", N)

3. What is the output of code corresponding to the following pseudocode?

    Main Program
        Write F(1, 2)
        Write G(–1)
        End Program
    Function F(X, Y) As Integer
        Set F = 5 * X + Y
        End Function
    Function G(X) As Integer
        Set G = X * X
        End Function

4. a. Write a function

        Function A (L, W) As Real

        that computes the area of a rectangle of length L and width W.

    b. Write an assignment statement that calls this function.

7.4 Recursion

When a subprogram calls itself, the process is called **recursion**, and the subprogram is said to be *recursive*. Some programming languages (such as Pascal and C++) allow recursion; others (such as Visual Basic) do not. Recursive algorithms (those that make use of recursive subprograms) can sometimes provide quick and simple solutions to complex problems.

To illustrate the concept of recursion, let's consider a simple programming problem: Given a positive integer N, write a function, Sum(N), that computes the sum of the first N positive integers. To solve this problem, we can follow the strategy given in Section 3.3, setting up a counter-controlled loop in which each successive integer is added to a running total. The pseudocode is:

```
Function Sum(N) As Integer
    Set Total = 0
    For K = 1 Step 1 Until N
        Set Total = Total + K
    End For
    Set Sum = Total
End Function
```

This pseudocode provides a *non*-recursive solution to the problem.

To solve this problem in a recursive manner, we ask the question "If we know the sum of the first N – 1 positive integers, how would we find the sum of the first N positive integers?" The answer is to add the integer N to the sum of the first N – 1 positive integers. In other words:

$$Sum(N) = [1 + 2 + ... + N - 1] + N$$
or $$Sum(N) = Sum(N - 1) + N$$

This is the key to the recursive solution of the problem. We have effectively replaced the original problem with a *smaller* problem, that of finding the sum of the first N – 1 positive integers; that is, finding Sum(N – 1). But, a similar argument gives us

$$Sum(N - 1) = Sum(N - 2) + N - 1$$

and we can continue in this manner until we reach

$$Sum(2) = Sum(1) + 2$$

Notice that we can't write Sum(1) = Sum(0) + 1, since Sum(0) makes no sense—we can't sum up the first 0 positive integers! However, since Sum(1) is the sum of the first 1 positive integers, we have:

$$Sum(1) = 1$$

Thus, we can define the function Sum(N) by the pair of formulas:

If N = 1, Sum(N) = 1
If N > 1, Sum(N) = Sum(N – 1) + N

We can then use these formulas to compute Sum(N) for any value of N. To illustrate the technique, let N = 4; that is, we will find Sum(4), the sum of the first four positive integers. To do so, we apply the formulas above with, successively, $N = 4$, $N = 3$, $N = 2$, and $N = 1$. The computation goes like this:

$N = 4$: $Sum(4) = Sum(3) + 4$

$N = 3$: $Sum(3) = Sum(2) + 3$

> Now, substituting this expression for Sum(3) into the line above gives:
> $Sum(4) = [Sum(2) + 3] + 4 = Sum(2) + 7$

$N = 2$: $Sum(2) = Sum(1) + 2$

> Substituting this expression for Sum(2) into the line above:
> $Sum(4) = [Sum(1) + 2] + 7 = Sum(1) + 9$

$N = 1$: $Sum(1) = 1$

> Substituting this value for Sum(1) into the line above:
> $Sum(4) = 1 + 9 = 10$

Compared to the straightforward way of finding Sum(4) presented earlier, the recursive solution shown here certainly seems awkward and even confusing. Remember, however, that you are looking at it from a human perspective. When a recursive solution is carried out in a program, the process often requires a small amount of code that is executed quickly.

EXAMPLE 8 The following pseudocode provides a recursive solution to the problem of summing the first N positive integers, where N is a given positive integer.

```
Function Sum(N) As Intéger
     If N = 1 Then
          Set Sum = 1
     Else
          Set Sum = Sum(N – 1) + N
     End If
End Function
```

Suppose that this function is called by the statement:

Set Total = Sum(4)

When this statement is executed, control transfers to the function Sum and N is set equal to 4. Execution then proceeds in the following way:

- *First call to the function*:

  Since $N = 4$, the Else clause is executed and the right side of the assignment statement

Set Sum = Sum(N – 1) + N

is evaluated, which gives

Sum(3) + 4

and causes a call to the function Sum with N = 3.

- *Second call to the function*:

The Else clause is executed with N = 3 and the right side of the assignment statement is evaluated, which gives

Sum(2) + 3

and causes the function to be called with N = 2.

- *Third call to the function*:

The Else clause is executed with N = 2 and the right side of the assignment statement is evaluated, which gives

Sum(1) + 2

and causes the function to be called with N = 1.

- *Fourth (last) call to the function*:

Since N = 1, the Then clause is executed, Sum is set equal to 1 (the function does *not* call itself), and execution of this call to the function is completed.

- Control now returns to the assignment statement,

Set Sum = Sum(1) + 2

in the *third call* to the function (where the last call to the function was made). Here, Sum(1) is replaced by 1 and Sum (on the left side) takes on the value 3. Execution of the third call is now complete.

- Control now returns to the assignment statement,

Set Sum = Sum(2) + 3

in the *second call* to the function. Here, Sum(2) is replaced by 3 and Sum (on the left side) takes on the value 6. Execution of the second call is now complete.

- Finally, control returns to the assignment statement,

Set Sum = Sum(3) + 4

in the *first call* to the function. Here, Sum(3) is replaced by 6 and Sum (on the left side) takes on the value 10. Execution of the first call is now complete and Total is set equal to 10.

The following table summarizes the action of the function Sum if it is called from the main program with N = 4.

Calling Sum(N) with N = 4	If Execution Is Here	Value of N	Value of Sum
	Start of execution of first call to Sum	4	Undefined
	Start of execution of second call to Sum	3	Undefined
	Start of execution of third call to Sum	2	Undefined
	Start of execution of fourth call to Sum	1	Undefined
	End of execution of fourth call to Sum	1	1
	End of execution of third call to Sum	2	3
	End of execution of second call to Sum	3	6
	End of execution of first call to Sum	4	10

Here is another example of recursion.

EXAMPLE 9   We will write a recursive function that finds the Nth power of the real number X, X^N, where N is a given positive integer. To do so, notice that $X^N = X * X^{N-1}$. Thus, if we call our function Power(X, N), then

> Power (X, N) = X * Power(X, N – 1)

if N > 1, and Power(X, 1) = X.

We can therefore replace the problem of finding the Nth power of X with that of finding the $(N – 1)^{st}$ power of X, which is the key to a recursive solution. Adapting the pseudocode of Example 8 to the current situation, we have

> Function Power(X, N) As Integer
>   If N = 1 Then
>   Set Power = X
>   Else
>   Set Power = Power(X, N – 1) * X
>   End If
>   End Function

Let us trace the execution of this function if it is called by the statement

> Set Answer = Power(5, 3)

(which will assign the value $5^3 = 125$ to the variable Answer). The assignment statement transfers control to the function Power, where X is set equal to 5 and N is set equal to 3. This is the first call to the recursive function, which calls itself a total of three times, as follows:

- *First call to the function*:

    Since N = 3, the Else clause is executed and the right side of the assignment statement

    > Set Power = Power(X, N – 1) * X

is evaluated, which yields

Power(5, 2) * 5

and causes a second call to the function Power with X = 5 and N = 2.

- *Second call to the function*:

    The Else clause is now executed with N = 2 and the right side of the assignment statement is evaluated, which yields

    Power(5, 1) * 5

    and causes Power to be called again with X = 5 and N = 1.

- *Third (last) call to the function*:

    Since N = 1 in this function call, the Then clause is executed, Power is set equal to 5 (the function does *not* call itself), and execution of the third call to the Power function is complete.

- Control now returns to the right side of the assignment statement,

    Set Power = Power(5, 1) * 5

    in the *second call* to the function (where the third call was made). Here, Power(5, 1) is replaced by 5 and Power (on the left side) takes on the value 25. Execution of the second call is now complete.

- Control now returns to the right side of the assignment statement,

    Set Power = Power(5, 2) * 5

    in the *first call* to the function. Here, Power(5, 2) is replaced by 25 and Power (on the left side) takes on the value 125. Execution of the first call is now complete and Answer is set equal to 125.

Self-Test 7.4

The *factorial* of a positive integer N is denoted by N! and defined to be:

If N = 1, N! = 1
If N > 1, N! = 1 × 2 × ... × N

Thus, 1! = 1, 2! = 1 × 2, 3! = 1 × 2 × 3 = 6, and so on.

1. Express N! in terms of (N − 1)!.
2. Write a recursive function, Factorial(N), that computes and returns N!.
3. Trace the action of the function Factorial(N), in a similar way to that of Example 9, if it is called by the statement:

    Set Answer = Factorial(3)

4. Write a non-recursive function, Fac(N) (using a For loop), that computes and returns N!.

7.5 *Focus on Problem Solving*

In this section, we will develop a program that not only makes use of the concept of subprogram parameters covered in this chapter, but also draws upon material from all prior chapters. In particular, this program is a menu-driven one that creates and modifies a sequential file with the aid of arrays.

A Grade Management Program

One of your instructors, Professor Allknowing, would like to have a program that creates an "electronic grade sheet" so that he can keep track of student scores in his classes. This program should allow the professor to enter the names of his students and their scores on three tests, compute the average test score for each student, and display this information any time he wants.

Problem Analysis This program needs a file, GRADES, to hold the required information—name, test scores, and test average—for each student in the class. Thus, this file must have records of the form:

name, test 1 score, test 2 score, test 3 score, average

To create this file, we must input the student names and test scores (not necessarily all at once) from the user and compute the test average for each student. This necessitates the use of the program variables Name, Score1, Score2, Score3, and Average. The output of this program is just a display of the contents of the GRADES file. (In creating and displaying the file, we will make use of the techniques described in Sections 5.3 and 5.4.)

Program Design   To determine the basic tasks that this program must perform, imagine that you are the instructor of this class. The first thing you would have to do is to create the file GRADES and enter the names of all students into this file. Then, after each test is given, the scores of all students on that test would be entered into the file. Moreover, at any time, you might want to compute the test average for each student and/or view the contents of the file. Thus, the program's basic tasks are:

1. Create the file GRADES, containing the names of the students in the class.
2. Enter scores for all students on a particular test into the file.
3. Compute the average test score for each student and enter these into the file.
4. Display the contents of the file GRADES.

In light of the nature of these tasks, we will design the program to be a menu-driven one with options corresponding to the four tasks listed above, as well as an option to "quit" the program. This necessitates another basic task, which must be performed prior to any of the others:

0. Allow the user to select an option from the menu.

In task 1, we only write data to GRADES; in tasks 2 and 3, we read each student name from GRADES and then write the corresponding test score or average to this file; and in task 4, we read and display the entire GRADES file. Thus, before executing task 2, 3, or 4, it would simplify the process if we loaded GRADES into arrays. Following this line of reasoning we will place tasks 2, 3, and 4 in a submodule, Retrieve Grade Sheet, that performs certain "housekeeping" tasks, such as opening GRADES for input, loading it into arrays, and closing it when done. This leads to the following modularization of this program:

> Main Module
> > Select from Menu module
> > Create Grade Sheet module
> > Retrieve Grade Sheet module
> > > Enter Test Scores module
> > > Compute Averages module
> > > Display Grade Sheet module

The hierarchy chart in Figure 3 on the next page pictures the relationships among these modules.

FIGURE 3

Hierarchy
Chart for
*A Grade
Management
Program*

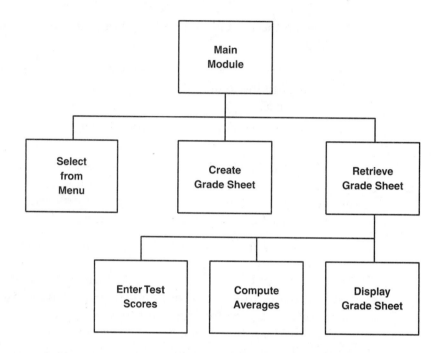

We now write a rough pseudocode outline for each module.

Main Module The main module, after displaying a welcome message, must call the Select from Menu module to determine which of its other submodules to call. Here is its rough pseudocode:

> Display a welcome message
> Call Select from Menu module
> Call either Create Grade Sheet or Retrieve Grade Sheet module
> End Program

Select from Menu module This module displays the menu of options and inputs the user's selection. (See Section 4.4 for information on menus.) A rough pseudocode outline is:

> Display menu options
> >   (Create Grade Sheet, Enter Test Scores,
> >   Compute Test Averages, Display Grade Sheet, Quit)
> Input user selection, Choice

This submodule exports (returns) the value of Choice to the main module.

Create Grade Sheet module This module creates the file GRADES used by this program; it inputs the student names and initializes (for each student) all three test scores and the test average to 0. (See Section 5.3 for information on creating a sequential file.) Its pseudocode is:

```
Open "GRADES" For Output As DataFile
Write "Enter student name; enter * when done."
Input Name
While Name <> "*"
     Write DataFile, Name, 0, 0, 0, 0
     Write "Enter student name; enter * when done."
     Input Name
End While
Close DataFile
```

(No data are imported or exported by this submodule.)

Retrieve Grade Sheet module   This module opens the existing file GRADES (for input), loads it into parallel arrays (one for student names, one for student averages, and a two-dimensional array for the three test scores), calls either the Enter Test Scores, Compute Averages, or Display Grade Sheet module (depending on the user's menu selection, Choice), and then closes the file when control returns from the called module. (Reading a sequential file and loading it into arrays are discussed in Sections 5.3 and 6.3, respectively.) Its pseudocode is:

```
Open "GRADES" For Input As DataFile
Declare Names[40], Averages[40], Scores[3,40]
Set Count = 0
While Not EOF(DataFile)
     Set Count = Count +1
     Read DataFile, Names[Count], Scores[1, Count],
          Scores[2, Count], Scores[3, Count], Averages[Count]
End While
Depending on value of Choice
     Call Enter Test Scores, Compute Averages,
          or Display Grade Sheet
Close DataFile
```

This submodule needs to import the value of Choice from the main module and export the value of Count (the number of students in the class) as well as possibly the arrays Names, Scores, and/or Averages to the submodule it calls.

Enter Test Scores module   This module determines which test (1, 2, or 3) is to be entered, then successively displays each student name and inputs the corresponding score.

```
Write "Enter the test number:"
Input TestNum
```

Write "When a name is displayed, enter the test score."
For K = 1 Step 1 To Count
    Write Names[K]
    Input Scores[TestNum, K]
End For

This submodule imports the value of Count and the array Names from the Retrieve Grade Sheet module and imports *and* exports the array Scores.

Compute Averages module   This module computes the test average for each student by summing up the three test scores and dividing by three.

For K = 1 Step 1 To Count
    Set Sum = Scores[1, K] + Scores[2, K] + Scores[3, K]
    Set Averages[K] = Sum / 3
End For

This submodule imports the value of Count and the array Scores from the Retrieve Grade Sheet module and exports the array Averages to this module.

Display Grade Sheet module   This module displays the contents of the file GRADES (which, when Display Grade Sheet is called, has already been loaded into arrays).

For K = 1 Step 1 To Count
    Write Names[K], Scores[1, K], Scores[2, K],
        Scores[3, K], Averages[K]
End For

This submodule imports the value of Count and the arrays Names, Scores, and Averages from the Retrieve Grade Sheet module. It does not export any data.

Referring to the comments (appearing at the end of each submodule's pseudocode) concerning the import and export of data, we turn the hierarchy chart of Figure 3 into the data flow diagram in Figure 4.

FIGURE 4

Data Flow
Diagram for
*A Grade
Management
Program*

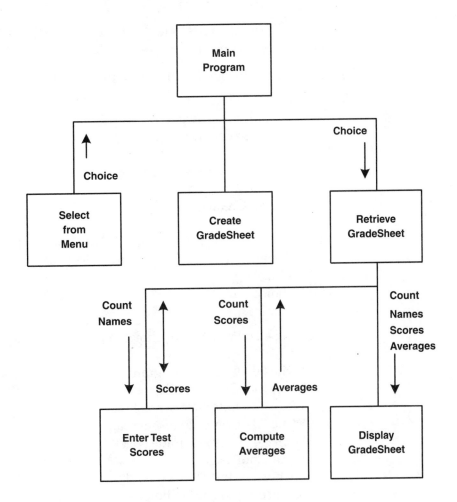

Refining the
pseudocode

We now refine the pseudocode for several of the program modules, making use of the subprogram arguments/parameters notation introduced in Sections 7.1 and 7.2. (Recall that variables *exported* from a subprogram must be indicated as reference, or "Ref", variables.) We will also indicate which subprogram variables are local by placing the appropriate Declare statements in the program modules. Here is a rundown on the refinements.

- In the main module (the main program), we place the calls to its submodules in a loop so that more than one task may be accomplished in each program run.

- In the Select from Menu module (subprogram), we validate the user's selection to ensure that it's in the proper range.

- In the Retrieve Grade Sheet subprogram, we explicitly specify which of its three submodules is called.

The refined pseudocode for the entire program follows.

```
Main Program
    Declare Choice As Integer
    Display a welcome message
    Repeat
        Call SelectFromMenu(Choice)
        If Choice = 1 Then
            Call CreateGradeSheet
        End If
        If (Choice = 2) Or (Choice = 3) Or (Choice = 4) Then
            Call RetrieveGradeSheet(Choice)
        End If
    Until Choice = 0
    End Program

Subprogram SelectFromMenu(Choice As Ref)
    Repeat
        Write "0 - Quit the program"
        Write "1 - Create grade sheet"
        Write "2 - Enter test scores"
        Write "3 - Compute test averages"
        Write "4 - Display grade sheet"
        Input Choice
    Until (Choice = Int(Choice)) And
        (Choice >= 0) And (Choice <= 4)
    End Subprogram

Subprogram CreateGradeSheet
    Declare Name As String
    Open "GRADES" For Output As DataFile
    Write "Enter student name; enter * when done."
    Input Name
    While Name <> "*"
        Write DataFile, Name, 0, 0, 0, 0
        Write "Enter student name; enter * when done."
        Input Name
    End While
    Close DataFile
    End Subprogram
```

```
Subprogram RetrieveGradeSheet(Choice)
    Open "GRADES" For Input As DataFile
    Declare Names[40], Averages[40], Scores[3,40]
    Declare Count As Integer
    Set Count = 0
    While Not EOF(DataFile)
        Set Count = Count +1
        Read DataFile, Names[Count], Scores[1, Count],
            Scores[2, Count], Scores[3, Count], Averages[Count]
    End While
    Select Case Of Choice
        Case 2 :
            Call EnterTestScores(Count, Names, Scores)
        Case 3 :
            Call ComputeAverages(Count, Scores, Averages)
        Case 4 :
            Call DisplayGradeSheet(Count, Names,
                Scores, Averages)
        End Case
    Close DataFile
    End Subprogram

Subprogram EnterTestScores(Count, Names, Scores As Ref)
    Declare TestNum, K As Integer
    Repeat
        Write "Enter the test number:"
        Input TestNum
    Until (TestNum = 1) Or (TestNum = 2) Or (TestNum = 3)
    Write "When a name is displayed, enter the test score."
    For K = 1 Step 1 To Count
        Write Names[K]
        Input Scores[TestNum, K]
    End For
    End Subprogram

Subprogram ComputeAverages(Count, Scores, Averages As Ref)
    Declare Sum, K As Integer
    For K = 1 Step 1 To Count
        Set Sum = Scores[1, K] + Scores[2, K] + Scores[3, K]
        Set Averages[K] = Sum / 3
    End For
    End Subprogram
```

Subprogram DisplayGradeSheet(Count, Names, Scores, Averages)
    Declare K As Integer
    For K = 1 Step 1 To Count
        Write Names[K], Scores[1, K], Scores[2, K],
            Scores[3, K], Averages[K]
    End For
End Subprogram

Program Code   The program code is now written using the design as a guide. At this stage, header comments and step comments (see Section 2.3) are inserted into each module, providing internal documentation for the program. Here are a couple of other points concerning the coding that are specific to this program:

- The main menu and the grade sheet should be displayed on blank screens. Recall that this is accomplished by using the programming language's "clear screen" statement. This statement should be the first statement in the Repeat-Until loop in the main program and the first statement in the DisplayGradeSheet subprogram.

- To display the contents of the GRADES file in a neat, readable fashion, the output produced by the Display Grade Sheet module must be *formatted*—the names, test scores, and averages should line up in columns. This can be accomplished using the programming language's special print formatting statements.

- Another way to improve the output's readability is to insert a blank line after displaying every few lines of student information. This can be done with the aid of the Int function (see Section 5.1) by changing the For loop in the DisplayGradeSheet subprogram to:

        For K = 1 Step 1 To Count
            Write Names[K], Scores[1, K], Scores[2, K],
                Scores[3, K], Averages[K]
            If Count / 3 = Int(Count /3) Then
                Write
            End If
        End For

This pseudocode causes a line to be skipped after every three lines of output.

- There is another, more subtle, problem with the display of the grade sheet. Immediately after it is displayed, control returns to the RetrieveGradeSheet subprogram and then to the main program. In the latter, the clear screen statement (see the first bullet, above) will remove the grade sheet from the screen, probably before it can be read. To delay returning from the DisplayGradeSheet subprogram, place the following statements at the end of this module (the corresponding text will appear under the grade sheet):

> Write "To return to the main menu, press the Enter key."
> Input Response

(The variable Response must be of type character or string.) Then, execution will pause until the user presses Enter, allowing the grade sheet to be viewed in a leisurely fashion.

Program Test   The best way to test this program is to imagine that you are the instructor of a very small class (say, two or three students), and use the program to create the grade sheet, enter scores for each of the three tests, and compute the test averages. After performing each of these tasks, display the grade sheet to check that the operation has been executed successively. In the course of doing this testing, you should also enter invalid values for the menu option (in the Select From Menu submodule) and the test number (in the Enter Test Scores submodule).

Self-Test 7.5

The following problems refer to the Grade Management program of this section.

1. Suppose we want to create a subprogram, DisplayStudentRecord, as a submodule of the Retrieve Grade Sheet module. This subprogram should input a student name from the user and display that student's name, test scores, and average.

   a. What data must be imported to and exported from this subprogram?

   b. Write pseudocode for this subprogram.

2. Suppose we want to create a subprogram, ChangeTestScore, as a submodule of the Retrieve Grade Sheet module. This subprogram should input a student name, test number (1, 2, or 3), and test score from the user and change the appropriate test score to the one input and correct the test average for that student.

   a. What data must be imported to and exported from this subprogram?

   b. Write the header for this subprogram.

Chapter Review and Exercises

Key Terms

Subprogram

Import data

Export data

Data flow diagram

IPO chart

Header (of subprogram)

Argument

Parameter

Value parameter

Reference parameter

Scope of a variable

Global variable

Local variable

Function

Built-in function

User-defined function

Recursion

Chapter Summary

In this chapter, we have discussed the following topics.

1. Parameters and arguments:

   - Data transmitted from one program module to another are *exported* from the former and *imported* by the latter.

   - A *data flow diagram* shows the relationships among the program modules and indicates the data imported and exported by each module. An *IPO chart* lists the data input and processed by, and exported from, each program module.

   - To pass data from a module to a submodule, the Call statement (in the former) contains *arguments* and the subprogram header (in the latter) contains *parameters*.

   - The number and type of arguments in a Call statement must be the same as the number and type of parameters in the corresponding header. The data are passed from an argument to a parameter based solely on their position in the argument or parameter list.

2. Value and reference parameters:

   - A change in the value of a *value parameter* in its subprogram does *not* affect the value of the corresponding argument; a change in the value of a *reference parameter* in its subprogram *does* change the value of the corresponding argument.

- Value parameters are used to import data into a subprogram; reference parameters are used to export (or to import *and* export) data from a subprogram.
- To indicate that a variable in a subprogram's parameter list is of reference type, this text follows its name by the symbols "As Ref".

3. Scope of a variable:
   - The *scope* of a variable is the part of the program in which that variable can be referenced (used).
   - The scope of a *global variable* is the entire program; the scope of *local variable* is the subprogram in which it is declared.
   - If the same variable is declared both locally and globally, it is treated as if it were two different variables, and the local declaration takes precedence.

4. Functions:
   - A *function* is a subprogram whose name returns a value to the calling subprogram; the function name may appear anywhere in the program that a constant of that type is valid.
   - *Built-in functions* are supplied with the programming language software; in this chapter, we introduced the following built-in functions:

     Abs(X) returns the absolute value of a number X
     Round(X) rounds X to the nearest whole number
     Str(X) converts X from a number to its string equivalent
     Val(S, N) converts the string S into a number

   - *User-defined functions* are functions created by the programmer; they are subprograms whose name may be assigned a value, and are called in the same way as built-in functions.

5. Recursion:
   - A *recursive subprogram* is a subprogram that calls itself.
   - To create a recursive function, F(N), which computes an expression that depends on a positive integer N:
     a. Express F(N) in terms of F(N − 1).
     b. Determine the value of F(1).
     c. In the function definition, use an If-Then-Else statement that sets F equal to F(1) if N = 1 and which involves F(N − 1) if N > 1.

Review Exercises

1. Fill in the blank: If a data item is transmitted from a subprogram to the main program, it is said to be returned to or _____ to the main program.

2. Fill in the blank: If a data item is transmitted from the main program to a subprogram, it is said to be _____ by the subprogram.

3. Fill in the blank: A diagram that shows the data transmitted between program modules is called a(n) _____.

4. Fill in the blank: A chart that lists the data imported and processed by, and exported from, each program module is called a(n) _____.

Exercises 5–10 refer to the following program:

```
Main Program
    Set X = 1
    Call Display (2 * X, X, 5)
    End Program

Subprogram Display (Num1, Num2, Num3)
    Write Num1, " ", Num2, " ", Num3
    End Subprogram
```

5. What data are passed from the main program to the subprogram?

6. What data are imported by the subprogram Display?

7. Draw a data flow diagram for this program.

8. Give an IPO chart for the subprogram Display.

9. If code corresponding to this pseudocode is run, what is the output of this program?

10. Suppose that in the subprogram, all occurrences of Num1, Num2, and Num3 were replaced by X, Y, and Z, respectively. If code corresponding to the resulting pseudocode were run, what would be the output now?

11. True or false: Changes to a value parameter in a subprogram affect the corresponding argument in the calling module.

12. True or false: Changes to a reference parameter in a subprogram affect the corresponding argument in the calling module.

13. Fill in the blank: The part of the program in which a given variable *can* be referenced is called the _____ of that variable.

14. Fill in the blank: The scope of a _____ variable is the entire program.

15. Write a subprogram called InputData that inputs two numbers from the user and exports their values to the main program.

16. Write a subprogram called Flip that imports two variables from the main program (into parameters X and Y), interchanges their values, and exports the results to the main program.

Exercises 17–20 refer to the following program (assume, as we have been doing in this text, that variables declared in the main program are global):

```
Main Program
      Declare X, Y As Integer
      Set X = 1
      Set Y = 2
      Call Sub(X, Y)
      Write X
      Write Y
      End Program
Subprogram Sub(Num1, Num2 As Ref)
      Declare X As Integer
      Set Num1 = 3
      Set Num2 = 4
      Set X = 5
      Write X
      End Subprogram
```

17. What is the scope of the variable

    a. Y, declared in the main program?

    b. X, declared in the subprogram?

18. List the local and global variables in this program.

19. What is the output of this program if code corresponding to this pseudocode is run?

20. Suppose the subprogram header is changed to:

    Subprogram Sub(Num1, Num2)

    If code corresponding to the new pseudocode is run, what is the output now?

21. Fill in the blank: A _____ is a type of subprogram whose name may be assigned a value.

22. Fill in the blank: A _____ function is one that is supplied by the programming language; its code does not appear in the program that uses it.

In Exercises 23–26, give the value returned by the built-in function. (These functions were introduced in Section 7.3.)

23. a. Abs(0)   b. Abs(–1.5)

24. a. Round(3.8)   b. Round(Abs(–1.5))

25. a. Str(10.5)   b. Val("ten", N)

26. a. Str(Val("–1.5", N))   b. Val(Str(87.6))

27. Suppose a program contains the function

        Function F(X) As Real
           Set F = X + 1
        End Function

     What is displayed when the statement

        Write F(3)

     in the main program is executed?

28. Suppose a program contains the function

        Function G(X, Y) As Real
           Set G = X + Y
        End Function

     What is displayed when the statement

        Write G(4, 5)

     in the main program is executed?

29. Write a function

        Function Average(Num1, Num2) As Real

     that finds the mean, (Num1 + Num2)/2, of the numbers Num1 and Num2.

30. Write a main module (main program) that inputs two numbers from the user, calls the Average function of Exercise 29 to find the mean of these numbers, and displays the result.

31. Fill in the blank: When a subprogram calls itself, the process is called _____.

32. Fill in the blank: If N = 2 and Sum(N) is a function with Sum(1) = 5, then the statement

        Set Sum = Sum(N–1) + N

     assigns the value _____ to the function Sum.

Exercises 33–36 refer to the following program:

```
Main Program
    Input K
    Set Result = F(K)
    Write Result
    End Program
Function F(N) As Integer
    If N = 1 Then
        Set F = 1
    Else
        Set F = N * F(N–1)
    End If
    End Function
```

33. What is the output of this program if K = 1?

34. If K = 3, how many times is the function F called?

35. What is the output of this program if K = 3?

36. Write a non-recursive function (using a For loop) that has the same effect as F.

37. Write a recursive function Mult(M, N) that multiplies the positive integers M and N by using the fact that:

$$M \times N = M + M + ... + M \quad (N \text{ times})$$

38. Write a non-recursive function (using a For loop) that has the same effect as the recursive function Mult(M, N) of Exercise 37.

Programming Problems

For each of the following problems, use the top-down modular approach and pseudocode to design a suitable program to solve it. In your program, make use of subprograms with parameters and arguments.

A. Input a list of positive numbers (terminated by 0) into an array, find the largest number in the array, and output the result. [Use a subprogram to input the numbers, a function to find the largest number, and a subprogram to output the result.]

B. Input a list of positive numbers (terminated by 0) into an array, find the mean (average) of the numbers in the array, and output the result. [Use a subprogram to input the numbers, a function to find the mean, and a subprogram to output the result.]

C. Load a sequential file, DRIVERLIST, containing records of the form

LicenseNumber (string), DriverName (string),
Tickets (integer)

into parallel arrays. Then, search the arrays for a license number input by the user, and display the corresponding name and number of tickets. [Use subprograms to load the file into arrays, input the desired license number, search the arrays, and display the required information.]

D. Rewrite the program of Problem C so that

- The user can input more than one license number in a single run.

- For each license, the program displays (based on a menu selection) *either* the corresponding driver name *or* the number of tickets.

[Use a subprogram to load the file into arrays, input the desired license number, display the menu and input the user's selection, and process each menu option.]

E. Load a sentence of text from a file TEXT into an array of characters. Then, determine the number of words in the sentence and display the results. *Hint*: To determine the number of words, search the array for the blank spaces between the words. [Use a subprogram to load the text, a function to count the words, and another subprogram to display the result.]

F. The *factorial* of a positive integer N, denoted by N!, is defined by:

$N! = 1$ if $N = 1$
$N! = 1 \times 2 \times ... \times N$ if $N > 1$

Input a positive integer from the user (checking that it *is* a positive integer), use a recursive function to compute N!, and display the result. [Use subprograms for the input and display operations.]

Data Files in the Everyday World (Revisited)

Remember the filing cabinet from a few chapters ago? That cabinet, filled with records and properly organized, is an indispensable tool in the modern office. To be truly useful, though, we have to be able to perform operations on those records (such as locating, adding, or deleting customers) reasonably quickly.

The key to performing file operations in a minimum amount of time is to have the records in some kind of order. Rather than just tossing all the customers' papers together at random, we can index them alphabetically, or by account number, or even by zip code if that makes sense. The payoff for all this sorting time and effort is a quick retrieval process. For example, we know that the "Bs" are near the top, so look there to find a file for someone whose name begins with B. Need a "K"? Go to somewhere near the middle of the stack. And a "Z"? That's near the end—guaranteed! This approach sure beats having to start at the beginning and go through all records one by one.

Unfortunately, there is a fly in the ointment. As long as the stack of records is small, this process is manageable. If our office has thousands and thousands of customers, however, the number of records is huge, and it's not practical to sift through the entire stack to find or insert a single record.

What to do? Simply stop worrying about having all the records in alphabetical order. Each time a new customer comes in, place his or her record at the end of the stack and give it a number. Then, the first person's record is #1, the second's is #2 and so on—regardless of their names. Now group the records together in reasonably-sized bunches—perhaps records #1 to #100 go in the first file drawer, records #101 to #200 in the second, and so on. But, then how do we know where things are? Easy. Keep a separate list of just the customers' names and the corresponding record numbers (an *index*), and update that list each time a customer comes or goes. Even with a huge number of people, the index contains a lot less information than the records themselves, so it's of manageable size. Even better, we now only have to keep the index, not the records themselves, in alphabetical order. For example, consider the vehicle registration information stored in your state's motor vehicle department. It may have over a million entries, each of which gives license number, type of vehicle, owner's name and address, etc., but it's still manageable. To locate a particular record, all a clerk needs to know is the vehicle license number—that's the index—and then the entire vehicle record is easily located.

Isn't this a handy tool for managing the records in a very large business? File that away for future reference!

8

More on Data Files

OVERVIEW   In Sections 5.3 and 5.4, we introduced the topic of sequential data files and described how to create, read data from, and modify these files. In this chapter, we will provide additional information on manipulating sequential files and also introduce *direct access files*. To be more specific, you will learn

1. To use efficient methods for searching and sorting files [Section 8.1].

2. How to merge two sequential files into a single file [8.2].

3. To create, read data from, and modify direct access files [8.3, 8.4].

4. To use indexed files [8.4].

Note that Sections 8.1 and 8.2 are independent of each other and of the material in the rest of the chapter. On the other hand, Section 8.4 requires the material covered in Section 8.3. As always, the Focus on Problem Solving section (8.5), is optional.

8.1 *Additional Searching and Sorting Techniques*

Because data files are stored on disk, they are relatively slow to access. For this reason, we usually copy, or *load*, files into memory (RAM) before manipulating them. Thus, to sort or search the data in a file, we normally begin by reading its records into parallel arrays, and then sort or search these arrays. (We have discussed loading files into arrays in Section 6.3.)

In Section 6.2, we described simple methods for searching and sorting arrays. However, because sequential files often contain huge amounts of data and these methods are not very efficient, they are not usually suitable for searching or sorting files. In this section, we will introduce more efficient searching and sorting techniques.

Binary Search

The **binary search** method is a good way to search a large amount of data for a particular item, the *search key*. It is considerably more efficient than the serial search technique, which was discussed in Section 6.2. A binary search does require, however, that the *table keys*, the array of data to be searched, be in numerical or alphabetical order.

To illustrate how the binary search method works, let us suppose you want to look up a certain word (the *target* word) in a dictionary. If you used a serial search to find it, starting with the first page and going through the dictionary word by word, it might take hours. A more reasonable approach would be to

1. Open the dictionary to the target word's approximate location.

2. Check the target word against an entry on that page to determine if you have gone too far or not far enough.

3. Repeat steps 1 and 2 until you have located the target word.

The technique just described gives the basic idea of the binary search procedure. We first compare the search key (the target) to the table key midway through the given array. Because the array data are ordered, we can then determine in which *half* of the array the search key lies. We now compare the search key to the table key in the middle of this half, and in so doing are able to determine in which *quarter* of the array the search key is located. We then look at the middle entry in this quarter, and so on, continuing this process until we find the search key.

<table>
<tr><td>The binary
search
pseudocode</td><td>Letting Key represent the item sought and Array the given array of N table keys, the following pseudocode performs a binary search (assuming that Array is sorted in ascending order). Recall that</td></tr>
</table>

- The function Int(X) produces the integer obtained by discarding the fractional part of X, if any.

- A program *flag* is a variable that indicates whether or not a specified action has taken place; typically, a flag value of 1 indicates that the action has occurred, a value of 0 indicates that it has not occurred.

In the pseudocode that follows, the variables Low and High represent, respectively, the smallest and largest array indexes in the part of the array currently under consideration. Initially, we are searching the entire array, so Low = 1 and High = N. However, after the first attempt at locating Key, we are either searching the first half or the last half of the array, so either Low = 1 and High = Int(N/2) or Low = Int(N/2) and High = N. The variable Index represents the middle element of the part of the array under consideration. Thus, Index is initially Int(N/2) and, in general, it is the average of Low and High: Index = Int((Low + High)/2).

```
Set Low = 1
Set High = N
Set Index = Int(N/2)
Set a flag (Found) = 0
While (Found = 0) And (Low <= High)
    If Key = Array[Index] Then
        Set Found = 1
    End If
    If Key > Array[Index] Then
        Set Low = Index + 1
        Set Index = Int((High + Low)/2)
    End If
    If Key < Array[Index] Then
        Set High = Index - 1
        Set Index = Int((High + Low)/2)
    End If
End While
```

After initializing the values of Low, High, Index, and Found, we enter the While loop. This loop will be reentered if

- The search key has still not been located, in which case Found = 0.

and

- There are still array elements to check, in which case Low <= High.

Within the loop, we deal with the three possible cases:

- If Key = Array[Index], we've located the search key, and Found is set equal to 1.

- If Key > Array[Index], then we've got to check the upper half of the remaining array elements, and Low is adjusted accordingly.

- If Key < Array[Index], then we've got to check the lower half of the remaining array elements, and High is adjusted accordingly.

In the first case, the loop is exited. In the last two cases, Index is reset to the middle of the remaining part of the array and the loop is reentered unless we've exhausted the array elements to be searched.

The following example illustrates how this procedure works.

EXAMPLE 1   In Table 8.1, a binary search is made for the word *House* in the given list. Here, N = 10, so on the first pass through the While loop, Index is 5. Now, "House" < Array[5], so High is set equal to 4 (Index − 1) and Index becomes $Int((1 + 4)/2) = 2$. The second pass is now made and this time "House" is greater than Array[Index], so we take Low = Index + 1 = 3, and replace Index by $Int((3 + 4)/2) = 3$. On the third pass, "House" is found.

TABLE 8.1

A Binary
Search for
the Word
House

Subscript	Word	First Pass	Second Pass	Third Pass
1	Book	Low	Low	
2	Dog		Index	
3	House			Low, Index
4	Job		High	High
5	Month	Index		
6	Start			
7	Top			
8	Total			
9	Work			
10	Zebra	High		

The next example shows how to search the records of a typical sequential file for data in a particular field.

EXAMPLE 2   Suppose that a business stores its customer data in a file called CUS-TOMER, which contains records of the form

> name (string), address (string), phone (string)

The first field contains the customer names in the form Last, First and the records are sorted in alphabetical order by last name. The following pseudocode opens this file, loads it into parallel arrays, and locates the telephone number of the customer named "Jones, Richard".

```
Declare Names[100], Addresses[100], Phones[100]
Open "CUSTOMER" For Input As DataFile
Set Count = 0
While Not(EOF(DataFile))
    Set Count = Count + 1
    Read DataFile, Names[Count], Addresses[Count],
        Phones[Count]
End While
Set Key = "Jones, Richard"
Set Low = 1
Set High = Count
Set Index = Int(Count/2)
Set Found = 0
While (Found = 0) And (Low <= High)
    If Key = Names[Index] Then
        Set Found = 1
        Set PhoneNumber = Phones[Index]
    End If
    If Key > Names[Index] Then
        Set Low = Index + 1
        Set Index = Int((High + Low)/2)
    End If
    If Key < Names[Index] Then
        Set High = Index - 1
        Set Index = Int((High + Low)/2)
    End If
End While
If Found = 0 Then
    Write Key, " not found."
Else
    Write "Phone number is ", PhoneNumber
End If
```

The first few statements in this pseudocode (through the While loop) declare the required (parallel) arrays, open the CUSTOMER file, and load this file into the arrays. The remainder of this pseudocode performs a binary search (as described earlier in this section) of the Names array for the name "Jones, Richard", which has been assigned to the variable Key. If and when the search key is found in the Names array, the corresponding element of the Phones array is assigned to PhoneNumber. Finally, when the search is complete:

- If the search key was found, the phone number is displayed.

- If the search key was not found, a message to this effect is displayed.

Selection Sort

The **selection sort** procedure is a more efficient way of sorting data stored in an array than the bubble sort technique presented in Section 6.2. The basic idea behind the selection sort is fairly simple. For example, here's how we would use it to sort an array in *ascending order*— from smallest to largest. We make several *passes* through the array:

- On the first pass, we locate the smallest array element and swap it with the first array element.

- On the second pass, we locate the smallest element after the first one and swap it with the second element of the array.

- On the third pass through the array, we locate the smallest element after the second one and swap it with the third element of the array.

And so on. If the array contains N elements, it will be completely sorted after at most N – 1 passes.

To illustrate the selection sort, we will first do a simple example by hand. Figure 1 demonstrates the process for a data set consisting of the numbers 9, 13, 5, 8, 6. It displays the given data in the first (leftmost) column and the results of the four passes through the data in the next four columns, using arrows to indicate which data values have been swapped.

FIGURE 1

Selection
Sort of the
Numbers: 9,
13, 5, 8, 6

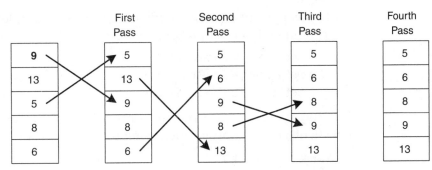

(On the fourth pass, no interchanges take place;
the numbers are sorted.)

To construct pseudocode that sorts an array, Array, containing N elements in ascending order, we use a loop whose iterations correspond to the *passes* described above:

```
For K = 1 Step 1 To N – 1
    Find the smallest, Min, of:
        Array[K], Array[K+1], ..., Array[N]
    If Min <> Array[K] Then
        Swap array elements Min and Array[K]
    End If
End For
```

Of course, each of the two statements in the For loop requires further explanation.

1. To find the smallest element, Min, in a set of numbers, we set Min equal to the first number and then compare Min, successively, to the remaining numbers. Whenever we find a number smaller than Min, we set that number equal to Min and record the current subscript, Index. Thus, this step in the pseudocode above becomes:

```
Set Min = Array[K]
Set Index = K
For J = K + 1 Step 1 To N
    If Array[J] < Min Then
        Set Min = Array[J]
        Set Index = J
    End If
End For
```

2. To swap array elements with subscripts K and Index, we use the technique described in Section 6.2:

> Set Temp = Array[K]
> Set Array[K] = Array[Index]
> Set Array[Index] = Temp

Thus, the refined pseudocode for sorting the array Array, consisting of N elements, in ascending order using the selection sort procedure is:

The pseudocode for selection sort

```
For K = 1 Step 1 To N – 1
    Set Min = Array[K]
    Set Index = K
    For J = K + 1 Step 1 To N
        If Array[J] < Min Then
            Set Min = Array[J]
            Set Index = J
        End If
    End For (J)
    If K <> Index Then
        Set Temp = Array[K]
        Set Array[K] = Array[Index]
        Set Array[Index] = Temp
    End If
End For (K)
```

The next example illustrates how the selection sort can be used to sort the records in a sequential file based upon the ordering of a specified field of that file.

EXAMPLE 3   Suppose that a business stores its employee telephone directory in a file called TELEPHONE, which contains records of the form

> name (string), phone number (string)

In the first field, the names are stored in the form Last, First. The following pseudocode opens this file, loads it into parallel arrays, and sorts the arrays in alphabetical order of employee last name.

```
Declare Names[100], Phones[100]
Open "TELEPHONE" For Input As DataFile
Set Count = 0
While Not(EOF(DataFile))
    Set Count = Count + 1
    Read DataFile, Names[Count], Phones[Count]
End While
```

```
For K = 1 Step 1 To Count – 1
    Set Min = Names[K]
    Set Index = K
    For J = K + 1 Step 1 To Count
        If Names[J] < Min Then
            Set Min = Names[J]
            Set Index = J
        End If
    End For (J)
    If K <> Index Then
        Set Temp = Names[K]
        Set Names[K] = Names[Index]
        Set Names[Index] = Temp
        Set Temp = Phones[K]
        Set Phones[K] = Phones[Index]
        Set Phones[Index] = Temp
    End If
End For (K)
```

The first seven statements of this pseudocode open the TELEPHONE file and load its records into two parallel arrays, Names and Phones. The remainder of the pseudocode performs a selection sort on the array Names, as outlined earlier in this section. Here, however, each time the smallest element is found, we must swap corresponding elements in *two* arrays, Names and Phones.

Other Types of Selection Sort   The selection sort procedure, illustrated in Example 3, can be used without modification to sort numeric or character data in ascending order. The changes needed to sort data in *descending* order are left as an exercise (see Self-Test 8.1).

Self-Test 8.1

1. Choose one answer. The binary search

    a   Requires that the list of table keys be ordered.

    b. Cannot be used if the list of table keys is ordered.

    c. Cannot be used with files that have more than one field.

    d. Cannot be used to locate a numeric search key.

2. Rewrite the binary search pseudocode given in this section to perform a search for an element Key in an array Array with N elements that has been sorted in *descending* order.

3. Choose one answer. The selection sort method

   a Requires that the given array already be ordered.

   b. Requires that the programming language contain a Swap statement.

   c. Cannot be used with files that have more than one field.

   d. Can be used to sort arrays of numbers in descending order.

4. What modifications must be made to the selection sort pseudocode to sort an array in descending order?

8.2 *Merging Sequential Files*

Section 5.3 introduces the topic of sequential files, and Section 5.4 describes how to how to *maintain* such a file—how to delete, insert, and change its records. In this section, we will discuss another operation on sequential files: **merging** (combining) the data from two files with the same types of records into a single file in a way that retains the desired ordering of the records.

We can think of the merging process as a form of file maintenance in which a series of insertions is to be made into one of the files, called the *master file*, with the new records input from the other file, the *update* file. We will therefore call the two files to be merged MASTER and UPDATE. To simplify the description of the process, we will initially assume that each file contains records consisting of a single field with the data sorted in ascending order.

We begin the merge process by loading the files into arrays (see Section 6.3). Since, at least for now, there is only one field per record, we need only one array for each file. We will call these arrays MasterArray and UpdateArray. (Due to our earlier assumption, each array consists of data sorted in ascending order.) So, to merge the given files, we need only create a new array, NewArray, whose entries are obtained from both MasterArray and UpdateArray, listed in ascending order. Once NewArray is created, it is copied to the file MASTER to complete the process.

In summary, to merge the files MASTER and UPDATE into the file MASTER:

A rough
outline of the
merge
process

1. Open both files for input.

2. Load the files into arrays MasterArray and UpdateArray.

3. Arrange all entries from both MasterArray and UpdateArray in order and call the resulting array, NewArray.

4. Copy NewArray to the file MASTER.

5. Close the files.

Of course, step 3 of this rough outline is the heart of the merge process, and needs a great deal of additional refinement.

To understand the basic idea behind merging the arrays MasterArray and UpdateArray (step 3 in the description above), let us see how the process begins. We first consider the first (smallest) elements of each array, and:

- If MasterArray[1] <= UpdateArray[1], assign MasterArray[1] to NewArray[1] and then compare MasterArray[2] and UpdateArray[1].

- If MasterArray[1] > UpdateArray[1], assign UpdateArray[1] to NewArray[1] and then compare MasterArray[1] and UpdateArray[2].

Pseudocode
for the
merge
process

To create the entire array NewArray, we continue this process, using a loop to move through the two given arrays, making comparisons, and assigning the proper elements to NewArray. Assuming that MasterArray has M elements and UpdateArray has N elements, the pseudocode for the array merge looks like this (here, I, J, and K are, respectively, the subscripts of MasterArray, UpdateArray, and NewArray):

```
Set I = 1
Set J = 1
Set K = 1
While (I <= M) And (J <= N)
    If MasterArray[I] <= UpdateArray[J] Then
        Set NewArray[K] = MasterArray[I]
        Set I = I + 1
    Else
        Set NewArray[K] = UpdateArray[J]
        Set J = J + 1
    End If
    Set K = K + 1
End While
```

The While loop is exited when we run out of elements in either MasterArray or UpdateArray. At this point, all of the elements in the other array have to be assigned to NewArray. For example, suppose that when we exit the loop, all MasterArray elements have been assigned to NewArray. Then, at this point, I = M + 1 and J < N. On the other hand, if the loop was exited because all UpdateArray elements had been assigned, I < M and J = N + 1. So, to complete the pseudocode for the array merge, add the following statements to the bottom of the pseudocode just given:

```
For Count = I Step 1 To M
    Set NewArray[K] = MasterArray[Count]
    Set K = K + 1
End For
For Count = J Step 1 To N
    Set NewArray[K] = UpdateArray[Count]
    Set K = K + 1
End For
```

Notice that only one of these For loops is executed while the other is skipped (depending on whether the While loop was exited because I = M + 1 or J = N + 1).

The following example puts together the pieces of the file merge process described above and shows how it works when the file records contain more than one field.

EXAMPLE 4   A company wants to merge two payroll files (PAYROLL1 and PAYROLL2) into a single file. Suppose that each record in these files has the form

employee number, employee name, rate of pay

and that the records are ordered by (ascending) employee number. We will read the records in each file into three parallel arrays, merge these two sets of three arrays into a set of three new parallel arrays, and then output the latter to a new file called PAYROLL. The following program performs the merge.

```
Open "PAYROLL1" For Input As File1
Open "PAYROLL2" For Input As File2
Open "PAYROLL" For Output As File3
Declare Nums1[100], Names1[100], Rates1[100]
Declare Nums2[100], Names2[100], Rates2[100]
Declare Nums[200], Names[200], Rates[200]
```

```
Set Count = 0
While Not EOF(File1)
    Set Count = Count + 1
    Read File1, Nums1[Count], Names1[Count], Rates1[Count]
End While
Set M = Count
Set Count = 0
While Not EOF(File2)
    Set Count = Count + 1
    Read File2, Nums2[Count], Names2[Count], Rates2[Count]
End While
Set N = Count
Set I = 1
Set J = 1
Set K = 1
While (I <= M) And (J <= N)
    If Nums1[I] <= Nums2[J] Then
        Set Nums[K] = Nums1[I]
        Set Names[K] = Names1[I]
        Set Rates[K] = Rates1[I]
        Set I = I + 1
    Else
        Set Nums[K] = Nums2[J]
        Set Names[K] = Names2[J]
        Set Rates[K] = Rates2[J]
        Set J = J + 1
    End If
    Set K = K + 1
End While
For Count = I Step 1 To M
    Set Nums[K] = Nums1[Count]
    Set Names[K] = Names1[Count]
    Set Rates[K] = Rates1[Count]
    Set K = K + 1
End For
For Count = J Step 1 To N
    Set Nums[K] = Nums2[Count]
    Set Names[K] = Names2[Count]
    Set Rates[K] = Rates2[Count]
    Set K = K + 1
End For
```

```
For Count = 1 Step 1 To K – 1
    Write File3, Nums[Count], Names[Count], Rates[Count]
End For
Close File1, File2, File3
```

This program follows the outline that precedes this example. The first part of the pseudocode opens the payroll files, declares the needed (parallel) arrays, and loads each of the two existing payroll files into three arrays. In the process, the number of elements in each set of parallel arrays is assigned to the variables M and N. The remainder of the pseudocode performs the merge of corresponding arrays (as described earlier in this section), creating a new set of parallel merged arrays, and then copies these arrays to the PAYROLL file.

Self-Test 8.2

1. True or false: To merge two existing sequential files, we must open *three* files—the existing ones for input and a new file for output.

2. True or false: To merge two sequential files, the records of both files must be arranged in the same order.

3. True or false: If we merge two sequential files, one with M records and the other with N different records, then the resulting file will contain M + N records.

4. What changes must be made to the pseudocode that precedes Example 4 to merge MasterArray and UpdateArray into NewArray, if the two given arrays are sorted in descending order?

8.3 *An Introduction to Direct Access Files*

In this section and the next, we will describe how to use direct access files. A **direct access** (or **random access**) **file** is one in which each data item can be read or written independently of the rest. For example, to read the 500th record in a direct access file, you do just that; you need not read the first 499 records to get to it, as you would with a sequential file. Thus, using a sequential file is analogous to listening to music on a cassette player—the tracks must be accessed in the order they appear on the tape; direct file access, on the other hand, is analogous to listening to a compact disc—here, you can quickly jump from track to track.

Setting Up a Direct Access File

A sequential file is a *text file* (see Section 5.3); it can be created, if you want, by simply typing its contents within a text editor and saving the result to disk. As you will soon see, creating a direct access file is a more complicated process.

In a sequential file, records are separated from one another by "carriage return" symbols and the fields within each record are separated by commas. A direct access file can also be divided into records and fields, but we use a different device for determining where one record or field ends and the next begins. In a direct access file, the corresponding fields in all records must have the same length. As a result, which record and field are currently being accessed can be determined by counting the number of *bytes* (characters) from the beginning of the file.

Direct access file structure
To illustrate the structure of a direct access file, suppose that it is set up (as described below) so that each record has the form:

student identification code, student name

Further suppose that each student ID code is 4 bytes long, and we want to allow 12 characters for each student name. Then, a certain file containing three records can be pictured as a sequence (or *stream*) of 48 bytes—16 for each record—like this:

```
A136Smith•John••C731Johnson•ElizG398Wong•Richard
```

In this representation, we have used the symbol • to represent a blank. In creating this file, a blank space is intentionally placed between the last and first names to separate them, and

- If the name does not fill the 12-character space allotted to it (as in the case of John Smith), then the programming language software automatically places *trailing blanks* after the name to fill up this space.

- If the name is too long to fit in the allotted 12-character space, it is automatically *truncated* to the 12-character limit (as in the case of Elizabeth Johnson).

Now, to read, say, the *name* field of the third record, a statement is executed that instructs the programming language software to move to the file's 37th byte. (The first 32 bytes hold the first two records, so the first field of the third record starts at the 33rd byte, and its second field starts four bytes after that.)

The Record Type statement

As usual, different programming languages use different statements for setting up the structure of a direct access file. In this text, to set up the file structure described in the preceding discussion, we will use the statement:

```
Record Type StudentInfo
    Code As String[4]
    Name As String[12]
End Record
```

This statement specifies that each record of type StudentInfo has two fields:

- The first field is called Code and is to contain a string of 4 characters.

- The second field is called Name and is to contain a string of 12 characters.

To access a file with records of the type StudentInfo, we will need a variable declared to be of this type; for example:

```
Declare Student As StudentInfo
```

Since StudentInfo is defined to have two string fields, Student can be assigned two string values, one for the Code field and one for the Name field. We will describe how this is done later in this section.

The Open statement for a direct access file

So far, we have defined a structure for our records and declared a variable of this type. We now must set up a file to hold the records. This is done using an Open statement that is similar to the one for sequential files (see Section 5.3). The Open statement assigns the file an external name (for the disk directory) and associates with it a mode and internal name (for use in the program). For the direct access file we are creating, we use the following Open statement:

```
Open "STUDATA" For Random As DataFile, Len = 16
```

As you can see, this statement resembles its sequential file counterpart (with *mode* given by Random), but unlike the latter:

- It does not specify an Input or Output mode; once opened, a direct access file can be written to, read from, or both.

- It specifies the length of each record (at the end of the statement). In place of Len = 16 in this Open statement, we could have used Len = Length(Student), where Length is the function (see Section 5.2) that gives the length of the string Student.

In summary, to set up our direct access file, we use the following statements:

```
Record Type StudentInfo
    Code As String[4]
    Name As String[12]
End Record
Declare Student As StudentInfo
Open "STUDATA" For Random As DataFile, Len =
Length(Student)
```

The record type StudentInfo defined above contains only string fields. To create a record structure with a numeric field, we will follow that field's name by the words **As Integer** or **As Real**. For example, suppose that the student code in StudentInfo is an integer. Then, the following statement would create the appropriate record layout:

```
Record Type StudentInfo
    Code As Integer
    Name As String[12]
End Record
```

For the sake of computing the record length, we will assume that:

- Numbers of type Integer require 2 bytes of memory.

- Numbers of type Real require 4 bytes of memory.

Thus, each record in this layout requires 14 bytes of memory—two for the integer field and 12 for the string field.

Transmitting Data to and from a Direct Access File

Once we have set up a direct access file for processing as described above, we can either write data to or read data from this file. In both cases, we make use of the variables defined in the Record Type and Declare statements to access the individual fields of a particular record. In this text, we will use, for this purpose, the variable obtained by inserting a period between the record and field names. For example, to refer to the first (Code) field of the Student record defined by the statements

```
Record Type StudentInfo
    Code As String[4]
    Name As String[12]
End Record
Declare Student As StudentInfo
```

we use the variable Student.Code. To refer to the second (Name) field of the record Student, we use the variable Student.Name. In general, to refer to a field with name FieldName in a record called RecordName, use the variable

> RecordName.FieldName

We call variables of this kind *field variables*.

A field variable may be used anywhere in a program that a variable of its type is allowed. In particular, a field variable can be assigned a value by an input, assignment, or file read statement and its value can be displayed by an output statement. Thus, both of the following statements are valid (assuming that they are preceded by the appropriate Record Type and Declare statements):

> Input Student.Name
> Write Student.Name

Writing data to a direct access file; the SeekPut statement

Writing data to a direct access file is a two-step process. We must

1. Assign the given data to field variables (using Input, Set, or Read).

2. Transmit the values of these variables to the file. To accomplish this, we will use a statement, called SeekPut (for "locate and place"), of the form:

> SeekPut *filename, record number, record variable*

Here, *filename* is the direct access file's internal name, *record number* is number of the record we are writing, and *record variable* is the name specified in the Declare statement.

For example, suppose that a direct access file has been set up using the statements:

> Record Type StudentInfo
>   Code As String[4]
>   Name As String[12]
> End Record
> Declare Student As StudentInfo
> Open "STUDATA" For Random As DataFile, Len =
>   Length(Student)

Then, the following statements input an ID code and name and write this data as the first record of the file STUDATA:

> Write "Enter a student's ID code: "
> Input Student.Code

Write "Enter the student's name (last name first): "
Input Student.Name
SeekPut DataFile, 1, Student

The two Input statements assign the user input to the field variables Student.Code and Student.Name. Then, the SeekPut statement writes this data to the first record of DataFile. For example, if the code and name input were the strings "A123" and "Doe John", respectively, then the first 16 bytes (4 for Code plus 12 for Name) of the file can be pictured as:

```
A123Doe•John••••
```

On the other hand, had the SeekPut statement in this pseudocode been

SeekPut DataFile, 2, Student

then the same data would have been written as the second record of the file STUDATA. Since each record occupies 16 bytes, this information would be positioned in bytes 17 to 32 of the file.

Reading data from a direct access file; the SeekGet statement

Reading data from a direct access file is a simpler process. All we need do is transmit the data from the file to the corresponding field variables. To do so, we will use a SeekGet ("locate and get") statement, which has a form similar to that of SeekPut:

SeekGet *filename, record number, record variable*

For example, assuming that the file STUDATA has been set up as described earlier, we read its fifth record using the statement

SeekGet DataFile, 5, Student

After this statement is executed, the field variable Student.Code contains the string made up of the first four bytes of the fifth record of STUDATA and Student.Name contains the string consisting of the remaining 12 bytes of this record. These variables can now be used as desired within the program.

The next example illustrates the process of setting up, writing data to, and reading data from a direct access file.

EXAMPLE 5   The following program creates and displays a direct access file with records of the form:

student ID (4-character string)
student name (12-character string)
units earned (integer)
grade point average (real)

```
Record Type StudentInfo
     Code As String[4]
     Name As String[12]
     Units As Integer
     GPA As Real
End Record
Declare Student As StudentInfo
Open "STUDATA" For Random As DataFile,
     Len = Length(Student)
Write "When prompted, enter"
Write "student ID, name, units earned, GPA"
Write "Enter  0,0,0,0  to quit."
Write "Enter data:"
Input Student.Code, Student.Name, Student.Units, Student.GPA
Set Count = 0
While Student.Code <> "0   "
     Set Count = Count + 1
     SeekPut DataFile, Count, Student
     Write  "Enter data:"
     Input Student.Code, Student.Name, Student.Units,
          Student.GPA
End While
For K = 1 Step 1 To Count
     SeekGet DataFile, K, Student
     Write Student.Code, Student.Name, Student.Units,
          Student.GPA
End For
Close DataFile
```

After the first few statements have described the record layout, declared
the record variable, and opened our direct access file, the While loop
inputs data from the user and writes it to the file. The counter Count
serves two purposes here: It counts the number of records so that a For
loop can be used to display them and it acts as a record index in the
SeekPut statement. Notice that a direct access file, unlike a sequential
one, need not be closed and reopened between the write and read operations. (It should, however, be closed at the end of the program using
a Close statement.) The For loop, toward the end of the program, displays the file records one line at a time.

Self-Test 8.3

1. What is one advantage and one disadvantage of using a direct access file instead of a sequential file?

2. Fields within a direct access file record are separated by (choose one):
   a. Commas
   b. Carriage returns
   c. Either *a* or *b*
   d. Neither *a* nor *b*

3. Give Record Type, Declare, and Open statements that could be used to set up a direct access file named INVLIST with records of the form:

   part number, part name, unit price, quantity

4. Give the statements needed to write the values

   123, "Handle", 5.69, 21

   to the third record in the file INVLIST of Exercise 3.

5. Write statements to display the fifth record of the file INVLIST of Exercise 3.

8.4 Using Direct Access Files; Indexed Files

A major advantage of direct access files over their sequential counterparts is the ease with which they can be modified. As you shall see, inserting, deleting, or changing a record in a direct access file (that is, *maintaining* the file) is a relatively quick and painless process. In this section, we will discuss these file maintenance procedures and also introduce *indexed files*, which simplify the retrieval of data stored in a direct access file.

Direct Access File Maintenance

We begin by introducing a function, LOF (length-of-file), that is useful in the file maintenance process. (This function is usually supported by programming languages that allow direct access files, but its name may differ from the one used here.) Our LOF function returns the number of bytes (characters) in the file; it has the form

LOF (*filename*)

where *filename* is the internal name of the file under consideration, as specified in the Open statement for that file.

The LOF function is usually used to determine the number of records in a file. This is done by dividing the total number of bytes in the file by its record length, as illustrated in the next example.

EXAMPLE 6   Suppose a direct access file named FULLNAME already exists on disk. The following statements display the number of records it contains.

```
Record Type NameInfo
    FirstName As String[12]
    LastName As String[20]
End Record
Declare Name As NameInfo
Open "FULLNAME" For Random As DataFile,
    Len = Length(Name)
Write "Number of records: ", LOF(DataFile) / Length(Name)
```

The statement

```
Write "Number of records: ", LOF(DataFile) / Length(Name)
```

displays the number of records—the number of bytes (LOF(DataFile)) divided by the record length.

Adding, Deleting, and Changing Records   Performing maintenance operations on a direct access file is relatively easy. We will describe how to add, delete, and change records with the help of examples that use a direct access file "STUDATA" set up by the following statements (see Example 5):

```
Record Type StudentInfo
    Code As String[4]
    Name As String[12]
    Units As Integer
    GPA As Real
End Record
Declare Student As StudentInfo
Open "STUDATA" For Random As DataFile,
    Len = Length(Student)
```

Adding a record   To *add* a record to a direct access file, we simply write it to the file, assigning it the next available record number. The next example illustrates this operation.

EXAMPLE 7   This program segment inputs data and appends it to the STUDATA file created in Example 5.

> Write "Enter data for new student in the form:"
> Write "ID Code, Name, Units Earned, GPA"
> Input Student.Code, Student.Name, Student.Units, Student.GPA
> Set Last = LOF(DataFile) / Length(Student)
> SeekPut DataFile, Last + 1, Student

After the data have been input and assigned to the field variables, the LOF function is used to determine the number of records in STUDATA. Then, the SeekPut statement writes the new record to the file and assigns it the next record number.

Deleting a record   To *delete* a record from a direct access file, we *overwrite* its contents with null strings and/or zeros. In other words, we delete the contents of the record, not the record itself. The next example shows how this is done.

EXAMPLE 8   This program segment "deletes" the record specified by the user from the file STUDATA created in Example 5.

> Write "Record number of record to be deleted:"
> Input Number
> Set Student.Code = ""
> Set Student.Name = ""
> Set Student.Units = 0
> Set Student.GPA = 0
> SeekPut DataFile, Number, Student

Don't Display Null Fields in a Direct Access File   When displaying the contents of a direct access file, check to see if a record contains null fields. If so, it was at some point "deleted" and should not be printed. For example, in the For loop of Example 5, the statement

Write Student.Code, Student.Name, Student.Units, Student.GPA
would read
> If Student.Code <> "" Then
> > Write Student.Code, Student.Name, Student.Units,
> > > Student.GPA
> End If

Modifying a record   To *modify* a record in a direct access file, we simply write it to the file with its fields changed as desired. The next example illustrates this operation.

EXAMPLE 9   This program segment changes the data in the units earned and GPA
             fields of the STUDATA file created in Example 5.

```
Write "Record number of record to be modified:"
Input Number
SeekGet DataFile, Number, Student
Write "Student name: ", Student.Name
Write "Enter total units earned, new GPA"
Write "or enter  0,0  to leave the record unchanged."
Input Student.Units, Student.GPA
If Student.Units <> 0 Then
     SeekPut DataFile, Number, Student
End If
```

After the record number is entered by the user, we read the corresponding record and display the student's name. This allows the user to check
that the correct record number was input. If not, the process is aborted
by entering 0,0. If the name *is* correct, new values of Units and GPA are
input and written to the file (by the SeekPut statement), overwriting
the previous values.

Indexed Files

One of the problems inherent in using direct access files is evident in
Examples 8 and 9. In order to access data in such a file, we must know
the relevant record number, which may not be readily available. It would
be more natural to locate a record by entering a *key item*, such as an ID
number or name. An **indexed file** allows the user to do just that.

To illustrate the concept of an indexed file, think of this book as a direct
access file in which the chapters are the records. To locate the topic of
arrays (for example), you don't have to know its chapter number. You
simply look in the table of contents, find *arrays*, get the corresponding
chapter number (6), and turn to that chapter. In this context, the chapter titles are the key items; the table of contents, which associates a key
item with a record number, is an **index file**; and the book together with
its table of contents forms an *indexed* file.

Simulating   In some programming languages (for example, COBOL), indexed files
an indexed   are built into the language. In most languages, however, we must *simu-*
file   *late* them using the existing structure. To simulate an indexed file, we
             use a combination of two files: a direct access file to store the data and
             a sequential file (the index file) to hold the list of key items. The *position*

of a key item in the sequential file gives its record number in the direct access file. The next example demonstrates how to create a (simulated) indexed file.

EXAMPLE
10

This program segment creates an index file, STUINDEX, for the existing direct access file STUDATA of Example 5.

```
Open "STUINDEX" For Output As IndexFile
Record Type StudentInfo
      Code As String[4]
      Name As String[12]
      Units As Integer
      GPA As Real
End Record
Declare Student As StudentInfo
Open "STUDATA" For Random As DataFile,
      Len = Length(Student)
Set Limit = LOF(DataFile) / Length(Student)
For K = 1 Step 1 To Limit
      SeekGet DataFile, K, Student
      Write IndexFile, Student.Code
End For
Close IndexFile, DataFile
```

The For loop reads the records one at a time from the direct access file and writes the key item (Student.Code) in each record to the sequential file. Thus the position of the key item in the latter is the same as the record number of the former. For example, suppose the file STUDATA contains the following data (for the sake of clarity, we have separated the fields by spaces):

Record 1　　A234 Johnson Samu 72 3.56
Record 2　　B567 Williams Ger 33 2.11
Record 3　　C368 Harding Jack 61 1.36

Then STUDATA will look like this (using the notation of Section 5.3):

```
"A234"<CR>"B567"<CR>"C368"<CR><EOF>
```

Suppose we want to make use of the indexed file created in Example 10 to display or modify a particular student's record. With our indexed file, the user need not know the corresponding record number to access this record; the user just enters the student's ID code and the program does the rest. More specifically, the process proceeds as follows:

1. Open STUINDEX (for Input) and STUDATA (for Random).

2. Input the student's ID code.

3. Read records of STUINDEX until the input code is found. The number of the resulting record in STUINDEX is the required record number for STUDATA.

4. Read this record from STUDATA.

5. Display it or modify its fields, as desired.

6. Close both files.

If a relatively large number of records are to be displayed and/or modified, it pays to first load the STUINDEX file into an array. In this case, the array is searched, and the subscript at which the student code is found becomes the required record number for STUDATA.

The next example supplies detailed pseudocode that carries out this process.

EXAMPLE 11

This program allows the user to display a specified record in the file STUDATA created in Example 5. It assumes that an index file, STUINDEX, has already been created, as in Example 10. The pseudocode given here follows the general outline described above.

```
Open "STUINDEX" For Input As IndexFile
Record Type StudentInfo
      Code As String[4]
      Name As String[12]
      Units As Integer
      GPA As Real
End Record
Declare Student As StudentInfo
Open "STUDATA" For Random As DataFile,
      Len = Length(Student)
Set Limit = LOF(DataFile) / Length(Student)
Write "Enter a student's ID code:"
Input IDCode
Set Found = 0
Set Counter = 0
While (Not(EOF(IndexFile)) And (Found = 0)
      Read IndexFile, Code
      Set Counter = Counter + 1
```

```
                    If Code = IDCode Then
                        Set Found = 1
                    End If
                End While
                If Found = 1 Then
                    SeekGet DataFile, Counter, Student
                    Write "ID Code: ", Student.Code
                    Write "Name: ", Student.Name
                    Write "Units: ", Student.Units
                    Write "GPA: ", Student.GPA
                Else
                    Write "Student code ", IDCode, " not found."
                End If
                Close DataFile, IndexFile
```

The first part of this program opens the STUINDEX and STUDATA files that make up our indexed file and specifies the structure of STUDATA. Then, the user enters the ID code for the record to be displayed, and the While loop searches the index file for this code. If the code is found, the corresponding record information is output; if not, an appropriate "error message" is displayed.

We will further illustrate the use of indexed files in Section 8.5.

Self-Test 8.4

1. Why are indexed files an improvement over direct access files?

    In Exercises 2–6, assume that a direct access file EMPLOYEE exists with records and fields defined by the statements:

    ```
    Record Type EmployeeInfo
        ID As String[5]
        Name As String[18]
        Pay As Real
    End Record
    Declare Worker As EmployeeInfo
    Open "EMPLOYEE" For Random As DataFile,
        Len = Length(Worker)
    ```

    Write statements that perform the indicated operation.

2. Display the number of records in EMPLOYEE.

3. Add a record (whose contents have already been input) to the file.

4. Delete the 25th record from the file.

5. Change the pay in record 18 to 13.90.

6. Create a sequential index file whose records consist of the ID fields of EMPLOYEE.

8.5 *Focus on Problem Solving*

In this section we will write a program that illustrates some of the material you have learned in this chapter. The program developed here displays and maintains a simulated indexed file.

A Parking Ticket Tracking Database

The State of Euphoria requires that its drivers pay all outstanding parking tickets before they can renew their vehicle registration. After unsuccessfully trying the honor system, the state has decided to use a computer program to keep track of unpaid tickets. When a motorist applies for a registration renewal, the clerk will enter the license plate "number" (a string of up to six characters), and if there are any unpaid tickets, the program should display the name of the vehicle's owner, the number of tickets outstanding, and the total amount owed. The program should also allow for the maintenance of the parking ticket *database* (the collection of all related information): a user should be able to add vehicle data to the list, delete vehicle data from the list, and make changes to the data on the list.

Problem Analysis   In the scenario described above, there are lots of data to be stored, but only small amounts will be accessed at any given time. We therefore use a direct access file (called REGDATA) to hold the parking ticket database; the collection of all vehicle data. Moreover, since the file records are to be accessed by entering a vehicle license number, we will make use of a sequential file (REGINDEX) that contains all license numbers; it will act as an index file to locate the appropriate record in the REGDATA file. We will assume that both files already exist on disk; our program will just maintain them and display their content. (In the Programming Problems at the end of this chapter, you are asked to write programs that create these files.)

The direct access file REGDATA has records with the following fields:

License plate number—License (string of length 6)
Registered owner—Owner (string of length 25)
Number of tickets—Tickets (integer)
Total amount owed—Amount (real)

The sequential file REGINDEX has one field, LicenseNum, to hold the vehicle license numbers. To speed up the search for a particular license number entered by the user (InputLicense), we will load the REGINDEX file into an array (see Section 6.3) called Licenses.

Thus, our program will acquire input from three sources: the file REGDATA containing all the vehicle data, the file REGINDEX containing the list of license numbers, and the license number, InputLicense, entered by the user. Its output consists of the record in the REGDATA file that corresponds to the license number input.

Program Design   The program will function as follows: The user enters a vehicle license number, and then indicates which operation is to be carried out on the corresponding vehicle information:

- Display all information (license number, owner name, number of tickets, total amount of fines) in the record for this vehicle.

- Add a new record to the database.

- Delete the record for this vehicle from the database.

- Modify the contents of the record for this vehicle; specifically, change the number of tickets and the total amount of the fines.

We will therefore design a menu-driven program (following the model given in Section 4.4) to display, add, delete, and change records in the indexed file consisting of REGDATA and REGINDEX. We take each of these four menu options to be a program module that is a submodule of the select-from-menu module (the module that inputs the user's choice of option). Moreover, since the display, add, delete, and change records modules all require a search for the license number input, our program will contain one additional module that carries out this search. The corresponding hierarchy chart is shown in Figure 2. Descriptions of the program modules follow.

FIGURE 2

The
Hierarchy
Chart for *A
Parking
Ticket
Tracking
Database*

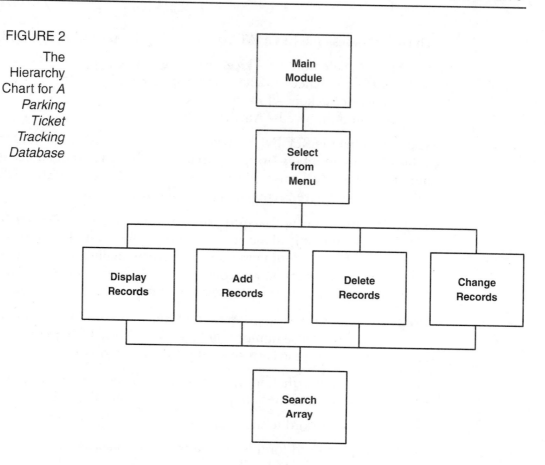

FIGURE 2

The Hierarchy Chart for *A Parking Ticket Tracking Database*

Main Module   The main module in this program design performs several small tasks. (It can therefore be further subdivided into submodules—see Self-Test 8.5.) The main module will:

Display a welcome message
Set up the sequential and direct access files (REGINDEX and
   REGDATA)
Load REGINDEX into the array Licenses
Call the Select from Menu module (which, in turn, will call the
selected option's module)
Copy the array Licenses to REGINDEX
Close the files
End Program

To be more specific, the pseudocode is as follows:

Display a welcome message
Set up the files REGINDEX and REGDATA:

```
Record Type VehicleInfo
    License As String[6]
    Owner As String[25]
    Tickets As Integer
    Amount As Real
End Record
Declare Vehicle As VehicleInfo
Open "REGDATA" For Random As DataFile,
    Len = Length(Vehicle)
Open "REGINDEX" For Input As IndexFile
Load REGINDEX into the array Licenses:
    Set Count = 0
    While Not EOF(IndexFile)
        Set Count = Count + 1
        Read IndexFile, Licenses[Count]
    End While
    Close IndexFile
Call Select from Menu module
Copy the array Licenses to REGINDEX:
    Open "REGINDEX" For Output As IndexFile
    For K = 1 Step 1 To Count
        Write IndexFile, Licenses[Count]
    End For
Close DataFile, IndexFile
End Program
```

(Updating REGINDEX toward the end of the main module is necessary because to this point all key item changes will have been made to the array Licenses, not to REGINDEX.)

Select from Menu module   Here's a rough outline for this module:

Display the menu options
Prompt for and input user selection
Call the appropriate module

Detailed pseudocode for this module is:

Display the menu options:
    Write "0 - Leave Program"
    Write "1 - Display a Vehicle's Information"
    Write "2 - Add a Vehicle"
    Write "3 - Delete a Vehicle"
    Write "4 - Change a Vehicle's Information"

Prompt for and input user selection:
　　Write "Selection?"
　　Input Choice
Call the appropriate module:
　　Select Case Of Choice
　　　　Case 1:
　　　　　　Call Display Records module
　　　　Case 2:
　　　　　　Call Add Records module
　　　　Case 3:
　　　　　　Call Delete Records module
　　　　Case 4:
　　　　　　Call Change Records module
　　End Case

The remaining modules make use of the Search Array module to locate the license number, InputLicense, that has been input. If InputLicense is located in the array Licenses at subscript Index, the variable Found is set equal to 1; if InputLicense is not located, Found is set equal to 0. The pseudocode for the Search Array module is given at the end of the program design.

Display Records module The pseudocode for Display Records is:
　　Write "To display a vehicle's information:"
　　Write "Enter the vehicle license number."
　　Write "Enter 0 to return to the main menu."
　　Input InputLicense
　　While InputLicense <> "0"
　　　　Call Search Array module
　　　　If Found = 1 Then
　　　　　　SeekGet DataFile, Index, Vehicle
　　　　　　Write "License:", Vehicle.License
　　　　　　Write "Owner:", Vehicle.Owner
　　　　　　Write "Number of Tickets:", Vehicle.Tickets
　　　　　　Write "Amount Owed:", Vehicle.Amount
　　　　Else
　　　　　　Write InputLicense, " not found."
　　　　End If
　　　　Write "Enter the vehicle license number."
　　　　Write "Enter 0 to return to main menu."
　　　　Input InputLicense
　　End While

Add Records module   The pseudocode for Add Records is:

> Write "To add a vehicle to the database:"
> Write "Enter the vehicle license number."
> Write "Enter 0 to return to the main menu."
> Input InputLicense
> While InputLicense <> "0"
>> Call Search Array module
>> If Found = 1 Then
>>> Write "Vehicle is already in the database."
>> Else
>>> Set Count = Count + 1
>>> Set Licenses[Count] = InputLicense
>>> Set Vehicle.License = InputLicense
>>> Write "Enter owner's name:"
>>> Input Vehicle.Owner
>>> Write "Enter number of tickets:"
>>> Input Vehicle.Tickets
>>> Write "Enter amount owed:"
>>> Input Vehicle.Amount
>>> SeekPut DataFile, Count, Vehicle
>> End If
>> Write "Enter the vehicle license number."
>> Write "Enter 0 to return to the main menu."
>> Input InputLicense
> End While

Delete Records module   The pseudocode for Delete Records is:

> Write "To delete a vehicle from the database:"
> Write "Enter the vehicle license number."
> Write "Enter 0 to return to the main menu."
> Input InputLicense
> While InputLicense <> "0"
>> Call Search Array module
>> If Found = 1 Then
>>> Set Licenses[Index] = ""
>>> Set Vehicle.License = ""
>>> Set Vehicle.Owner = ""
>>> Set Vehicle.Tickets = 0
>>> Set Vehicle.Amount = 0
>>> SeekPut DataFile, Index, Vehicle
>> Else

Write InputLicense, " not found."
End If
Write "Enter the vehicle license number."
Write "Enter 0 to return to the main menu."
Input InputLicense
End While

Change Records module   This module allows the user to change, for a particular vehicle, the number of tickets and the amount of fines owed. Its pseudocode is:

Write "To change a vehicle's ticket information:"
Write "Enter the vehicle license number."
Write "Enter 0 to return to the main menu."
Input InputLicense
While InputLicense <> "0"
    Call Search Array module
    If Found = 1 Then
        SeekGet DataFile, Index, Vehicle
        Write "Enter number of additional tickets:"
        Input AddTickets
        Set Vehicle.Tickets = Vehicle.Tickets + AddTickets
        Write "Enter additional amount of fines:"
        Input AddAmount
        Set Vehicle.Amount = Vehicle.Amount + AddAmount
        SeekPut DataFile, Index, Vehicle
    Else
        Write InputLicense, " not found."
    End If
    Write "Enter the vehicle license number."
    Write "Enter 0 to return to the main menu."
    Input InputLicense
End While

Search Array module   This module performs a serial search (see Section 6.2) of the array Licenses for the element InputLicense. If InputLicense is located, Found is set equal to 1 and Index is set equal to the corresponding array subscript.

Set Found = 0
Set Index = 0
While (Index < Count) And (Found = 0)
    Set Index = Index + 1

```
        If Licenses[Index] = InputLicense
            Set Found = 1
        End If
    End While
```

Program Code The program code is now written using the design as a guide. At this stage, header comments and step comments (see Section 2.3) are inserted into each module, providing internal documentation for the program. Here are a couple of other points concerning the coding that are specific to this program:

- The display of the menu (in the Select from Menu module) and the vehicle records (in the Display Records module) would benefit from formatting; it would make them more readable and professional looking. This can be accomplished using the programming language's special print formatting statements.

- To simplify the pseudocode, we have not used defensive programming techniques in the program design. In particular, in coding the program, you should validate input data. For example, in the Select from Menu module, the statements

    ```
    Write "Selection?"
    Input Choice
    ```

    should be placed in a loop:

    ```
    Repeat
        Write "Selection?"
        Input Choice
    Until (Choice = 0) Or (Choice = 1) Or (Choice = 2)
        Or (Choice = 3) Or (Choice = 4)
    ```

- Data should be passed among the program modules using subprogram parameters and arguments (see Sections 7.1 and 7.2).

Program Test To test this program, you would have to create simple REGDATA and REGINDEX files (see Programming Problems E and F), containing just a few records each. Then, you can check the code by adding, deleting, and changing records in the REGDATA file. After each of these operations, display the file records (using the appropriate menu option) to make sure that the operation was performed correctly. As part of this testing process, you should also enter improper data (for example, a negative number for the number of outstanding tickets) to check that the data validation code works properly.

Self-Test. 8.5

These exercises refer to the Parking Ticket Tracking Database program of this section.

1. The main module of this program performs several small tasks (for example, displaying a welcome message, loading the index file into an array, and updating the index file) as described in the Program Design subsection. Redesign the main module so that these tasks are performed by submodules. Specifically:

   a. Break the main module into submodules and draw the new hierarchy chart.

   b. Rewrite the pseudocode for the main module.

2. The Search Array module makes use of the serial search technique. How would the array Licenses have to be modified before performing a binary search on it?

Chapter Review and Exercises

Key Terms

Binary search   Random access file
Selection sort   Indexed file
Merge data files   Index file
Direct access file

Chapter Summary

In this chapter, we have discussed the following topics.

1. More efficient search and sort procedures:

   • Binary search for the element Key in an array called Array containing N elements and sorted in ascending order:

           Set Low = 1
           Set High = N
           Set Index = Int(N/2)
           Set Found = 0
           While (Found = 0) And (Low <= High)
               If Key = Array[Index] Then
                   Set Found = 1
               End If

```
                    If Key > Array[Index] Then
                        Set Low = Index + 1
                        Set Index = Int((High + Low)/2)
                    End If
                    If Key < Array[Index] Then
                        Set High = Index – 1
                        Set Index = Int((High + Low)/2)
                    End If
                End While
```

- Selection sort of the array Array (containing N elements) in ascending order:

```
            For K = 1 Step 1 To N – 1
                Set Min = Array[K]
                Set Index = K
                For J = K + 1 Step 1 To N
                    If Array[J] < Min Then
                        Set Min = Array[J]
                        Set Index = J
                    End If
                End For (J)
                If K <> Index Then
                    Set Temp = Array[K]
                    Set Array[K] = Array[Index]
                    Set Array[Index] = Temp
                End If
            End For (K)
```

2. Merging sequential files. To merge two sequential files:
   - Open both files for input.
   - Load the files into arrays MasterArray and UpdateArray.
   - Arrange all entries from both MasterArray and UpdateArray in order and call the resulting array, NewArray.
   - Copy NewArray to the file.
   - Close the files.

3. Direct access files:
   - Setting up a direct access file using the Record Type, Declare, and Open statements
   - Writing to a direct access file using the SeekPut statement
   - Reading a direct access file using the SeekGet statement

- Adding a record to, deleting a record from, and modifying a record in a direct access file with the aid of the LOF (length-of-file) function

4. Indexed files:

   - An indexed file is simulated by a pair of files—the given direct access file and a sequential file (the *index file*), whose records contain the contents of a key field of the direct access file.

   - To locate a key item in an indexed file, locate that item in the (sequential) index file; its position in this file will be the desired record number in the direct access file.

Review Exercises

1. True or false: The binary search procedure can only be used with numeric data.

2. True or false: A binary search requires that the data be sorted before beginning the search.

Exercises 3–6 refer to the following pseudocode, used to perform a binary search of the names Arnold, Drake, Gomez, Johnson, Smith, Wong (stored in Array), for the name Gomez:

```
Set N = 6
Set Key = "Gomez"
Set Low = 1
Set High = N
Set Index = Int(N/2)
Set Found = 0
While (Found = 0) And (Low <= High)
    If Key = Array[Index] Then
        Set Found = 1
    End If
    If Key > Array[Index] Then
        Set Low = Index + 1
        Set Index = Int((High + Low)/2)
    End If
    If Key < Array[Index] Then
        Set High = Index - 1
        Set Index = Int((High + Low)/2)
    End If
End While
```

3. On entering the While loop for the first time, what is the value of Index?

4. After the first pass through the While loop, what are the values of Low and High?

5. How many passes are made through the While loop?

6. After the While loop is exited, what is the value of Found?

Exercises 7–10 refer to the following pseudocode, used to perform a selection sort of the names Wong, Smith, Johnson, Gomez, Drake, and Arnold (stored in Array) in ascending order:

```
Set N = 6
For K = 1 Step 1 To N − 1
    Set Min = Array[K]
    Set Index = K
    For J = K + 1 Step 1 To N
        If Array[J] < Min Then
            Set Min = Array[J]
            Set Index = J
        End If
    End For (J)
    If K <> Index Then
        Set Temp = Array[K]
        Set Array[K] = Array[Index]
        Set Array[Index] = Temp
    End If
End For (K)
```

7. How many passes are made through the outer For loop?

8. After the first pass through the inner For loop, what is the value of Index?

9. After the first pass through the outer For loop, which name is stored in Array[1]?

10. What changes must be made to this pseudocode to sort an array of six names in descending order?

11. True or false: After merging two sequential files that are sorted in ascending order, the resulting merged file will also be sorted in ascending order.

12. True or false: To merge two sequential files, they must first be loaded into arrays.

Exercises 13–18 refer to the following pseudocode, which *partially* merges the arrays MasterArray and UpdateArray. Assume that the contents of these arrays are:

MasterArray—"Corinne", "Marjorie", "Shirley", "Tamara"
UpdateArray—"Arthur", "Michael", "Sam"

```
Set I = 1
Set J = 1
Set K = 1
While (I <= 4) And (J <= 3)
    If MasterArray[I] <= UpdateArray[J] Then
        Set NewArray[K] = MasterArray[I]
        Set I = I + 1
    Else
        Set NewArray[K] = UpdateArray[J]
        Set J = J + 1
    End If
    Set K = K + 1
End While
```

13. After the first pass through the While loop, what are the value of I, J, and NewArray[1]?

14. When the While loop is exited, what are the values of I and J?

15. When the While loop is exited, what are the contents of NewArray?

16. Which names must be added to the end of NewArray to complete the merging of the two arrays?

17. If MasterArray and UpdateArray had been sorted in descending order, what changes would have to be made to this pseudocode to merge these arrays?

18. If MasterArray and UpdateArray had been sorted in descending order and the pseudocode were changed as in Exercise 17, what would be the contents of NewArray after the While loop is exited?

19. True or false: A direct access file is also known as a random access file.

20. True or false: A direct access file is a type of text file.

21. True or false: The fields in a record of a direct access file are separated from each other by commas.

22. True or false: The lengths of all records in a direct access file must be the same.

Exercises 23–28 refer to a direct access file CARDATA that has been set up using the following statements:

```
Record Type CarInfo
    Make As String[15]
    Model As String[10]
End Record
Declare Car As CarInfo
Open "CARDATA" For Random As DataFile, Len = Length(Car)
```

23. What is the length of each record in the file CARDATA?

24. Fill in the blank: The second field of the third record of CARDATA begins with the _____ byte of this file.

25. Fill in the blanks: The field variables for this file are denoted by _____ and _____.

26. Write a sequence of statements (Set and SeekPut) that writes the data Chevrolet and Corvair to the first and second field, respectively, of the first record of CARDATA.

27. Fill in the blank: To read the second record of CARDATA, we would use the statement _____.

28. Suppose that the first record of CARDATA contains the data Chevrolet and Corvair in its first and second fields, respectively. Write statements that read this record and display the make and model information.

29. Fill in the blank: A(n) _____ file allows the user to locate a record by entering a key item rather than a record number.

30. Fill in the blank: When an indexed file is simulated by creating a sequential file containing the key items of the given direct access file, that sequential file is known as an _____ file.

Exercises 31–35 refer to a direct access file CARDATA that has been set up using the following statements:

```
Record Type CarInfo
    Make As String[15]
    Model As String[10]
End Record
Declare Car As CarInfo
Open "CARDATA" For Random As DataFile, Len = Length(Car)
```

31. Write a statement that displays the number of records in the file.

32. Write statements that add a record (whose contents have already been input into field variables) to the file.

33. Write statements that delete the fourth record from the file.

34. Write statements that change the model of record 10 to "Explorer".

35. Write statements that create a sequential index file, CARINDEX, whose records consist of the Model fields of CARDATA.

36. Using the simulated indexed file consisting of the direct access file CARDATA (of Exercises 31–35) and the sequential file CARINDEX (of Exercise 35), write statements that delete the record corresponding to the car model "Camry".

Programming Problems

For each of the following problems, use the top-down modular approach and pseudocode to design a suitable program to solve it.

A. Ramon Descartes teaches French at Polytechnic High School. He stores his grades in a sequential file GRADES with the following fields:

student name, test 1 score, test 2 score

Write a program that sorts the records of the GRADES file in ascending order by student name using a selection sort method.

B. Write a program that uses the binary search method to locate a student name (input by the user) in the GRADES file of Problem 1, and then displays that name and test scores.

C. Create an indexed file to hold the data of Problem 1 by reading all the data from the file GRADES into a direct access file GRADES1 and reading the data in its first field (student name) into a sequential file GRADES2.

D. The Last National Bank has two branches, each of which uses a sequential file containing a summary of customers' checking accounts in the form

account number, customer name, balance

The files, which are called ACCOUNT1 and ACCOUNT2, are ordered by account number, and both files are terminated by sentinel records with account number 0. (Assume that no two account numbers are the same.) Due to financial reverses, one of the branches must be closed, and the two files need to be merged into a single one called ACCOUNT3. Write a program to perform this operation.

E. Write a program that could be used to create the REGDATA direct access file of Section 8.5 by inputting the required data from the user. The records in this file have fields of the form:

> License plate number—License (string of length 6)
> Registered owner—Owner (string of length 25)
> Number of tickets—Tickets (integer)
> Total amount owed—Amount (real)

F. Write a program that creates the REGINDEX index file of Section 8.5, which contains the license plate numbers (from the first field) of REGDATA (see Problem E).

Objects in the Everyday World

The chapter you're about to read is about objects, and you're probably wondering what on earth that means. The answer is simple: Anything that has properties and a function (or functions) is an object. Objects are all around us—the chair you're sitting on is an object, this book is an object, and so is the washing machine you use to clean your clothes. Even *you* are an object.

Consider the washing machine. It certainly has properties—it's made of metal and has a tub, motor, and gearbox, has certain dimensions, and weighs a few hundred pounds. After writing a long list of its properties, we may know what a washing machine looks like (which is fine), but we don't yet know enough to define it. We also have to talk about its functions, the processes it carries out: The machine turns on, fills with water, agitates, empties, rinses, spins, and turns off. Finally, we need to know what our object "works on"; in this case, clothes. Put together all these pieces—properties, functions, and something to work on—and we can completely describe a useful object.

Here are a couple of other important aspects of a washing machine or, for that matter, any useful object:

- You don't have to know how it works internally to be able to use it.
- If someone has already built a suitable one, and it's available for purchase (or, better yet, for free), you don't have to build it yourself.

As another example, consider the chair mentioned above. Here's how we could describe one of these objects:

- Properties: Made of wood, has four legs, has a seat, has a back, is light brown
- Functions: Holds up a weight applied to the seat and back
- Works on: A person

In programming, objects containing properties (data) and functions (processes) provide "packaged solutions" to help us solve our programming problems. Defining and creating objects may initially seem unnecessarily complicated, but their use leads to elegant and efficient ways to handle complex problems. Moreover, by their very nature, objects ultimately simplify the programming process and ensure that we don't have to re-invent the wheel (or washing machine or chair).

9

More on OOP and GUIs

OVERVIEW   Throughout this text, we have used a single approach in developing our more complicated programs: top-down, modular design. In this chapter, we will discuss two other approaches to program design—object-oriented and event-driven programming. In Section 2.5, we provided a brief introduction to these topics; here, we will explore them in more depth. We will first discuss the basic concepts that underlie object-oriented programming (OOP) and then apply this material to the objects that make up a typical graphical user interface (GUI). To be more specific, you will learn

1. The basic terminology used in object-oriented programming [Section 9.1].

2. How to define classes and create objects [9.1].

3. About the inheritance and polymorphism features of OOP [9.2].

4. About object-oriented program design [9.2].

5. About the objects used in creating a graphical user interface [9.3].

6. How to handle events in programming for a GUI [9.4].

7. About event-driven program design [9.4, 9.5].

9.1   Classes and Objects

As you may recall from Section 2.5, an **object** is a structure comprised of data (or *attributes*) and processes (or *methods)* that perform operations on that data. **Object-oriented programming** (or **OOP,** for short) refers to an approach to program design and coding that places an emphasis on the objects needed to solve a given problem and the relationships among them. In this section, we will discuss some basic concepts underlying object-oriented programming.

Some Terminology

When learning a new subject, coming to grips with its special terminology is not always easy. In the case of object-oriented programming, we have the additional complication that there are often several terms that describe the same concept. On the other hand, as you will see, many of the new terms and concepts are analogous to ones with which you are already familiar.

Classes of objects
The fundamental entity in object-oriented programming is the *class*. A **class** is a data type that allows us to create objects; it provides the definition for a collection of objects by describing its **attributes** (data) and specifying the **methods** (operations) that may be applied to those data. For example, consider the following definition of the class "televison":

- Its attributes include brand name, model number, dimensions, screen size, and cabinet color.

- Its operations include turn it on, change channels, change volume, and turn it off.

This "televison class" just describes what a television *is* and what can be done with it; a "televison object," on the other hand, is a particular example of a televison, such as a Sony XBR32S.

So, to put it simply, the purpose of defining a class is to allow us to create objects; an object is just a particular *instance* of its class. The relationship between a class and its objects is analogous to the relationship between a data type and variables of that type. For example, when we write

Declare Number As Integer

the type Integer states what *kind* of data we are dealing with and what operations (+, −, etc.) can be performed on it. The variable Number is a particular instance of the type Integer. It can be assigned a specific integer value to be used within the program.

Other-object-related terminology

Let us now take a closer look at the objects themselves. As you know, objects are made up of two components: data and operations on that data. (We say that an object *encapsulates*—packages together—data and operations.) The operations are specified in the class definition; the data are specific to the particular object under consideration (although the *type* of data is also specified in the class definition). Be aware that there are several alternate names for the two components that make up an object:

- An object's data are also known as its *attributes, properties,* or *state*.
- An object's operations are also called *methods, behaviors, services, procedures,* or *functions*.

In this text, we will usually use the terms *attributes* (for data) and *methods* (for operations).

Defining Classes and Creating Objects

In Section 8.3, we showed how to define the structure of a direct access file and declare a record variable for that file using statements such as:

```
Record Type StudentInfo
      Code As String[4]
      Name As String[12]
      Units As Integer
      GPA As Real
End Record
Declare Student As StudentInfo
```

In this pseudocode, the Record Type statement defines the record layout called StudentInfo. But, StudentInfo is a data type, and cannot be referenced in the program. Thus, we use a Declare statement to create a variable (Student) of this type—an *instance* of the type StudentInfo—whose fields can be assigned values in the program.

We will use similar pseudocode to define a class and create objects of that class. The following example illustrates the process.

EXAMPLE 1 Recall that a *cube* is a box-shaped solid in which all sides are of equal length and whose volume is equal to the third power of the length of a side. Suppose we want to define a class called Cube that will have

- Attributes: the length of a side (Side) and the volume (Volume) of the cube

- Methods that:

  assign a value to the side (SetSide)
  compute the volume of the cube (ComputeVolume)
  return the value of the side to the program (GetSide)
  return the volume of the cube to the program (GetVolume)

(We will discuss these methods later in this section.)

To define the class Cube, we use the following pseudocode:

```
Class Cube
    Side As Real
    Volume As Real
    Subprogram SetSide(NewSide)
        Set Side = NewSide
    End Subprogram
    Subprogram ComputeVolume()
        Set Volume = Side ^ 3
    End Subprogram
    Function GetVolume() As Real
        Set GetVolume = Volume
    End Function
    Function GetSide() As Real
        Set GetSide = Side
    End Function
End Class
```

The Function and Subprogram notation we have used in this pseudocode was introduced in Chapter 7. The symbols "()" following the name of a subprogram indicate that it has no parameters.

Data hiding In Example 1, the methods SetSide, GetSide, and GetVolume, are called *access methods*. They provide the rest of the program with access to the object's attributes. SetSide imports a value of the attribute Side from the main program. GetSide and GetVolume allow the main program to make use of the values of Side and Volume. This raises the question:

Why not just pass the values of the variables Side and Volume back and forth to the program as parameters? The answer to this question is one of the keys to understanding OOP: We normally want to keep the class variables completely "hidden" from the rest of the program. This practice of *data hiding* has a two-fold purpose:

1. It enhances the security of the object's data—the data cannot be altered except by the means intended, namely, by using one of the object's methods.

2. It helps shield the inner workings of the object from the programmer. In OOP, objects work like "black boxes." Although their interface with the outside programming world (their methods) is made public, the way in which a method gets its job done and the variables with which it works are kept private.

Programming Pointer

To explicitly state which members (attributes and/or methods) of a class are **public** (available to code outside an object of that class) and which are **private** to the class (not available outside the class), programming languages use the keywords Public and Private. The relevant keyword, placed in front of the variable or method name, specifies the status of that class member. For example, in Example 1, to specify all variables as private and all methods as public, we would rewrite the pseudocode as:

```
Class Cube
      Private Side As Real
      Private Volume As Real
      Public Subprogram SetSide(NewSide)
            Set Side = NewSide
            End Subprogram
      Public Subprogram ComputeVolume()
            Set Volume = Side ^ 3
            End Subprogram
      Public Function GetVolume() As Real
            Set GetVolume = Volume
            End Function
      Public Function GetSide() As Real
            Set GetSide = Side
            End Function
End Class
```

Attributes are normally declared to be Private (to protect their integrity). Methods are declared as Public if they are part of the interface between the object and program, and as Private if they are only used internally—within the class itself.

After we have defined a class, we need to create one or more objects of that class. (In OOP language, we need to create an *instance* of the class; that is, we must perform an *instantiation* operation.) This is typically done by means of a declaration statement placed in the main program. For example, in this text, we use the statement

Declare Cube1, Cube2 As Cube

to create two objects, named Cube1 and Cube2, of the class Cube.

Once they are created, we can make use of the objects Cube1 and Cube2 in our program. To refer to an object's attributes or methods, we use the "dot notation" introduced in Section 8.3 for referring to the fields of a record in a direct access file. For example, in this text, to assign a value of 10 to the Side attribute of Cube1 (see Example 1), we will use the statement:

Call Cube1.SetSide(10)

Or, to display the Volume attribute of Cube1, we will use

Write Cube1.GetVolume

In general, to refer to a public member (attribute or method) called MemeberName, of an object called ObjectName, we use the notation:

ObjectName.MemberName

EXAMPLE 2   The following program makes use of the Cube1 object. It inputs a number from the user and displays the volume of the corresponding cube.

Main Program
    Declare Cube1 As Cube
    Write "Enter a positive number:"
    Input Side1
    Call Cube1.SetSide(Side1)
    Call Cube1.ComputeVolume
    Write "The volume of a cube of side ", Cube1.GetSide
    Write "is ", Cube1.GetVolume
    End Program

Notice that there are four calls in this pseudocode to the methods of the object Cube1; two subprogram calls (to SetSide and ComputeVolume) and two function calls (to GetSide and GetVolume). In OOP language, each of these calls is a **message** to the appropriate method.

Programming Pointer

In Example 2, a program error will result if the main program calls the function ComputeVolume before its Side attribute is given a value. To prevent this (and for other reasons, as well), object-oriented programming languages supply an easy way, through the use of a *constructor*, to initialize an object's attributes. A **constructor** is a special method included in the class definition that automatically performs specified setup tasks (such as initializing the object's attributes) when an object is created.

Self-Test 9.1

1. What are the two major components of an object?

2. What is the relationship between a class and objects in that class?

3. What is the difference between public and private class members?

4. Define a class called InAndOut that has one attribute named Value (of type Real) and two methods:

   - SetValue imports a value of the attribute Value from the main program.

   - GetValue returns the value of the attribute Value to the main program.

5. What is a constructor?

9.2 More on Object-oriented Programming

In this section, we will continue our discussion of object-oriented programming (OOP). We will describe additional features that provide OOP with versatility and power, and also discuss the process of object-oriented program design.

Inheritance and Polymorphism

In contrast to OOP, the approach to programming that makes use of top-down modular design is known as **procedural programming**. Most early programming languages, such as FORTRAN and BASIC, did not support the use of classes and objects, and are known as *procedural languages*. Most modern languages, on the other hand, allow the programmer to make use of objects (in addition to providing the tools found in a procedural language). However, to take full advantage of the power of OOP—to truly support object-oriented programming—a language must include the following features:

Character-
istics of an
object-
oriented
language

- **Encapsulation**—The incorporation of data and operations on that data into a single unit in such a way that the data can only be accessed through these operations. This is the fundamental idea behind classes and objects.

- **Inheritance**—The ability to create new classes that are based on existing ones. The methods (operations) and attributes (data) of the original class are incorporated into the new class, together with methods and attributes specific to the latter.

- **Polymorphism**—The ability to create methods that perform a general function, which automatically adapts itself to work with objects of different classes.

Some Benefits of Object-oriented Languages   Object-oriented programming tools have been in use for several decades, but only started to gain great popularity in the late 1980s. There are two basic reasons for this development:

- During the 1980s, programs became more complex as demand grew for sophisticated applications such as word processors, graphics programs, and computer games. Programs of this sort had so many options and possible outcomes that keeping track of their subprograms became a nightmare. Due to the self-contained nature of objects and the properties of inheritance and polymorphism, OOP is better equipped than procedural programming to deal with these extremely complex programs.

- The graphical-user-interface (GUI), popularized by the Apple Macintosh in the mid-1980s, slowly became almost universal for computers. A GUI is comprised of objects (windows, boxes, buttons, etc.), so OOP became the natural way of programming for these interfaces.

The concept of encapsulation was discussed in Section 9.1; inheritance and polymorphism will be described below.

Inheritance   In everyday life, we often classify things. For example, trucks and cars are both kinds of vehicles, and station wagons, convertibles, and sedans are all types of cars. In a more mathematical way, we can say that the set of cars is a subset of the set of vehicles, and the set of convertibles is a subset of the set of cars. To picture the relationships among these sets, we can use a kind of hierarchy chart, as shown in Figure 1.

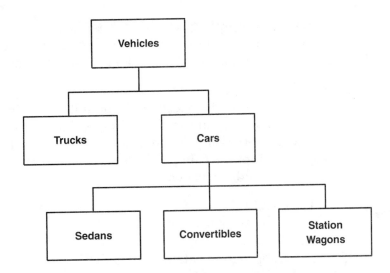

FIGURE 1

A Hierarchy
of Vehicles

Classifying objects can help explain what they are and how they operate. For example, if we know what a car is, then in describing a convertible, we don't have to explain the attributes and functions that it has in common with (that it has *inherited from*) a car. We just state that a convertible is a car, and present the special features of a convertible that distinguish it from a car.

This concept of classification and inheritance also works in object-oriented programming. Object-oriented languages allow us to create a *subclass* of an existing class. In this case, the existing class is called the **base class** (or *parent class*) and the subclass is called the **derived class** (or *child class*). In creating a subclass, the attributes and methods of the base class automatically become members of the derived class, together with any additional attributes and methods defined specifically for the latter.

In OOP, the derived class may or may not be a special type (a subset) of the base class. Rather, a derived class is created to take advantage of the methods that have already been defined in an existing class. As an example, recall the "Cube" class of Section 9.1. Its attributes and methods are:

- Attributes—Side, Volume

- Methods—SetSide, ComputeVolume, GetSide, GetVolume

We may consider a cube to be a special type of box—one in which all sides are equal. If we want to define a class that models another kind of box, one with a square base but whose height is *not* the same as the sides of its base, we need not start from scratch; we can define this new class to be a subclass of Cube. The next example demonstrates how to do this.

EXAMPLE 3   The following pseudocode gives the definitions of the class Cube (from Section 9.1) and its subclass, SquareBox. The SquareBox class makes use of all attributes and methods of the Cube class (although it changes the definition of the ComputeVolume method) and adds an attribute and two methods of its own.

```
Class Cube
    Side As Real
    Volume As Real
    Subprogram SetSide(NewSide)
        Set Side = NewSide
        End Subprogram
    Subprogram ComputeVolume()
        Set Volume = Side ^ 3
        End Subprogram
    Function GetVolume() As Real
        Set GetVolume = Volume
        End Function
    Function GetSide() As Real
        Set GetSide = Side
        End Function
End Class

Class SquareBox As Cube
    Height As Real
    Subprogram SetHeight(NewHeight)
        Set Height = NewHeight
        End Subprogram
    Function GetHeight() As Real
        Set GetHeight = Height
        End Function
    Subprogram ComputeVolume()
        Set Volume = Side ^ 2 * Height
        End Subprogram
End Class
```

Notice that we specify SquareBox to be a subclass of Cube with the statement:

Class SquareBox As Cube

(Of course, each programming language has its own way of defining subclasses.) The derived class SquareBox has the following members:

- Its attributes are Side and Volume, both inherited from Cube, and Height.

- Its methods are SetSide and GetSide, inherited from Cube, and SetHeight, GetHeight, and ComputeVolume.

A statement (elsewhere in the program) like

Declare Box As SquareBox

creates an object called Box of the class SquareBox that can take advantage of all these attributes and methods. For example, the following statements assign the values 10 and 20 to the Side and Height attributes, respectively:

Call Box.SetSide(10)
Call Box.SetHeight(20)

Overriding a method   In Example 3, notice that a ComputeVolume method appears in both the base class Cube and the derived class SquareBox. In such a case, for an object in the derived class, the definition in the derived class *overrides* (is used instead of) the one in the base class. The next example clarifies this notion.

EXAMPLE 4   With the definition of the SquareBox class as given in Example 3, the following pseudocode inputs values for the side and height of a box from the user and computes and displays its volume.

```
Main Program
    Declare Box As SquareBox
    Write "For a box with a square base and arbitrary height,"
    Write "enter the length of the sides of its base:"
    Input BoxSide
    Call Box.SetSide(BoxSide)
    Write "Enter the height of the box:"
    Input BoxHeight
    Call Box.SetHeight(BoxHeight)
    Call Box.ComputeVolume
    Write "The volume of the box is ", Box.GetVolume
End Program
```

When the message

    Call Box.SetSide(BoxSide)

is sent, the computer "looks in" the class definition SquareBox (the class of the object Box) for the method SetSide. Not finding it there, the computer looks in the parent class Cube for this method and applies it to the object Box, setting Box.Side equal to the value input. On the other hand, when the subprogram SetHeight is called, this method *is* found in the definition of SquareBox, and invoked. Similarly, when the message

    Call Box.ComputeVolume

is sent, it is received by the method ComputeVolume defined in SquareBox. Thus, the correct formula, Volume = Side ^ 2 * Height, is applied at this point.

Polymorphism   In a hierarchy of classes, it is often the case that some methods are common to several classes, but that their definitions may differ from class to class. For example, the ComputeVolume method of Example 3 calculates the volume of a cube in the base class Cube and the volume of a box with a square base in the derived class SquareBox. More generally, a module might contain definitions of many three-dimensional objects—cubes, boxes, spheres, cylinders, etc.—each of which has a volume given by a different formula. It would be convenient if a programmer were able to use a single method, ComputeVolume, to calculate the volume of any of these objects. Polymorphism allows for this kind of flexibility.

The word *polymorphism* means "many shapes." In programming, it allows a method to take on many definitions when applied to objects in a hierarchy of classes. Although this OOP feature is implemented differently in various object-oriented languages, the next example shows the general way in which it works.

EXAMPLE 5   The following pseudocode shows how a method can take on different forms when applied to different objects. It makes use of the class definitions given in Example 3 (earlier in this section).

    Main Program
        Declare Box1 As Cube
        Declare Box2 As SquareBox
        Write "Enter the length of the side of a cube:"
        Input Side1
        Call Box1.SetSide(Side1)

Call Box1.ComputeVolume
Write "The volume of this cube is ", Box1.GetVolume
Write "For a box with a square base and arbitrary height,"
Write "enter the length of the sides of its base:"
Input Side2
Call Box2.SetSide(Side2)
Write "Enter the height of the box:"
Input Height2
Call Box2.SetHeight(Height2)
Call Box2.ComputeVolume
Write "The volume of this box is ", Box2.GetVolume
End Program

The Declare statements create the objects Box1 and Box2 as instances of the classes Cube and SquareBox, respectively. Thus, for all statements that refer to Box1, the Cube class definition is referenced. In particular, when the first message is sent to the method ComputeVolume, the formula used is Volume = Side ^3. On the other hand, for statements that refer to Box2, the SquareBox class definition is referenced; the parent Cube definition is used only when an attribute or method definition is not found in SquareBox. Thus, when the second message is sent to ComputeVolume (this time, preceded by "Box2."), the definition in SquareBox is used, providing the formula Volume = Side ^ 2 * Height, as desired.

Object-oriented Program Design

As you know, the top-down modular approach to program design (procedural programming) places an emphasis on determining the subprograms (procedures) that are needed in a program.

Object-oriented program design, on the other hand, places an emphasis on determining the objects needed to solve the given problem. In fact, in most cases in which OOP is better-suited to solve a given problem (such as in programming for a graphical user interface), there is no strong hierarchy of program modules.

Viewed in terms of the program development cycle of problem analysis, program design, program coding, and program testing, it is the analysis phase that differs the most between the two approaches. In developing an OOP program, the analysis phase entails:

1. Identifying the classes to be used in the program.

2. Determining the attributes needed for these classes.

3. Determining the methods needed for these classes.

4. Determining the relationships among the classes.

The manner in which these steps are carried out is not so different from that of the top-down approach. The program designer works with the program specifications, imagining what kinds of situations the program will encounter—what types of specific cases it must handle—and determines the needed objects, attributes, and methods from these scenarios.

In carrying out these steps, there is a natural transition into the design phase of the program development cycle. Here, as in the top-down technique, the methods (subprograms) must be defined. Although this is easy to *say*, in real-life programs, there may be hundreds or even thousands of methods. Encapsulating them in objects generally makes it easier to manage them. Finally, although the coding and testing phases proceed as in procedural programming, here too, a benefit of OOP emerges. It is likely that some pre-existing objects can be recycled in this new program; making use of this *reusable code* speeds up both coding and testing.

The next example illustrates the analysis phase of an object-oriented design.

EXAMPLE 6   Suppose we want to create a grade management program (like the one in Section 7.5) to input and store student names and test scores, and compute test averages for each student. An object-oriented solution to this problem would begin as follows:

1. In analyzing the problem, we decide to use two classes of objects:

   - A Student class, whose objects are the students enrolled in the course.

   - A Test class, whose objects are the test scores and averages for each student.

2. The attributes of the Student class are Name and ID number. (There could be others, such as Major and Rank—Freshman, Sophomore, etc.). The attributes of the Test class are an array of Scores and AverageScore.

3. The methods for the Student class allow access to its attributes; they are SetName, GetName, SetID, and GetID. The methods for the Test class are those that allow access to its attributes together with a subprogram, ComputeAverage, that calculates the average test score.

4. The classes Student and Test are related; each test score and average refers to a particular student. Thus, we take Test to be a class derived from the parent class Student, so that the former inherits the attributes and methods of the latter.

Now that we have determined the classes, attributes, and methods needed to solve this problem, we must design, code, and test the corresponding subprograms, as well as the program itself. (Section 9.5 presents a GUI solution to the grade management problem.)

Self-Test 9.2

1. Fill in the blank: In contrast to object-oriented programming, the top-down modular approach to programming is referred to as _____ programming.

2. Identify each of the following OOP features using a single word:

   a. The incorporation of data and operations on that data into a single unit in such a way that the data can only be accessed by making use of these operations.

   b. The ability to create new classes that are based on existing ones and to make use of their data and attributes.

   c. The ability to create methods that perform a general function which automatically adapts to work with certain related classes.

3. Fill in the blanks: When we create a subclass of an existing class, the new class is called the _____ class; the original is the _____ class.

4. List the fundamental steps taken in analyzing a problem to be solved using object-oriented program design.

5. What is one advantage of OOP over procedural programming?

9.3 Graphical User Interfaces Revisited

One of the important applications of object-oriented programming (OOP) is to create programs that employ a graphical user interface. A **graphical user interface** (or **GUI**) is comprised of **windows** that contain components such as menus, buttons, boxes, etc., which allow users to make choices and issue commands in a simple, intuitive way. In Section 2.5, we introduced some basic GUI concepts. In this section and the next, we will explore this topic in greater detail.

Window Components

Figure 2 displays a typical dialog box window (the Print dialog box for the Microsoft Windows GUI). Its buttons, boxes, and other elements are collectively known as **window components** (or *controls*). From a programming point of view, both windows and window components are objects. The names and functions of common window components are described below; their attributes and methods are discussed later in this section and in Section 9.4.

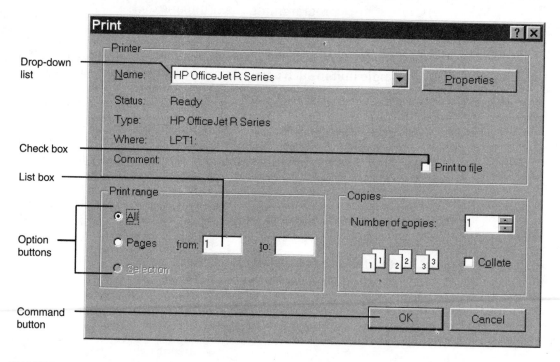

FIGURE 2 A Typical Dialog Box

- **Command buttons**, like the Properties, OK, and Cancel buttons in Figure 2, are represented by labeled rectangles. When you *click* a command button (when you position the mouse pointer over it and tap the mouse button), it initiates an action. For example, clicking the command button labeled OK in Figure 2 closes the dialog box (removes it from the screen) and sends part or all of the current document to the printer. The Cancel button closes the dialog box without performing any action and returns all items within it to the values they had when the box was opened.

- A **check box**, like the "Print to file" check box in Figure 2, is represented by a small square, which may or may not contain a check mark. When the check mark is present (indicating that the specified option is in effect), we say that the check box is *selected*; when the check mark does not appear (indicating that this option is not in effect), the check box is said to be *deselected* or *cleared*. For example, the deselected check box in Figure 2 indicates that the document will *not* "Print to file." To select a check box, the user clicks on it; to clear it, the user clicks on it again.

- A **text box**, like the "from" and "to" text boxes in Figure 2, allows the user to input text or a number into the dialog box. A text box is symbolized by a rectangle which is either blank or contains the *current value* for that object—the text or number that is used if it is not changed. (In Figure 2, the current value for the "from" box is 1.) To enter data into a text box, the user clicks inside it, deletes the current value (if any), and then types the desired letters or digits.

- **Option buttons**, which are represented by small circles, always appear in groups (like the "Print range" group in Figure 2). These kinds of buttons are sometimes called *radio buttons* because they work like the station selection push buttons on a radio—when the user clicks on one of them, that button is *selected* (turned on) and the others are automatically *deselected* (turned off). For this reason, in a group of option buttons, only one of the corresponding options can be selected at any given time. The currently selected option button is indicated by a *bullet* within the corresponding circle. For example, in Figure 2, the "All" option is selected; it contains the bullet. If the user clicks on the "Pages" option button, it will acquire the bullet and become the current selection.

- A **drop-down list box**, like the one labeled Name in Figure 2, is used to display a list of items. The current value of this object ("HP OfficeJet R Series" in Figure 2) is the only item initially visible. To display the rest of the list, the user clicks on the downward-facing triangle at the right end of the box. Then, to select an item from the list, the user clicks on that item—the list will close and the new item will become the current value.

- A **list box** (not shown in Figure 2) is like a drop-down list box, but displays the entire list of items, with the current value at the top. Again, to select an item from the list so that it becomes the current value (and moves to the top), the user clicks on that item.

- A **label** is text in the dialog box that is not part of another window component. It is often located near a component to help identify it. For example, in Figure 2, Printer, Name, Status, and Ready are all labels.

Creating GUI Objects in a Program

The major OOP languages have built-in classes (*class libraries*) that supply the objects needed to write programs for a graphical user interface. Thus, there is no need to define windows, command buttons, etc. The way that these objects are created within a program depends on the language used:

- In some programming languages, GUI objects are created in the same way as any other objects, as instances of the class to which they belong.

- In other programming languages, GUI objects are selected from a menu or toolbar and "drawn" on the screen.

For example, in the Java programming language, we add a command button to a window by using a "new" statement to create the object and an "add" statement to place it in the window. In Visual Basic, on the other hand, we click on the command button icon on a toolbar and then draw the button (using the mouse) in the window; these actions create code that adds the button to the window. For simplicity's sake, in this text we will assume that windows and window components can be created in the Visual Basic way, without explicitly writing any code.

Typical properties of GUI objects

Each window and window component (command button, text box, etc.) in a GUI has a set of attributes, or *properties*, such as name, position, and size. Here are some examples of GUI object properties.

- The properties of a *window* include:
    Name (by which it's known in the program)
    Height and Width, (usually in *pixels*, the tiny dots that make up the screen image)

Title ("Area Calculator" in Figure 3)
Title Font—the typeface and size of the window title
Visible (True or False)—whether or not the window
     appears on the screen

- *Command button* properties include:
     Name (by which it's known in the program)
     Caption ("Done" or "Calculate" in Figure 3)
     Position—distance (in pixels) from the left and top
          edges of the window
     Enabled (True or False)—whether the button is active or
          inactive (the Calculate button is inactive, or "grayed
          out," and will not respond to a mouse click; the Done
          button is active)

- *Text boxes* (like the two in Figure 3) have properties similar to those
  of command buttons, but text boxes have a Text property (holding
  the string that currently appears inside the box) instead of a Caption property.

- *Labels* (like the two in Figure 3) have properties that are very similar to those of text boxes, except that the user cannot change the
  text of a label.

- *Option button* properties include:
     Name (by which it's known in the program)
     Caption ("All," "Pages," or "Selection" in Figure 2)
     Enabled (True or False)—whether the button is active or
          inactive (grayed out)
     Value (True or False)—whether or not the option button
          has a bullet

FIGURE 3

A Simple
Window

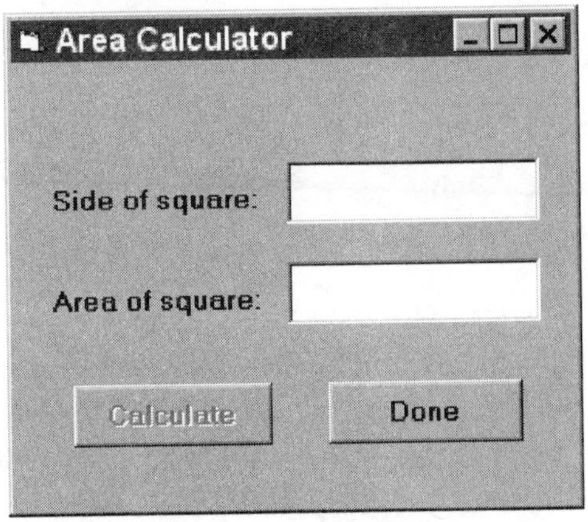

Since windows and components are objects, their properties can be assigned values, just like the attributes of any object. Most GUI properties have *default values*—those that are automatically used unless new ones are assigned. To change these default values, we can make use of assignment statements; for example, in the Area Calculator window of Figure 3:

- If the name of the window is MainWindow, then the statements
    Set MainWindow.Title = "Area Calculator"
    Set MainWindow.Height = 100
specify that the title of the window is "Area Calculator" and that the height of the window is 100 pixels.

- If the name of the right command button is QuitButton, then the statements
    Set QuitButton.Caption = "Done"
    Set QuitButton.Enabled = False
label it as "Done" and cause it to be grayed out when the window is opened.

**Programming
Pointer** Remembering the names of all the possible properties of all window components isn't easy. To simplify matters, some languages allow you to specify properties by selecting items from menus or entering values into dialog boxes.

As objects, windows and their components also have methods (procedures) associated with them. We will discuss this aspect of GUI programming in the next section.

Self-Test 9.3

1. Identify each of the following window components as either a command button, an option button, a check box, or a text box.
    a. It can receive data input by the user.
    b. When clicked, it initiates an action.
    c. It allows the user to select one choice from a group of related choices.

2. What is the difference between a list box and a drop-down list box?

3. Give two properties of each of the following objects:
    a. A window   b. A text box   c. An option button

4. A command button has the name OKbutton. Write assignment statements that set its Caption property equal to "OK" and its Enabled property equal to False.

9.4   *Event-driven Programming*

Thus far in this chapter we have discussed object-oriented programming (OOP) and some of the objects used in creating a graphical user interface (GUI). In this section, we will continue this discussion, returning to the concepts of events and event-driven program design that were touched on briefly in Section 2.5.

Handling Events

In a procedural (top-down) program, the flow of execution is determined by the code and the data that it makes use of. Although the user can influence the flow through the input of data, it is the data that make the difference, not the fact that the user entered those data. However, in many programs nowadays, the *actions* of the user (such as clicking the mouse) or system-related circumstances (such as the state of a timer) determine the flow of execution. These actions are called **events** and the resulting program is said to be **event-driven**. Although event-driven programs need not be written for a GUI or be object-based, the prime examples of event-driven programs are object-oriented and employ a graphical user interface.

To illustrate the concept of events and how they are handled by a program, let us return to the simple window displayed in Figure 3 of Section 9.3. (For the sake of convenience, it is reproduced here in Figure 4.) We will use this window and the components it contains as the interface for an event-driven program.

FIGURE 4

A GUI
Interface

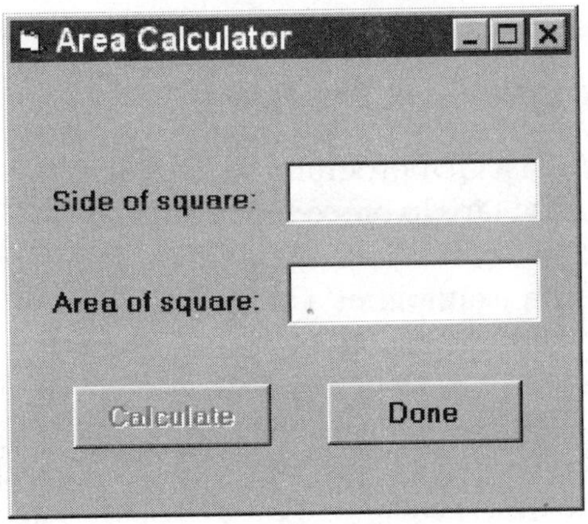

As you know from Section 9.3, windows and the components contained within them are objects that have various attributes. Also associated with each object is a set of events and methods called *event-handlers* or *event procedures* that enable the objects to carry out their functions. For example, the basic function of a command button is to allow the user, by clicking that button, to call for a specified action. Thus, the command button object needs a method to handle this event—to recognize the click and then call the appropriate subprogram. The programming language software ensures that this is done automatically. However, the programmer must design and write the code for this subprogram so that it performs the proper action when called.

Some methods for GUI objects

Here is a list of some typical methods associated with the objects in a GUI. (As usual, the names we use here will probably differ from those in an actual programming language.)

- Methods for a window include:
    - Open—opens the window
    - StartUp—programmer-written procedure that executes automatically when the window is opened
    - Close—closes the window

- Command button methods include:
    - Click—executes automatically when the button is clicked

- Text box methods include:
    - Click—executes automatically when the box is clicked
    - Change—executes automatically when the text within the box is changed

- Option button methods include:
    - Click—executes automatically when the button is clicked

A Simple GUI Program

When a GUI program is run, the initial window appears on the screen and a StartUp procedure, if any, for this window is executed. From that point on, the flow of execution is determined by the events that occur. As an example of a simple GUI program and how it works, we will present the pseudocode used to create an area calculator.

EXAMPLE 7 To use the Area Calculator shown in Figure 4, the user types a number (representing the side of a square) into the upper text box. When this is done, the Calculate button becomes active (it is no longer grayed out) so that it can respond to a mouse click. The user then clicks this button to display the area of the square in the lower text box. To calculate another area, the user clicks inside the upper text box, which clears the numbers in both text boxes, grays out the Calculate button, and allows the process to be repeated. When done calculating areas, the user clicks the Done button, which closes the window and ends the program. Here is the pseudocode that defines the methods and sets some of the attributes for the objects in this program (attributes for GUI objects are described in Section 9.3):

Window
    Name = MainWindow
    Title = "Area Calculator"

Upper Label
    Text = "Side of Square"

Lower Label
    Text = "Area of Square"

Upper Text Box
    Name = InputBox
    Text = ""
    Subprogram InputBox.Click()
        Set InputBox.Text = ""
        Set OutputBox.Text = ""
        Set CalculateButton.Enabled = False
        End Subprogram
    Subprogram InputBox.Change()
        Set CalculateButton.Enabled = True
        End Subprogram

Lower Text Box
    Name = OutputBox
    Text = ""

Left Command Button
    Name = CalculateButton
    Caption = "Calculate"
    Enabled = False
    Subprogram CalculateButton.Click()
        Set OutputBox.Text = Val(InputBox.Text) ^ 2
        End Subprogram

Right Command Button
    Name = DoneButton
    Caption = "Done"
    Subprogram DoneButton.Click()
        Call MainWindow.Close
        End Program
        End Subprogram

When the program is started, the window shown in Figure 4 appears on the screen. (All object properties, including those specified in the pseudocode above, are assigned when the program is compiled.) Since there is no StartUp procedure defined for this window, execution pauses until an event occurs. The program works as described at the beginning of this example; to make sense out of the pseudocode, imagine that you are running the program, and when you "perform an action," read the corresponding subprogram. Also, note that:

- The Val function converts string data into numeric data; it is described in Section 7.3.

- The End Program statement in the last subprogram halts execution.

Event-driven Program Design

One of the striking differences between top-down programming and event-driven programming is that the latter has no main program, no "master controller." Execution begins by displaying the program's initial window and running its StartUp procedure, if any. But, from then on, execution moves from subprogram to subprogram depending on the events that take place. Execution terminates when an End Program statement is encountered.

The analysis phase of an event-driven program design is similar to that of an object-oriented program (see Section 9.2). Here are the basic steps involved:

1. Identify the windows needed in the program.

2. Determine the relationships among the windows; for example, which window can open another (so that the latter appears on the screen). Such relationships can be pictured in a flow diagram (see Figure 5). In a flow diagram, an arrow pointing from one window to another (as from Window 6 to Window 2 in Figure 5) means that

the first can open or reactivate the second; a "double arrow," pointing in both directions (as with Windows 2 and 3 in Figure 5) means that either window can open or reactivate the other.

3. For each window:

- Determine the components (command buttons, text boxes, etc.) needed for that window.
- Draw a rough sketch of the resulting window.
- Determine the properties and methods needed for the window and each of its components. (The methods need not be "fleshed out" in this phase.)

The third step of this process leads us into the design phase of the program development. Here, the methods for each object (and perhaps additional properties) are defined. We will illustrate the design process in more detail in Section 9.5.

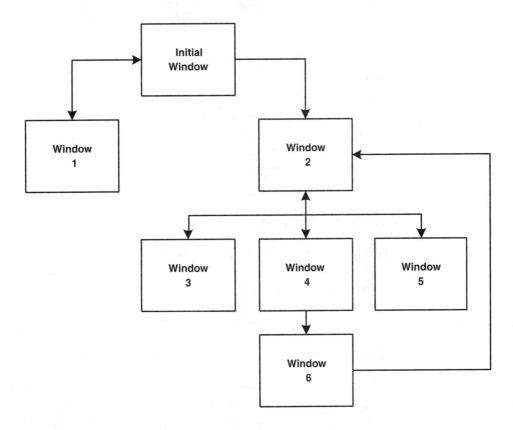

FIGURE 5   An Example of a Flow Diagram for a GUI Program

Self-Test 9.4

1. Is each of the following statements true or false?

   a. When the user clicks a command button during program execution, that action is considered to be an event.

   b. Event-driven programs must make use of a graphical user interface.

2. Which method would you use to respond to data being typed into a Text box—its Click method or its Change method?

3. How would you modify the Area Calculator program of this section to

   a. Display the number 0 in both text boxes when the program starts?

   b. Display the message "Invalid input" in the bottom text box if the user enters a negative number into the top text box and clicks the Calculate button? (*Hint:* Use an If-Then-Else statement in the CalculateButton.Click subprogram.)

4. Which of the following is the first step in developing an event-driven program?

   a. Write the main program code.

   b. Write the "click" subprograms.

   c. Determine which windows are needed.

   d. Determine which buttons are needed.

9.5   Focus on Problem Solving

In this section, we will develop an event-driven program for a problem we originally solved in Section 7.5 using a traditional top-down modular approach. Our new program uses the material covered in this chapter, but will be easier to understand if you first review Section 7.5.

The Grade Management Program Revisited

One of your instructors, Professor Allknowing, would like to have a program that creates an "electronic grade sheet" so that he can keep track of student scores in his classes. This program should allow the professor to enter the names of his students and their scores on three tests, compute the average test score for each student, and display this information any time he wants.

Problem Analysis We first want to determine the windows we will need to handle this problem. To do so, we imagine that we are teaching this class, and think about the kinds of things we will do with this program.

1. We must create a file (GRADES) to hold the grade sheet information, namely the name, test scores, and test average for each student in the class. In the process of creating the file, we enter the names of students in the class.

2. Once the GRADES file has been created, we need to be able to retrieve the file to display its information, enter test scores, or compute test averages.

Thus, the initial window should allow the user to select from two options: create the grade sheet or retrieve the grade sheet.

Now that we have determined the contents of the initial window, it is clear that we need at least two additional windows:

- A *Create Grade Sheet* window

- A *Retrieve Grade Sheet* window

The latter window would allow users to specify the particular task that they want to perform: display the grade sheet, enter test scores, or compute test averages. This leads to at least three more windows:

- A *Display Grade Sheet* window

- An *Enter Test Scores* window

- A *Compute Test Averages* window

Now, to see if additional windows are needed, we imagine that we were using the program to perform its stated functions. In doing so, we realize that when entering test scores, the first thing the program must know is whether those scores are for test 1, test 2, or test 3. For this reason, we create one more window, a *Select Test* window, to precede the actual entering of test scores.

Figure 6 displays an execution flow diagram that shows the windows described above and their relationship to one another. Recall that an arrow from one window to another means that execution can move from the first window to the second.

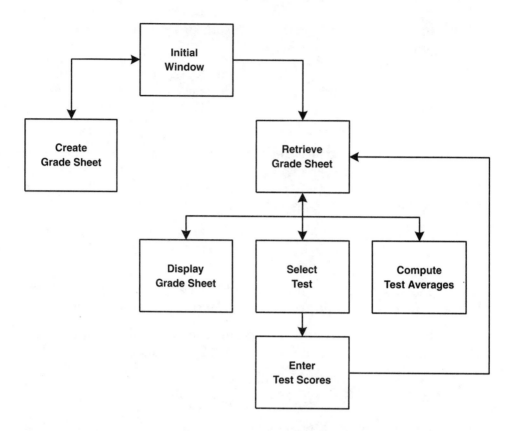

FIGURE 6   Execution Flow Diagram for the Grade Management Program

Program Design   The program design consists of two stages. For each window indicated in Figure 6, we must

1. Determine the objects (window components) needed to implement the user interface for that window.

2. Write pseudocode that describes the attributes (properties) and methods (subprograms) for that window.

(Due to the space required to present these descriptions, we will not supply detailed pseudocode for every aspect of this program.)

Initial Window

We will use the following window components for the initial window:

- A label to describe the options that follow.

- Two option buttons to allow selection of the display grade sheet or retrieve grade sheet option.

- A command button (OK) to put the selected option into effect.
- A command button (Quit) to allow the user to end the program.

A sketch of this window (that the program designer might draw) and the actual window are shown in Figures 7 and 8, respectively. Here is the pseudocode for this window's option buttons and command buttons:

FIGURE 7

A Sketch of the Initial Window

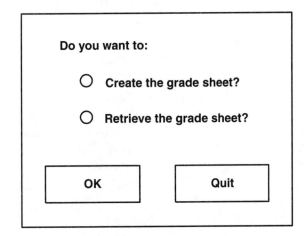

FIGURE 8

The Actual Initial Window

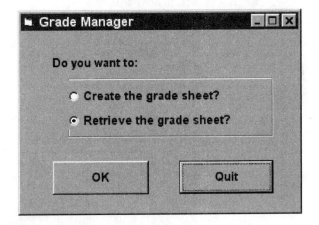

```
Top option button:
     Name = Option1
     Caption = "Create the grade sheet?"
     Value = False  [no bullet]
     Subprogram Option1.Click()
          Set Option1.Value = True
          Set Option2.Value = False
     End Subprogram
```

Bottom option button:
    Name = Option2
    Caption = "Retrieve the grade sheet?"
    Value = True [*bullet*]
    Subprogram Option2.Click()
        Set Option1.Value = False
        Set Option2.Value = True
        End Subprogram

Left command button:
    Name = OKbutton
    Caption = "OK"
    Subprogram OKbutton.Click()
        Set InitialWindow.Visible = False
        If Option1.Value = True Then
            Call Create.Open
        Else
            Call Retrieve.Open
        End If
        End Subprogram

Right command button:
    Name = QuitButton
    Caption = "Quit"
    Subprogram QuitButton.Click()
        End Program
        End Subprogram

Create Grade Sheet Window

The window components are shown in Figure 9. The pseudocode needed to implement this window involves:

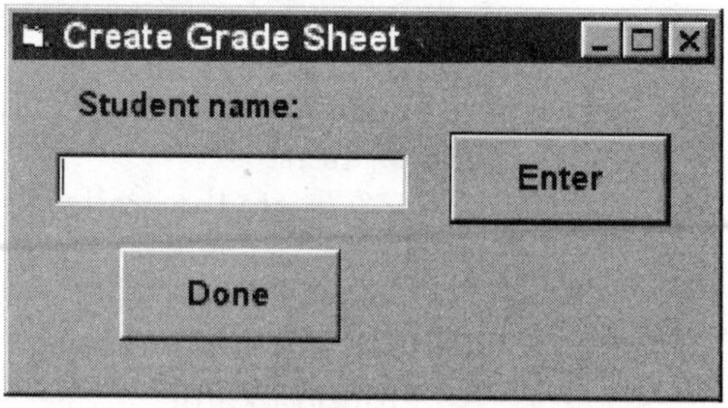

FIGURE 9

The *Create Grade Sheet* Window

1. Opening a file (for Output) to hold the required information—name, test scores, and test average—for each student in the class. Thus, this file must have records of the form:

   student name, test 1 score, test 2 score, test 3 score, average

2. Inputting the student names from the user.

3. Writing the names to the file and, at the same time, initializing all test scores and averages in the file to 0.

4. Closing the file.

The pseudocode for opening the file is housed in this window's StartUp method. This method also initializes a counter, StudentCount, that will hold the number of students in the class for use by several other subprograms. If the current window has the Name attribute Create, then the pseudocode for StartUp is:

```
Subprogram Create.StartUp()
      Open "GRADES" For Output As GradeFile
      Set StudentCount = 0
      End Subprogram
```

To input a student name, the user types it in the text box and clicks the Enter command button. Thus, all the code to input names and write the corresponding file records can be housed in the Enter command button's Click method. (In this pseudocode, we assume that the Name attribute of the text box is InputBox.) This method also increments the counter StudentCount that was initialized in the window's StartUp method.

```
Subprogram Enter.Click()
      Write GradeFile, InputBox.Text, 0, 0, 0, 0
      Set StudentCount = StudentCount + 1
      Set InputBox.Text = ""
      End Subprogram
```

Finally, the file is closed when the user clicks the Done button, which also closes the Create Grade Sheet window and reactivates (makes visible) the initial window.

```
Subprogram Done.Click()
      Close GradeFile
      Call Create.Close
      Set InitialWindow.Visible = True
      End Subprogram
```

Retrieve Grade Sheet window

This window and its methods have several functions:

1. When the window is opened, its StartUp method opens the file GRADES for Input and loads it into three parallel arrays—two one-dimensional arrays to hold the student names (Names) and test averages (Averages) and a two-dimensional array (Scores) to hold the scores on the three tests (see Section 7.5).

2. The window allows the user to choose one of three options—display the grade sheet, enter test scores, or compute test averages.

3. The window allows the user to elect to exit the program, and then copies the arrays back to the GRADES file (see Section 7.5), closes this file, and halts execution.

To implement these actions, we use

- A label object at the top displaying the text "Select an option and click OK."

- Three option buttons with captions "Display the grade sheet," "Enter test scores," and "Compute test averages."

- Two command buttons at the bottom: One labeled OK, which transfers execution to the proper window; the other labeled Exit Program, which closes the GRADES file and halts execution.

We leave the sketch of this window and the pseudocode for its components as an exercise (see Self- Test 9.5).

Display Grade Sheet Window

When opened, this window displays the contents of the grade sheet (the Names, Scores, and Averages arrays) in the window itself. (The code to do this is located in the window's StartUp method.) It also contains a single command button (labeled OK) that closes this window and reactivates the Retrieve Grade Sheet window.

Select Test Window

The Select Test window (with Name = SelectTest) allows the user to specify, by clicking the appropriate option button, whether he or she wants to enter scores for test 1, test 2, or test 3 into the Scores array. This window also contains OK and Cancel command buttons. Clicking the OK button records the user's selection, closes the window, and opens the Enter Test Scores window. Clicking the Cancel button closes the window and reactivates the Retrieve Grade Sheet window. The pseudocode for this window is:

Top option button:
    Name = Option1
    Caption = "Enter scores for test 1"
    Value = False
    Subprogram Option1.Click()
        Set Option1.Value = True
        Set Option2.Value = False
        Set Option3.Value = False
        End Subprogram

Middle option button:
    Name = Option2
    Caption = "Enter scores for test 2"
    Value = False
    Subprogram Option2.Click()
        Set Option1.Value = False
        Set Option2.Value = True
        Set Option3.Value = False
        End Subprogram

Bottom option button:
    Name = Option3
    Caption = "Enter scores for test 3"
    Value = False
    Subprogram Option3.Click()
        Set Option1.Value = False
        Set Option2.Value = False
        Set Option3.Value = True
        End Subprogram

Left command button:
    Name = OKbutton
    Caption = "OK"
    Subprogram OKbutton.Click()
        If Option1.Value = True Then
            Set TestNum = 1
        End If
        If Option2.Value = True Then
            Set TestNum = 2
        End If

```
                    If Option3.Value = True Then
                         Set TestNum = 3
                    End If
                    Call EnterScores.Open
                    Call SelectTest.Close
                    End Subprogram

          Right command button:
                Name = CancelButton
                Caption = "Cancel"
                Subprogram CancelButton.Click()
                    Set Retrieve.Visible = True
                    Call SelectTest.Close
                    End Subprogram
```

Enter Test Scores Window

The Enter Test Scores window contains two text boxes and a command button. The student names are displayed, one by one, in the upper text box. After each name is displayed, the user types the corresponding score in the lower text box and clicks the Enter button. When all student scores have been entered, this window closes automatically and the Retrieve Grade Sheet window is displayed. (The Enter Test Scores window is shown in the Programming Problems section at the end of this chapter. In that section, you are asked to create a program that inputs test scores.)

Compute Test Averages Window

When the "Compute test averages" option in the Retrieve Grade Sheet window is activated (by clicking the OK button in that window after this option button has been selected), the average score for each student is calculated and written to the Averages array. This pseudocode (which you are asked to provide in Self-Test 9.5) is located in the Compute Test Averages StartUp method. The window itself is very simple—it consists of the message (label) "Average test scores have been computed!" and a single command button labeled OK. When the latter is clicked, the window closes and the Retrieve Grade Sheet window is reactivated.

Program Code   The program code is now written using the design as a guide. Even though this is not a procedural (top-down) program, it still needs documentation (see Section 2.3). Header comments are used to help explain the general purpose of the program, each window, and the more complicated subprograms; step comments are used to explain the purpose of certain variables, properties, and statements. Here are a couple of other points concerning the coding of this program:

- Keep in mind that some languages, although providing built-in class definitions for GUI objects, require you to write code that creates these objects and adds them to the appropriate window. You may also have to, in code, specify an object's position, size, and many other attributes not mentioned in the pseudocode in this text.

- To display the contents of the GRADES file in a neat, readable fashion, the output produced in the Display Grade Sheet window must be *formatted*—the names, test scores, and averages should line up in columns. This can be accomplished using the programming language's special print formatting statements.

Program Test   This program is tested in a way similar to that of its top-down counterpart in Section 7.5: Imagine that you are the instructor of a very small class (say, three students), and use the program to create the grade sheet, enter scores for each of the three tests, and compute the test averages. After performing each of these tasks, display the grade sheet to check that the operation has been executed successively. Moreover, as you perform the testing, examine each window and ask yourself if it could be improved in any way: Could it look better? Could it be made more intuitive? Could it be simplified?

Self-Test 9.5

These exercises refer to the Grade Management Program developed in this section.

1. Draw a sketch of the Retrieve Grade Sheet window.

2. Suppose that the (internal) name for the Retrieve Grade Sheet window is Retrieve, that the names of its option buttons are Option1, Option2, and Option3, and that the name of its "OK" command button is OKbutton.

    a. Write a Click procedure for Option1 that causes it to acquire the bullet (and causes the other two option buttons to be bullet-less).

    b. Write a Click procedure for OKbutton that "hides" the Retrieve Grade Sheet window and opens the window named Display,

SelectTest, or ComputeAverages, depending on the state of the option buttons.

3. The StartUp procedure for the ComputeAverages window uses the data in the Scores array to calculate the average test score for each student, and writes this data to the Averages array. Write a subprogram called ComputeAverages.StartUp that does this. Recall that

- The variable StudentCount holds the number of students in the class.

- The array Scores has entries of the form Scores[*testnum, studentnum*]; for example, Scores[2, 15] holds the score of student 15 on test 2.

Chapter Review and Exercises

Key Terms

Object	Derived class
Object-oriented programming	Graphical user interface
OOP	GUI
Class (of objects)	Window
Attributes (of an object)	Window component
Methods (for a class)	Command button
Public member	Check box
Private member	Text box
Message (to a method)	Option button
Constructor	Drop-down list box
Procedural programming	List box
Encapsulation	Label
Inheritance	Event
Polymorphism	Event-driven program
Base class	

Chapter Summary

In this chapter, we have discussed the following topics:

1. Classes and objects:

- A class is a data type that defines a structure consisting of attributes (data) and methods (procedures). We use a Class ... End Class statement to define a class.

- An object is an instance of a class. We use a Declare statement to create an object.

2. Characteristics of an object-oriented programming language:

- Encapsulation—the combining of data and operations on that data into a single package.
- Inheritance—the ability to create a subclass (derived class) that automatically contains the attributes and methods of its (base) class.
- Polymorphism—the ability of a method to work with objects of different classes.

3. Object-oriented program design; in analyzing the problem:

- Identify the classes to be used in the program.
- Determine the attributes needed for these classes.
- Determine the methods needed for these classes.
- Determine the relationships among the classes.

4. Objects in a graphical user interface include:

- Windows—to act as containers for other objects
- Command buttons—to initiate actions
- Check boxes—to allow the user to select or deselect a single option
- Text boxes—to receive input or display output
- Option buttons—to allow the user to select from among several options
- List boxes—to allow the user to select an item from a list

5. A GUI object has:

- Properties (attributes) that include its name, its caption or text, its value, whether or not it is enabled (active or inactive), the font of its text, and so on.
- Methods that include responding to a click and other events, depending on the particular object.

6. Event-driven programs:

- Respond to user or system events (actions).
- Are designed in a manner similar to an OOP program, but put the emphasis on the windows, rather than on the general objects, needed to solve the given problem.

Review Exercises

1. Fill in the blank: A(n) _____ is a data type comprised of attributes and methods.

2. Fill in the blank: A(n) _____ is an instance of a class.

3. True or false: The attributes of an object include the name of the class to which it belongs.

4. True or false: The methods of an object are the operations that can be performed on that object's data.

5. True or false: Attributes are also known as subprograms, procedures, or functions.

6. True or false: Methods are also known as services or behaviors.

Exercises 7–10 refer to the following pseudocode, which defines a class called Square.

```
Class Square
    Side As Real
    Area As Real
    Subprogram SetSide(NewSide)
        Set Side = NewSide
        End Subprogram
    Subprogram ComputeArea()
        Set Area = Side ^ 2
        End Subprogram
    Function GetArea() As Real
        Set GetArea = Area
        End Function
    Function GetSide() As Real
        Set GetSide = Side
        End Function
End Class
```

7. List the attributes of the class Square.

8. Give the names of the methods of the class Square.

9. Fill in the blank: To specify that the variable Side may not be referenced from outside this class, place the keyword _____ in front of it (in the first line of the class definition).

10. Fill in the blank: To specify that Subprogram SetSide may be called from outside this class, place the keyword _____ in front of it (in the third line of the class definition).

In Exercises 11–14, write a (main program) statement that uses the class Square (defined above Exercise 7) to perform the indicated operation.

11. Create an object Square1 in the class Square.

12. Set the length of the side of Square1 equal to 20.

13. Compute the area of Square1.

14. Display the area of Square1.

15. Fill in the blank: The property of OOP that refers to the incorporation of data and operations into a single unit is called _____.

16. Fill in the blank: The property of OOP that allows the creation of new classes based on existing ones is called _____.

17. Fill in the blank: The property of OOP that allows a method to be applied to objects of different classes is called _____.

18. Fill in the blank: When a subclass is created based on an existing class, the original class is called the _____; the new class is called the _____.

Exercises 19–22 refer to the following pseudocode, which uses the class Square defined above Exercise 7.

```
Class Rectangle As Square
      Height As Real
      Subprogram SetHeight(NewHeight)
            Set Height = NewHeight
            End Subprogram
      Function GetHeight() As Real
            Set GetHeight = Height
            End Function
      Subprogram ComputeArea()
            Set Area = Side * Height
            End Subprogram
End Class
```

19. List *all* attributes of an object in the class Rectangle.

20. List the names of *all* methods for an object of the class Rectangle.

21. Suppose Square1 is an object in the class Square and the statement

    Call Square1.ComputeArea

    appears in the main program. Which formula for area is used in the execution of the subprogram ComputeArea?

    a. Area = Side ^ 2
    b. Area = Side * Height
    c. Neither of these formulas is used.

22. Suppose Rectangle1 is an object in the class Rectangle and the statement

    Call Rectangle1.ComputeArea

    appears in the main program. Which formula for area is used in the execution of the subprogram ComputeArea?

    a. Area = Side ^ 2
    b. Area = Side * Height
    c. Neither of these formulas is used.

23. True or false: When contrasted to OOP, the approach to programming that uses top-down, modular program design is called procedural programming.

24. True or false: In designing an object-oriented program, the emphasis is placed on the procedures, rather than on the objects, needed to solve a given problem.

25. For the window shown in Figure 10, give the captions (labels) for its

    a. Command buttons
    b. Option buttons

FIGURE 10

The Window for Exercises 25–28

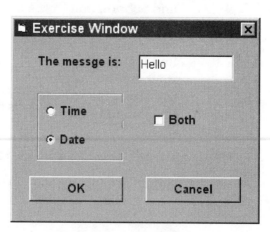

26. For the window shown in Figure 10, give the text appearing in its
    a. Text boxes
    b. Label objects

27. In the window shown in Figure 10, is the check box selected or clear?

28. In the window shown in Figure 10, which option button is selected?

29. Which of the following GUI objects is most commonly used to allow the user to initiate an action?
    a. Check box
    b. Command button
    c. Option button
    d. Text box

30. Which of the following GUI objects is most commonly used to receive input from the user?
    a. Check box
    b. Command button
    c. Option button
    d. Text box

31. Which of the following GUI objects is most commonly used to allow the user to select or deselect a single option?
    a. Check box
    b. Command button
    c. Option button
    d. Text box

32. Which of the following GUI objects is most commonly used to allow the user to make one choice from a group of choices?
    a. Check box
    b. Command button
    c. Option button
    d. Text box

33. True or false: The attributes of objects that make up a GUI are also called properties.

34. True or false: All window components have the same attributes.

35. List three properties of a window.

36. List three properties common to command buttons, option buttons, and text boxes.

37. True or false: From a programming point of view, when you click a command button, it is an event.

38. True or false: An event-driven program must make use of the mouse.

39. True or false: Command buttons, option buttons, and text boxes all have Click events associated with them.

40. True or false: The programming language supplies the code for the action that takes place when the user clicks a command button.

41. Write a subprogram called Abutton.Click that sets the text in the text box named Text1 equal to "Hello" and grays out the command button named Bbutton.

42. Write a subprogram called OKbutton.Click that opens a window named Window1 or a window named Window2, depending on whether option buttons named Option1 or Option2, respectively, contain a bullet.

43. Write a subprogram called Option1.Click that places a bullet in an option button named Option1 and removes the bullet from an option button named Option2.

44. Write a subprogram called EnterButton.Click that adds the number in a text box named NumberBox to a variable Sum and then clears the text box.

Programming Problems

For Problems A and B, use pseudocode to write an object-oriented program consisting of a class definition and a main program (like those in Sections 9.1 and 9.2) to solve the given problem.

A. Write a program that inputs (from the user) the number of hours worked and hourly pay rate for employees and outputs their total pay. The program should process an arbitrary number of employees; the user will terminate input by entering 0 for both hours worked and rate of pay. Use a class called Worker with

- Attributes: Hours, Rate, Total
- Methods: ComputeTotal (and access methods for each of the attributes)

B. Write a program that displays the income tax due (in a certain state) on a taxable income entered by the user, according to the following table:

TAXABLE INCOME		TAX DUE	
From	To		
$0	$50,000	$0 + 5%	of amount over $0
$50,000	$100,000	$2,500 + 7%	of amount over $50,000
$100,000	. . . .	$6,000 + 9%	of amount over $100,000

The program should allow the user to enter a series of incomes, terminated by 0. Use a class called Tax, with attributes Income and TaxDue and methods that include ComputeTax.

In Problems C–F, use pseudocode to write an event-driven program (like those in Sections 9.3–9.5) according to the given specifications. If a picture of a window is not shown, sketch it before writing the pseudocode.

C. Write a program for an interface that consists of a single window entitled Greeting, containing an unlabeled text box and two command buttons (Respond and Done). When the program starts, the text box contains the word *Hello*. If the user clicks the Respond button, the word changes to *Goodbye*. When the user clicks the Done button, the program terminates.

D. Using the window shown in Figure 11, write a temperature conversion program. To use this program, the user selects an option, types a temperature into the appropriate text box, and clicks the Convert command button. The corresponding temperature then appears in the other text box. Clicking on the Done button ends the program. *Hint:* Use the formulas:

$C = 5 * (F = 32) / 9$ to convert from Fahrenheit to Celsius;
$F = 9 * C / 5 + 32$ to convert from Celsius to Fahrenheit.

FIGURE 11
The Window for Problem D

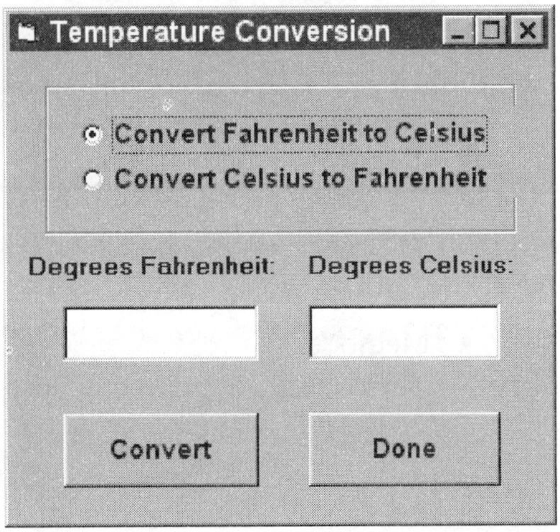

E. Write a program that displays the names of the students in a certain class, one by one, and allows the user to enter a test score for that student. The student names and scores are contained in one-dimensional arrays called Names and Scores, respectively. Assume that both arrays have already been declared and that the Names array contains N entries.

The window for this program is shown in Figure 12. When the program starts, the first student name is displayed in the upper text box. The user types the test score for that student in the lower text box and clicks the Enter button. This action assigns that number to the first element of the array Scores, displays the next name in the upper text box, and empties the lower text box so that the next score can be entered. When all student scores have been entered (and assigned to the corresponding elements of Scores), the window closes automatically and the program terminates.

F. Write a program that searches a sequential file called CUSTOMER, with records of the form

name (string), phone number (string)

for a specified name and then displays the corresponding phone number. The interface consists of a window entitled "Customer Phone Numbers" that contains two text boxes (an upper one labeled "Customer name:" and a lower one labeled "Phone number:") and three command buttons (labeled Find, Clear, and Done).

The CUSTOMER file is opened in the window's StartUp method. To use this program, the user types the customer name into the upper text box, clicks on the Find command button, and

• If the name is found in the file, the corresponding phone number appears in the lower text box.

- If the name is not found, the lower text box displays "Name not found."

Clicking the Clear button removes the text in the upper and lower text boxes. Clicking the Done button closes the file and terminates the program.

Answers to Self-Tests

Chapter 1

Self-Test 1.1

1. a. High speed, stores a large amount of data, and programmable
   b. High speed and stores a large amount of data

2. a. program   b. ENIAC
   c. supercomputers   d. Internet

3. a. true   b. true   c. false   d. true

4. Babbage—Analytical Engine; Eckert—ENIAC; Jobs—Apple II

Self-Test 1.2

1. CPU, internal memory, mass storage devices, input devices, output devices

2. a. It executes logical and arithmetic operations and controls the operation of the other components.
   b. They store all data and programs to be used on the computer.

3. a. true   b. false   c. true   d. false

4. a. Keyboard, mouse (also microphone, joystick, track ball, etc.)
   b. Monitor, printer, speakers, etc.

5. Advantages—faster, better output, lower cost of operation
   Disadvantages—higher price, especially for color

Self-Test 1.3

1. Applications software refers to the programs used by people for education, entertainment, and business purposes; system software are programs used to run the computer and manage its resources.

2. See the list on page 14.

3. High-level, assembly, and machine languages

4. Assembly language provides more control over, and more efficient use of, computer resources.

5. FORTRAN; developed in the mid-1950s.

6. Over time, languages have been created to perform general or certain specific programming tasks better than their predecessors.

Self-Test 1.4

1. Input, processing, and output

2. Write "Enter a temperature in degrees Fahrenheit:"
   Input F

3. a. The input data are: Amount invested, rate of interest, length of time
   b. InitialAmount, Rate, Term

4. All variables are of numeric type.

Self-Test 1.5

1. 35 degrees Celsius

2. a. 12   b. 11   c. 12

3. 7

4. a. Write "The price of the item is ", DollarPrice, " dollars"
   b. Write "The price in pounds is ", PoundPrice
      Write "The price in dollars is ", DollarPrice

5. Write "Enter a temperature in degrees Fahrenheit:"
   Input F
   Set C = 5 * (F − 32) / 9

Write "Temperature in degrees Fahrenheit: ", F
Write "Temperature in degrees Celsius: ", C

Chapter 2

Self-Test 2.1

1. Analysis, design, coding, testing

2. *Analysis*—understand the problem; identify the output and input, and determine how to get from the given input to the desired output.

   Design—create a language-independent outline of the program-to-be.

   Coding—create the program code in a particular programming language.

   Testing—run the program to ensure that it works correctly; correct errors if it doesn't.

3.   a. false   b. true   c. false

4. Input variable: C; output variable: F;
    Formula: F = 9 * C / 5 + 32

Self-Test 2.2

1. See the list on page 41.

2. See the list on page 42.

3. Write " Compound Interest Calculations"
   Write
   Write "Investment principal (in dollars): ", Principal
   Write "Rate of interest (in percent): ", PercentageRate
   Write "Term of investment (in years): ", Term
   Write "Number of times per year compounded: ", Frequency
   Write
   Write "Value of investment at maturity: ", FinalValue

4.   a. The first statement of the Cancer Cure module
     b. The Write statement

5. See Figure 1 (on the next page).

FIGURE 1

Hierarchy
Chart for
Self-Test 2.2
Problem 5

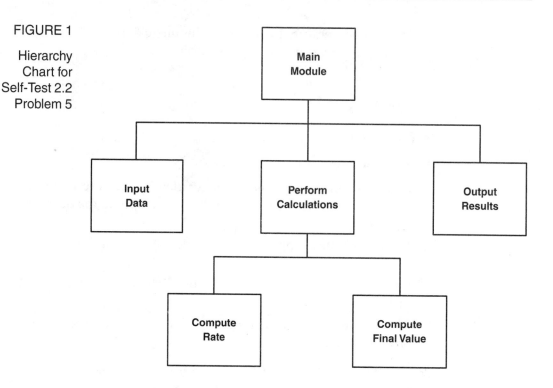

Self-Test 2.3

1. Header comments appear at the beginning of a program or program module, and give general information; step comments appear with, and explain, specific portions of code.

2. External documentation is help for the *user* of the program in the form of a user guide or on-screen help.

3. tested (or run)

4. A syntax error violates the programming language's rules for statement structure; a logic error results from program code that does not achieve its intended purpose.

Self-Test 2.4

1. Follow the steps of the program development cycle; design the program in a top-down modular fashion; use the appropriate control structures in the proper way; use good programming style (among others).

2. a. Process: b. Decision: c. Input/output:

3. Sequential, loop (repetition), and selection (decision)

4. Good programming style makes the program code easier to understand and the program itself easier to use.

5. See the list on page 56.

Self-Test 2.5

1. graphical user interface

2. In an event-driven program, the actions of the user (such as pressing a key or clicking the mouse) determine the flow of execution.

3. See the list on pages 58 and 59.

4. Its attributes (data) and methods (procedures)

5. For example, a door has attributes such as height, width, number of hinges, and whether or not it can be locked; its methods include opening it, closing it, and locking it.

Chapter 3

Self-Test 3.1

1. a. 2   b. 2
       4   4

2. a. true   b. false   c. false   d. true   e. false   f. true

3. a. false   b. true   c. true

4. See page 77.

5. Insert Input Number after Write Number

Self-Test 3.2

1. a. 3 3   b. 10
       3 4   8
       3 5

2. a. No output

   b. Hooray
      Hooray
      Hooray

3. For Count = 1 Step 1 To 3
     Write 10 * Count
  End For

4. For Num = 1 Step 1 To 10
     Input Response
     Write Response
  End For

Self-Test 3.3

1. Repeat
     Write "Enter a character; enter * to quit."
     Input Char
  Until Char = "*"

2.   a. Prompt for and input Num
      While Num <= 100
        Prompt for and input Num
      End While

   b. Repeat
        Prompt for and input Num
      Until Num > 100

3. Set Sum = 0
  For K = 1 Step 1 To 100
     Set Sum = Sum + K
  End For

4. Add the following statement after End For:
     Set Average = Sum / 100

Self-Test 3.4

1. 2 2   2. 1
    2 3   1
    3 2   1
    3 3   7
    4 2   7
    4 3   7

3. See Figure 2.

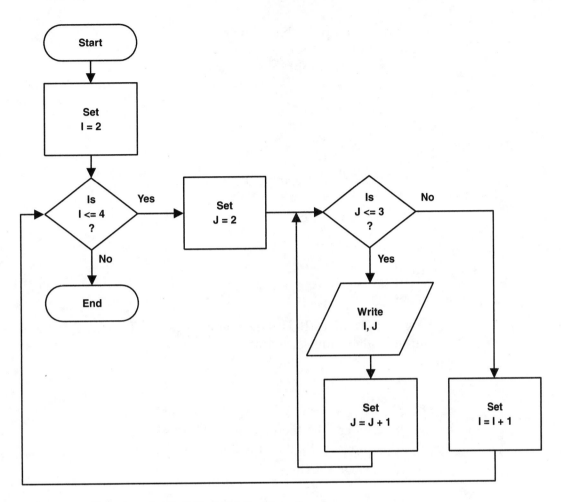

FIGURE 2   Flowchart for Self-Test 3.4 Problem 3

4. Repeat
        Repeat
            Input X
        Until X > 0
    Until X < 10

Self-Test 3.5

1. a. Cost = 100,000, Revenue = 0, Profit = –100,000
    b. Cost = 110,800, Revenue = 9000, Profit = –101,800

2. a. Spacing = 1000; X = 0, 1000
    b. Spacing = 10; X = 0, 10, 20, ..., 100

3. Input and prompt for NumRows
    While NumRows <= 1
        Input and prompt for NumRows
    End While

4. Set X = 0
    While X <= MaxX
        Set Cost = 100000 + 12 * X
        • • •
        Write X, Cost, Revenue, Profit
        Set X = X + Spacing
    End While

Chapter 4

Self-Test 4.1

1. Single-alternative (If-Then), dual-alternative (If-Then-Else), and multiple-alternative structures

2. a. 5   b. -1
        5

3. a. 5   b. 1

4. a. If Number = 10, then the output is: Yes
        If Number = –10, then the output is: No

    b. If Number > 0 Then
            Write "Yes"
        Else
            Write "No"
        End If

Self-Test 4.2

1. a. relational   b. arithmetic   c. logical

2. a. true   b. false   c. true   d. false

3. a. true   b. false   c. false   d. false

4. Input Num
    If Not ((Num > 0) And (Num < 100)) Then
        Write "Correct"
    End If

Self-Test 4.3

1. If X = 0 Then
        Write "Low"
    End If
    If (X = 1) Or (X = 2) Then
        Write "Medium"
    End If
    If (X >= 3) And (X <= 10) Then
        Write "High"
    End If

2. If X = 0 Then
        Write "Low"
    Else
        If (X = 1) Or (X = 2) Then
            Write "Medium"
        Else
            Write "High"
        End If
    End If

3. Select Case Of X
        Case 0:
            Write "Low"
        Case 1, 2:
            Write "Medium"
        Case 3-10:
            Write "High"
    End Case

4. If (Choice = "y") Or (Choice = "Y") Then
        Call YesAction module
    Else
        If (Choice = "n") Or (Choice = "N") Then
            Call NoAction module
        Else
            Write "Signing off"
            Write "Goodby"
        End If
    End If

Self-Test 4.4

1. a. 2 b. 3

2. If (A >= 0) And (B <> 0) Then
        Set C = Sqrt(A) / B
    Else
        Write "A must be nonnegative and B cannot be 0"
    End If

3. a. R = 1

    b. If R <> 1 Then
            Set S = (1 – R)^N / (1 – R)
        Else
            Write "S cannot be found because R = 1"
        End If

4. a. true b. true

5. Write "   Menu"
    Write
    Write "1 - Order hamburger"
    Write "2 - Order hotdog"
    Write "3 - Order tuna salad"
    Write "   Selection: "
    Input Choice

Self-Test 4.5

1. For the Compute Engine Cost module:
        If EngineChoice = "S" Then
            Set EngineCost = 150
        End If
        If EngineChoice = "E" Then
            Set EngineCost = 425
        End If
        If EngineChoice = "D" Then
            Set EngineCost = 750
        End If

2. In the main module, replace the Write and Input statements by:
        Call Compute Base Price
    Compute Base Price module
        Write "Enter the model: X, Y, or Z:"

```
Input ModelChoice
If ModelChoice = "X" Then
        Set BasePrice = 20000
End If
If ModelChoice = "Y" Then
        Set BasePrice = 25000
End If
If ModelChoice = "Z" Then
        Set BasePrice = 28000
End If
```

Chapter 5

Self-Test 5.1

1. a. 2   b. 1

2. a. –34500   b. .0000123

3. a. 1, 2, 3, 4   b. 4, 5

4. For K = 1 Step 1 To 100
        Set Num = Random(11) + 9
        Write Num
    End For

Self-Test 5.2

1. a. true   b. true   c. false

2. a. false   b. false

3. a. true   b. false

4. Input Name1, Name2
    If Name1 <= Name2 Then
        Write Name1
    Else
        Write Name2
    End If

5. Step-by-Step

Self-Test 5.3

1. a. A text file is one that consists solely of ASCII symbols.

   b. Its simplicity—it is easier to create and can be read by virtually any computer system.

2. In a sequential file, the records must be read in the order in which they were created; in a direct access file, any record can be read independently of the others.

3. Open "EMPLOYEE" For Input As DataFile
   While Not EOF(DataFile)
      Read DataFile, Name
      Write Name
   End While
   Close DataFile

4. Open "EMPLOYEE" For Output As DataFile
   Write "Enter name; enter * when done."
   Input Name
   While Name <> "*"
      Write DataFile, Name
      Write "Enter name:"
      Input Name
   End While
   Close DataFile

Self-Test 5.4

1. Open "PAYROLL" For Input As DataFile
   Open "SCRATCH" For Output As TempFile
   While Not EOF(DataFile)
      Read DataFile, Number, Name, Rate
      If Number <> 138 Then
         Write TempFile, Number, Name, Rate
      End If
   End While
   Close DataFile, TempFile
   Copy SCRATCH onto PAYROLL

2. Open "PAYROLL" For Input As DataFile
   Open "SCRATCH" For Output As TempFile
   While Not EOF(DataFile)
      Read DataFile, Number, Name, Rate
      If Number = 456 Then
         Write TempFile, Number, Name, 7.89
      Else

          Write TempFile, Number, Name, Rate
      End If
End While
Close DataFile, TempFile
Copy SCRATCH onto PAYROLL

3. Open "PAYROLL" For Input As DataFile
Open "SCRATCH" For Output As TempFile
Read DataFile, Number, Name, Rate
While (Not EOF(DataFile)) And (Number < 167)
      Write TempFile, Number, Name, Rate
      Read DataFile, Number, Name, Rate
End While
If Number > 167 Then
      Write TempFile, 167, "C.Jones", 8.50
      Write TempFile, Number, Name, Rate
Else
      Write TempFile, Number, Name, Rate
      Write TempFile, 167, "C.Jones", 8.50
End If
While Not EOF(DataFile)
      Read DataFile, Number, Name, Rate
      Write TempFile, Number, Name, Rate
End While
Close DataFile, TempFile
Copy SCRATCH onto PAYROLL

Self-Test 5.5

1. Insert, at the beginning of the module:

      Write "Enter month and year of sales report,"
      Write "separated by commas."
      Input Month, Year

2. Insert, after the third Write statement:

      Write Month, " ", Year
      Write

3. The first value is 1, the last value is 3.

4. None

Chapter 6

Self-Test 6.1

1. 10
    1
    2

2. F
    O
    O

3. The first statement should be

    Declare X[100]

4. Declare Numbers[20]
    For K = 1 Step 1 To 20
        Input Numbers[K]
    End For
    For K = 20 Step -1 To 1
        Write Numbers[K]
    End For

5. Arrays can reduce the number of variable names used, eliminate
    the need to reenter data, and create more general and more effi-
    cient programs.

Self-Test 6.2

1. c

2. Declare Client[100]
    Set Found = 0
    For K = 1 Step 1 To 100
        If Client[K] = "Smith" Then
            Set Found = 1
        End If
    End For
    If Found = 1 Then
        Write "FOUND"
    Else
        Write "NOT FOUND"
    End If

3. Three interchanges

4. Declare Client[100]
    Set Sorted = 0
    While Sorted = 0
        Set Sorted = 1

```
        For K = 1 Step 1 To 99
            If Client[K] > Client[K + 1] Then
                Interchange Client[K] and Client[K + 1]
                Set Sorted = 0
            End If
        End For
    End While
```

Self-Test 6.3

1. a. false
    b. false

2. Set FirstChar = Name[1]
    Set LastChar = Name[Length(Name)]

3. Declare String1[25] Of Characters
    Declare String2[25] Of Characters
    Input String1
    For K = 1 Step 1 To Length(String1)
        Set String2[K] = String1[K]
    End For

4. Declare Numbers[100], Names[100], Rates[100]
    Open "PAYROLL" For Input As DataFile
    Set Count = 0
    While Not EOF(DataFile)
        Set Count = Count + 1
        Read DataFile, Numbers[Count], Names[Count],
            Rates[Count]
    End While
    Close DataFile
    Open "PAYROLL" For Output As DataFile
    For K = 1 Step 1 To Count
        If Numbers[K] = 456 Then
            Set Rates[K] = 7.89
        End If
        If Numbers[K] <> 138 Then
            Write DataFile, Numbers[K], Names[K], Rates[K]
        End If
    End For
    Close DataFile

Self-Test 6.4

1. a. 50   b. 110

2. a. Fog[1, 2] = 10, Fog[2, 3] = 35
    b. Fog[1, 3] = 15, Fog[2, 1] = 25

3. 3 3 4

4. 60

5. Set Max = 0
    For Row = 1 Step 1 To 3
        For Col = 1 Step 1 To 5
            If X[Row, Col] > Max Then
                Set Max = X[Row, Col]
            End If
        End For (Col)
    End For (Row)

Self-Test 6.5

1. The invoice will contain a title, the customer's name, column headings, and the amount due will be 0, but no parts will be listed.

2. All the statements in the While loop will remain the same, but they are preceded by

        If Num <> 0 Then
            Repeat
    and followed by

            Until Num = 0
        End If

3. *Welcome Message* module:

        Write "THE LEGENDARY LAWNMOWER COMPANY"
        Write "   Invoice Preparer"
        Write
        Write "This program prepares an invoice for lawnmower"
        Write "parts ordered by a customer. The customer's name"
        Write "and the part numbers are input from the keyboard;"
        Write "the price data are input from the file PRICELIST."

    To implement this module, in the Main Module, replace the statement

> Display a welcome message

by the statement

> Call Welcome Message module

Chapter 7

Self-Test 7.1

1. See Figure 3.

2. Main Program
   > Write "Enter a name:"
   > Input Name
   > Call DisplayName(Name)
   > Call DisplayName(Name)
   > Call DisplayName(Name)
   > End Program
   Subprogram DisplayName(Name)
   > Write Name
   > End Subprogram

3. 213

4. a. Replace Num1, Num2, and Num3 in the Write statement by, respectively, B, C, and A.

   b. No changes need be made.

FIGURE 3

Data Flow Diagram for Exercise 1

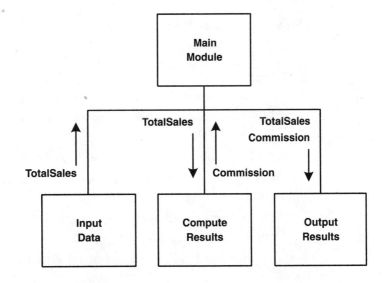

Self-Test 7.2

1. 321
    456
    623

2. 321
    456
    623

3. a. 321   b. 321
        456   456
        123   654

4. X, Y, and Z are global variables. There are no (declared) local variables.

5. a. 1   b. 0

Self-Test 7.3

1. a. 2   b. 3

2. a. 0   b. 4   c. "0.1"   d. –32

3. 7
    1

4. a. Function A(L,W) As Real
            Set A = L * W
            End Function

    b. Set Area = A(5, 10)

Self-Test 7.4

1. N! = (N – 1)! * N

2. Function Factorial(N) As Integer
            If N = 1 Then
                    Set Factorial = 1
            Else
                    Set Factorial = Factorial(N – 1) * N
            End If
            End Function

3. When N = 3, the function Factorial is called three times:

    • On the first call, we get Factorial(2) * 3, and Factorial is called again.

    • On the second call, we get Factorial(1) * 2, and Factorial is called again.

    • On the third call, Factorial is set equal to 1, completing this call, giving a value for Factorial in the second call of 1 * 2 = 2, and finally giving a value of Factorial in the first call of 2 * 3 = 6.

Thus, the value 6 is assigned to Answer.

4. Function Fac(N) As Integer
    Set Product = 1
    For K = 1 Step 1 To N
        Set Product = Product * K
    End For
    Set Fac = Product
    End Function

Self-Test 7.5

1. a. The arrays Names, Scores, and Averages, and the variable Count must be imported to this subprogram; no data are exported.

   b. Subprogram DisplayStudentRecord(Count, Names,
        Scores, Averages)
     Write "Enter a student's name:"
     Input Name
     Set Found = 0
     Set K = 0
     While (Found = 0) And (K < Count)
        Set K = K + 1
        If Name = Names[K] Then
           Set Found = 1
           Write Names[K], Scores[1, K], Scores[2, K],
             Scores[3, K], Averages[K]
        End If
     End While
     If Found = 0 Then
        Write Name, " not found."
     End If
     End Subprogram

2. a. The arrays Names, Scores, and Averages and the variable Count must be imported by this subprogram. The arrays Scores and Averages are exported from it.

   b. Subprogram ChangeTestScore(Count, Names, Scores As Ref,
        Averages As Ref)

Chapter 8

Self-Test 8.1

1. a

2. Just interchange the two lines:
        If Key > Array[Index] Then
        If Key < Array[Index] Then

3. d

4. Replace Min by Max wherever it appears and replace
        If Array[J] < Min Then
   by If Array[J] > Max Then

Self-Test 8.2

1. false   2. true   3. true

4. Just replace the statement
        If MasterArray[I] <= UpdateArray[J] Then
   by If MasterArray[I] >= UpdateArray[J] Then

Self-Test 8.3

1. Advantage: Records in a direct access file can be accessed more quickly.

   Disadvantage: A direct access file is not a text file; it cannot be created or displayed in a text editor.

2. d

3. Record Type PartInfo
        Number As Integer
        Name As String[12]
        Price As Real
        Quantity As Integer
   End Record
   Declare Part As PartInfo
   Open "INVLIST" For Random As PartFile, Len = Length(Part)

4. Set Part.Number = 123
   Set Part.Name = "Handle"
   Set Part.Price = 5.69
   Set Part.Quantity = 21
   SeekPut PartFile, 3, Part

5. SeekGet PartFile, 5, Part
   Write Part.Number, Part.Name, Part.Price, Part.Quantity

Self-Test 8.4

1. With indexed files, we use a key item to locate desired information; the record number for that information need not be known.

2. Write LOF(DataFile) / Length(Worker)

3. Set Last = LOF(DataFile) / Length(Worker)
   SeekPut DataFile, Last + 1, Worker

4. Set Worker.ID = ""
   Set Worker.Name = ""
   Set Worker.Pay = 0
   SeekPut DataFile, 25, Worker

5. SeekGet DataFile, 18, Worker
   Set Worker.Pay = 13.90
   SeekPut, DataFile, 18, Worker

6. Open "EMPINDEX" For Output As IndexFile
   Set Limit = LOF(DataFile) / Length(Worker)
   For K = 1 Step 1 To Limit
       SeekGet DataFile, K, Worker
       Write IndexFile, Worker.ID
   End For

Self-Test 8.5

1. a. See Figure 4 (on next page).

   b. *Main Module*

      Call Welcome Message module
      Call Set Up Files module
      Call Select from Menu module
      Call Copy Array to Index File module
      End Program

2. It would have to be sorted; put in order.

FIGURE 4

Hierarchy
Chart for
Exercise 1

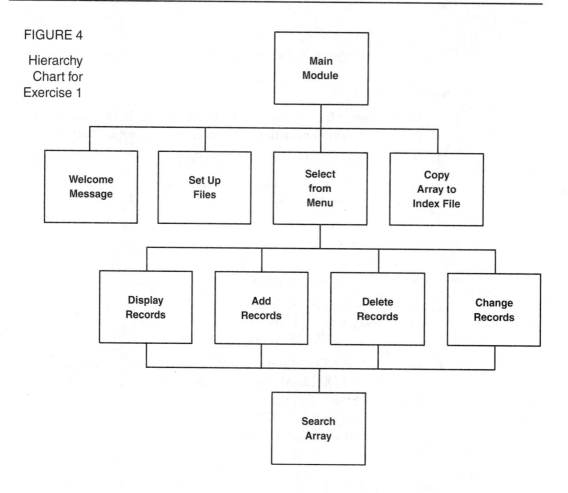

Chapter 9

Self-Test 9.1

1. data (attributes) and operations (methods)

2. A class provides the definition for its objects; the objects are instances of the class.

3. Private members cannot be accessed from outside the class; public members can.

4. InAndOut As Class
        Value As Real
        Subprogram SetValue(Num)
            Set Value = Num
        End Subprogram

```
Function GetValue() As Real
    Set GetValue = Value
End Function
End Class
```

5. A constructor is a special method included in the class definition that automatically performs specified setup tasks when an object is created.

Self-Test 9.2

1. procedural

2. a. encapsulation   b. inheritance
   c. polymorphism

3. derived (child) / base (parent)

4. • Identify the classes to be used in the program.
   • Determine the attributes needed for these classes.
   • Determine the methods needed for these classes.
   • Determine the relationships among the classes.

5. Advantages of OOP include: the security offered by data hiding, the ability to create reusable code, the relative ease of developing extremely complex programs, and the relative ease of developing programs that make use of a GUI.

Self-Test 9.3

1. a. text box   b. command button   c. option button

2. Both types of list boxes allow the user to select one item from a list. A list box displays the entire list. A drop-down list box initially only displays the current item; to see the others, one must click on a down-facing triangle symbol.

3. a. Name, title, title font, title bar color, visible or not, enabled or not, size, position on the screen, etc.

   b. Name, text, text font, text color, position in the window, size, etc.

   c. Name, caption (label), position, size, value (bullet or not), enabled or not, etc.

4. Set OKbutton.Caption = "OK"
   Set OKbutton.Enabled = False

Self-Test 9.4

1. a. true   b. false

2. Change

3. a. In the Text Box 1 and Text Box 2 sections, replace
       Text = ""
    by Text = "0"

   b. Rewrite the following subprogram as indicated:
      Subprogram CalculateButton.Click()
          Set Num = Val(InputBox.Text)
          If Num > 0 Then
              Set OutputBox.Text = Num ^ 2
          Else
              Set OutputBox.Text = "Invalid input"
          End If
      End Subprogram

4. c

Self-Test 9.5

1. See Figure 5.

FIGURE 5

The Window
Sketch for
Exercise 1

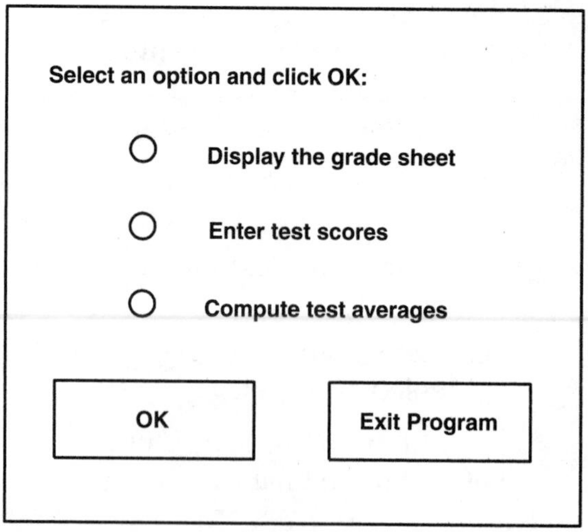

Select an option and click OK:

○   **Display the grade sheet**

○   **Enter test scores**

○   **Compute test averages**

OK   **Exit Program**

2. a. Subprogram Option1.Click()
        Set Option1.Value = True
        Set Option2.Value = False
        Set Option3.Value = False
        End Subprogram

   b. Subprogram OKbutton.Click()
        Set Retrieve.Visible = False
        If Option1.Value = True Then
            Call Display.Open
        End If
        If Option2.Value = True Then
            Call SelectTest.Open
        End If
        If Option3.Value = True Then
            Call ComputeAverages.Open
        End If
        End Subprogram

3. Subprogram ComputeAverages.StartUp()
     For K = 1 Step 1 To StudentCount
        Set Averages[K] =
            (Scores[1, K] + Scores[2, K] + Scores[3, K]) / 3
     End For
     End Subprogram

Answers to Odd-numbered Review Exercises

Chapter 1

1. Charles Babbage
3. transistor
5. b, a, d, c
7. c, b, a, d
9. hardware
11. 8
13. CD-ROM *or* DVD *or* tape
15. true
17. true
19. false
21. d
23. b
25. a
27. operating system
29. b
31. FORTRAN
33. processing
35. a. 4   b. 100

Chapter 2

1. program development cycle
3. true
5. b
7. main module
9. hierarchy chart
11. c
13. false
15. false
17. header
19. false
21. syntax
23. true

25. false   27. c

29. a   31. a

33. graphical user interface   35. true

37. object-oriented programming

39. Attributes include height, width, number of hinges, lockable or not lockable, etc.
    Methods include open it, close it, lock it, etc.

41. false

Chapter 3

FIGURE 1

Flowchart for Exercise 9

1. a. true   b. true   c. false

3. a. true   b. true   c. false

5. a. post-test

   b. Write Num
      Set Num = Num - 1

   c. Num = 0

7. a. pre-test

   b. Write Num
      Set Num = Num - 1

   c. Num <> 0

9. See Figure 1.

11. false

13. false

15. a. K

    b. Initial value = 3;
       increment = 2;
       limit value = 8.

17. negative

19. sentinel value

21. Repeat
       Write "Enter a"
       Write "negative number"
       Input Num
    Until Num < 0

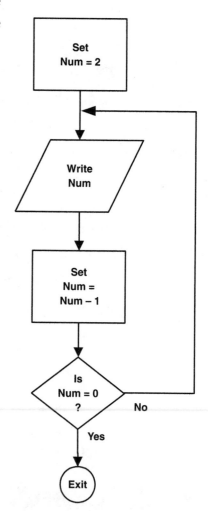

23. a. A   b. B

25. Set A = 0
    Set B = 1
    While B <= N
         Set A = A + 2 * B - 1
         Set B = B + 1
    End While

27. pre-test loop

29. 4
    5
    8
    10
    12
    15

31. true

33. false

Chapter 4

1. =, <>, <, <=, >, >=

3. a. false   b. true

5. a. true   b. false   c. false

7. a. N <= 0   b. (N < 0) Or (N > 5)

9. If-Then

11. a

13. false

15. Input Num
    If (Num = 1) Or (Num = 2) Then
         Write "Yes"
    End If

17. See Figure 2.

19. Input Num
    If Num = 1 Then
         Write "Yes"
    Else
         Write "No"
    End If

21. Input X

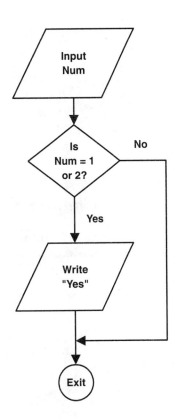

FIGURE 2

Flowchart for Exercise 17

```
If X > 0 Then
      Set Answer = 1 / Sqrt(X)
      Write Answer
Else
      If X = 0 Then
            Write "Error: Division by zero"
      Else
            Write "Error: Square root of negative number"
      End If
End If
```

23. Multiple-alternative structure

25. Input Score
```
If (Score >= 7) And (Score <= 10) Then
      Write "Pass"
Else
      If (Score = 5) Or (Score = 6) Then
            Write "Retest"
      Else
            Write "Fail"
      End If
End If
```

27. 5
    Not
    And

29. a. 1   b. 2   c. 3
       DONE   DONE   DONE

31. Change the first line to:
    If Grade = "A" Then

Chapter 5

1. integer / real (floating point)   3. floating point

5. a. 5   b. 4   7. Yes

9. a. 1, 2, 3, 4, 5   11. For K = 1 Step 1 To 25
   b. 4, 5, 6, 7, 8   Set N = Random(2)
                                      Write N
                                  End For

13. true   15. *a* and *b* are true

17. a. true   b. true   19. 9

21. file   23. text (or ASCII)

25. sequential

27. a. true   b. true

29. a. false   b. true

31. "A", 25<CR><EOF>

33. "A", 25<CR>"E", 15<CR><EOF>

35. "A", 25<CR>"C", 75<CR>"E", 15<CR><EOF>

37. control break processing

Chapter 6

1. true

3. true

5. 4
   1 9

7. false

9. Replace the While statement by:
       While (Found = 0) And (Index < N)
   In the If-Then structure, replace "Set Found = 1" by:
       Set Found = 0

11. 20

13. Write Name[1], Name[10]

15. Declare Score1[25], Score2[25], Score3[25]

17. Open "TEST" For Input As DataFile
    For K = 1 Step 1 To 25
        Read DataFile, Score1[K], Score2[K], Score3[K]
    End For
    Close DataFile

19. true

21. Declare X[5, 5]
    For I = 1 Step 1 To 5
        For J = 1 Step 1 To 5
            Write "Enter a number."
            Input X[I, J]
        End For (J)
    End For (I)

23. 1
    0
    0
    1

Chapter 7

1. exported
3. data flow diagram
5. The value of X
7. See Figure 3.
9. 2 1 5
11. false
13. scope
15. Subprogram InputData(Num1 As Ref,
          Num2 As Ref)
      Write "Enter two numbers"
      Input Num1, Num2
    End Subprogram
17. a. The entire program
    b. The subprogram Sub
19. 5
    1
    4
21. function
23. a. 0
    b. 15
25. a. "10.5"
    b. 0
27. 4
29. Function Average(Num1, Num2) As Real
      Set Average = (Num1 + Num2) / 2
    End Function
31. recursion
33. 1
35. 6
37. Function Mult(M, N) As Integer
      If N = 1 Then
          Mult = M
      Else
          Mult = Mult(N – 1, M) + M
      End If
    End Function

FIGURE 3

Data Flow Diagram for Exercise 7

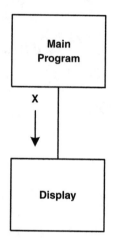

Chapter 8

1. false
3. 3
5. 1
7. 5
9. Arnold
11. true
13. I = 1, J = 2, and NewArray[1] = "Arthur"

15. "Arthur", "Corinne", "Marjorie", "Michael", "Sam"

17. *Replace*   If MasterArray[I] <= UpdateArray[J] Then
    by   If MasterArray[I] >= UpdateArray[J] Then

19. true   21. false

23. 25 bytes (characters)   25. Car.Make / Car.Model

27. SeekGet DataFile, 2, Car

29. indexed

31. Write LOF(DataFile) / Length(Car)

33. Set Car.Make = ""
    Set Car.Model = ""
    SeekPut DataFile, 4, Car

35. Open "CARINDEX" For Output As IndexFile
    Set Limit = LOF(DataFile) / Length(Car)
    For K = 1 Step 1 To Limit
        SeekGet DataFile, K, Car
        Write IndexFile, Car.Model
    End For
    Close IndexFile

Chapter 9

1. class   3. false

5. false   7. Side, Area

9. Private   11. Declare Square1 As Square

13. Call Square1.ComputeArea   15. encapsulation

17. polymorphism   19. Area, Side, Height

21. a   23. true

25.   a. OK, Cancel   b. Time, Date

27. clear   29. b

31. a   33. true

35. Name, Title, Title Font, Enabled (Active), Visible, etc.

37. true   39. true

41. Subprogram Abutton.Click()
        Set Text1.Text = "Hello"
        Set Bbutton.Enabled = False
        End Subprogram

43. Subprogram Option1.Click()
        Set Option1.Value = True
        Set Option2.Value = False
    End Subprogram

Index